COOKING

from the

GARDEN

COOKING
from the
GARDEN

Best Recipes from KITCHEN GARDENER

EDITED BY RUTH LIVELY

The Taunton Press

The Taunton Press
Inspiration for hands-on living®

The Taunton Press, Inc., 63 South Main Street, PO Box 5506, Newtown, CT 06470-5506

e-mail: tp@taunton.com

....

Editors: **RUTH LIVELY** *and* **COURTNEY JORDAN**

Copy editor: **NINA RYND WHITNAH**

Indexer: **JAY KREIDER**

Cover designer: **ERICA HEITMAN-FORD** *for* **MUCCA DESIGN**

Interior designer: **ERICA HEITMAN-FORD** *for* **MUCCA DESIGN**

Illustrator: **CHRIS SILAS NEAL**

....

Library of Congress Cataloging-in-Publication Data

Cooking from the garden : best recipes from Kitchen gardener / editors and contributors of Kitchen gardener.

    p. cm.

  Includes index.

  ISBN 978-1-60085-247-3

  1. Cookery. I. Fine gardener.

  TX714.C654322 2010

  641.5--dc22

                    2009047190

Printed in the United States of America

10 9 8 7 6 5 4 3 2 1

Table of Contents

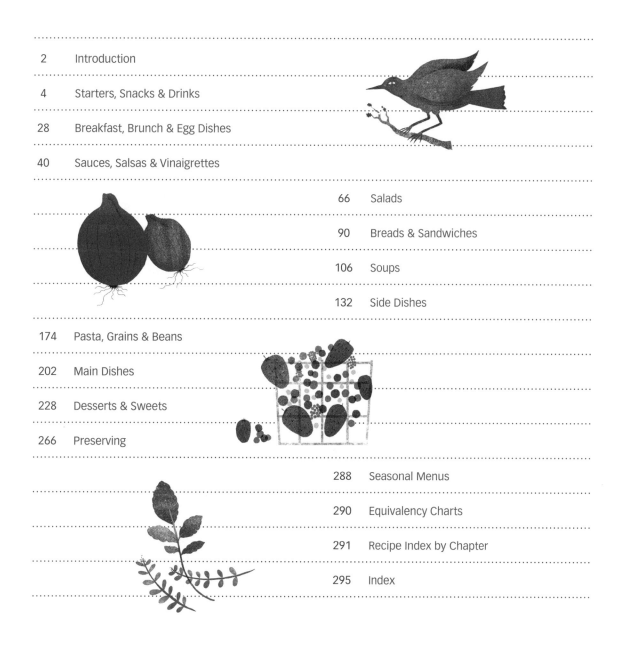

Introduction

Cooking from the Garden celebrates finding delicious food close to home, and showcases how innovative and tasty meals come almost effortlessly to the plate when made with fresh and seasonal ingredients. The recipes in this collection are mouthwatering, unfussy and uncomplicated, and made with style and expertise—the best of what *Kitchen Gardener*, the magazine dedicated to edible gardening, had to offer.

Published from 1996 to 2001, *Kitchen Gardener* showed how to grow great ingredients, and what to do with them once they were in the kitchen. We focused on appealing recipes that made good use of the things we were growing in our gardens. The recipes came from many different hands: culinary professionals—chefs, bakery owners, and cookbook authors; foodies from the garden and the kitchen; and others who were simply good home cooks, often gardeners who were writing about what they grew. The recipes in *Cooking from the Garden* are the best of those offerings; from people who all love great food and have learned the universal culinary secret: that it is the fresh ingredients that make any dish a success.

So you won't find recipes made with fancy, can't-find, or super-expensive ingredients. Instead, what makes *Cooking from the Garden* recipes a cut above the rest are the ripe and ready-for-eating fruits and vegetables they're made with.

These honest, straightforward dishes really show off how to make the most of those treasures from the earth.

But cooking from the garden doesn't necessarily mean you need a garden to cook this way—it's not an all-or-nothing proposition. Buy from farm stands or the local farmer's market; have a membership in a community-supported farm; or simply shop at the best local produce vendor you can find. However you bring it to the table, you're coming with fresh produce, and that immediacy—of cooking and eating—is what it's all about, whether you're a seasoned gardener or you just know that cooking with fresh ingredients feels right.

So let the spirit of the garden permeate your cooking. When there's an abundance of an ingredient, use it generously. If the tomatoes are coming on thick and fast, that's the time to slow-roast a big pan of them until they collapse and their flavors concentrate. If scarcity is the order of the day, look for ways to turn small quantities of vegetables into a meal. That's the time to gather the few things you have in the garden and make a vegetable soup or stir-fry. Or pull out that jar of chunky tomato sauce you've been waiting all autumn to use in your next meal.

Always remember that what you have on hand may be the unexpected makings of your next flavorful, exciting meal. If the escarole is bolting or you've used all the tender white leaves of the head you bought, cut the remaining dark green outer leaves into ribbons and sauté with a few seasonings for a delicious side or savory pizza topping. Or take the dark green leek tops that most cooks—good ones, too!—discard. Slice and tuck them underneath the next chicken you roast; they will season the pan juices beautifully and turn into the most irresistibly delicious caramelly bits. Collect your vegetable trimmings to make a simple stock or to boost the flavor of a store-bought one. This is the kind of creative cooking that our recipes will guide and inspire in you—nothing is wasted and you are never left wanting. Because great food will out—just give your ingredients a chance to show you what they can do.

And there are so many ways to get to a great dish—be flexible. The recipes in *Cooking from the Garden* offer substitutions and highlight alternative ingredients, so even if you don't have the vegetable or herb or fruit called for, the dish is always within your means.

Here, you'll find recipes for every meal of the day—from breakfast and brunch to salads, soups, main dishes, desserts, and all the fixings in between; from quick and easy weekday meals to prize dishes for holiday fêtes. And with a whole chapter dedicated to jams, preserves, and pickles, you can turn summer's bounty into tasty treats to enjoy throughout the year or to give as gifts.

Seek out the *Fresh from the garden* listings; just about every recipe has one, and there you will find the vegetables, fruits, and herbs called for in the recipe that can be grown pretty much anywhere in the country. Use the list to help you find recipes to match what's in your garden—or your crisper drawer.

Depending on where you live, there may be even more ingredients that can come from your garden or a local grower—citrus, avocados, pecans, walnuts, and hazelnuts. And by letting some of your herbs flower and

set seed, you can harvest your own spices. Cilantro (also called coriander), fennel, dill, and mustard seed are easy to harvest this way, and the flavor of freshly ground spices beats that of pre-ground hands down.

In keeping with the celebration of seasonal bounty, we've drawn up chic, surefire menus for every season of the year. Among them you'll find an early spring dinner, a summer appetizer menu for entertaining, a vegetarian feast, and a harvest dinner, plus others (p. 288).

To get the most out of the recipes, please read the entire recipe before you start, including the nutritional information, which is listed per serving (unless otherwise specified). That way you won't be surprised by a required overnight rest in the fridge or have to make a frantic search for an ingredient at the last minute. Before starting to cook, gather your ingredients, and scrub, soak, peel, slice, and dice whenever appropriate. Unless otherwise specified, assume that butter is unsalted; eggs are large; flour is unbleached, all-purpose; salt is table salt; sugar is white granulated; fresh herbs, greens, and lettuces are washed and dried; garlic, onions, and fresh ginger are peeled. If a recipe calls for adding water, it generally won't be listed in the ingredients; you'll find it in the directions. Also, pay attention to how an ingredient is described; for example, "1 cup flour, sifted" isn't the same as "1 cup sifted flour."

Sitting down to a meal of simple, freshly cooked food—dishes made with fresh ingredients, perhaps grown by you or someone you know—is immensely satisfying and nourishing on so many levels. Eating seasonally and locally is a reward in itself, and more and more of us are coming to understand that truth. At its heart, *Cooking from the Garden* is cooking seasonally and locally, so enjoy this book, a celebration of the best that the garden has to offer.

—*Ruth Lively, editor*

STARTERS, SNACKS & DRINKS

You'll find lots of tasty possibilities for appetizers and meal openers in this chapter, ranging from rustic to elegant, from light to substantial, from simple to involved. Some are small plates—little dishes that can be eaten as a first course or paired with a salad or cup of soup for a light meal. There are several tasty spreads like Baba Ghanoush and White Bean and Herb Spread that you can make up and keep on hand for impromptu entertaining or healthful snacks. Plus there are lots of good things to drink—smoothies, herbal teas, and a refreshing and somewhat unusual Watermelon Milkshake with Cardamom.

Many of these could become staples in your kitchen. Green Olive Tapenade and Oil-Simmered Garlic are some of my favorites. Not only do they make terrific spreads on their own, but they also can be used as ingredients in so many ways that I'd never want to be without them. I mash the garlic into vinaigrettes, pan sauces, or just with olive oil and herbs for a simple pasta sauce. The tapenade can be stuffed into chicken breasts or lamb roasts, used as a sauce for grilled fish, or as a sandwich condiment. The Shallots Braised in Sherry are another example of versatility. They work as an appetizer or a condiment; try them with a holiday ham or roast pork, or simply alongside a sandwich.

Spicy Carrot Fritters with Fresh Salsa

If you're looking for something different to make with carrots, try these quick fritters. Topped with a traditional salsa made with fresh tomatoes, red onion, and cilantro, these fritters are perfect for a first course or a sassy side, or paired with a salad for a tasty lunch.

....

Fresh from the garden: TOMATOES, RED ONION, JALAPEÑO, CILANTRO, CARROTS, POTATO, SCALLIONS
Makes 10 fritters | *150 calories, 10g fat, 140mg sodium**

....

FOR THE SALSA

3 tomatoes, diced

1 small red onion, diced

1 jalapeño, minced

2 tablespoons finely chopped
    fresh cilantro

Salt to taste

FOR THE CARROT FRITTERS

2 cups shredded carrots

1 large potato, grated

¼ cup chopped scallion tops

3 eggs, lightly beaten

¼ cup heavy cream

¼ cup flour

1 teaspoon crushed red pepper flakes

½ teaspoon salt

¼ cup vegetable oil for frying

....

MAKE THE SALSA | Combine all the ingredients for the salsa and set aside.

MAKE THE FRITTERS | Combine all the ingredients for the fritters. The batter will be loose. In a large frying pan, heat ¼ cup of oil over high heat, but don't let the oil smoke. Use a ¼-cup measuring cup to scoop out the batter. Put as many fritters in the pan as will fit without crowding. Cook them until golden brown on both sides. Remove the fritters from the frying pan and place them on a paper towel to drain. Repeat with the remaining mixture until all the fritters are cooked. Top with salsa and serve.

— *Recipe by
Rosemary Campiformio*

** Nutritional information is calculated
per serving except where otherwise noted.*

Small Tomatoes in Shallot-Flavored Cream

One and a half minutes on the cut side of the tomato and one minute on the other side is all it takes to put this side together. Quick and easy, but oh, so elegant, this recipe is a perfect use for tomatoes that are too small to slice.

Fresh from the garden: SHALLOTS, SMALL TOMATOES, PARSLEY
4 servings | *290 calories, 18g fat, 580mg sodium*

4 ounces Parmigiano-Reggiano
4 shallots (¼ pound), minced
1 tablespoon flour
1⅓ cups half-and-half

Pinch of freshly grated nutmeg
8 small tomatoes (1 pound),
  cut in half

Salt and freshly ground
  white pepper
Handful of chopped fresh parsley

Whirl the cheese to tiny nubbins in a food processor. Warm a large nonstick frying pan over medium-high heat. Add the shallots and sauté, stirring until browned, about 2 minutes. Whisk in the flour, then slowly whisk in the half-and-half. Add the nutmeg and whisk until thick.

Place the tomatoes cut sides down in the half-and-half, turn the heat to high, sprinkle with salt and pepper, and cook 1½ minutes. Use a spatula to turn the tomatoes. Cook the tomatoes until they begin to exude juices and the sauce is pink, about 1 minute. Spoon into small heated bowls and sprinkle with the cheese and parsley.

— Recipe by Sylvia Thompson

Eggplant "Sandwiches" on Crisp Greens with Sherry-Shallot Vinaigrette

Oven-roasted slices of eggplant replace bread in this twist on grilled cheese sandwiches. Peppery greens like arugula, frisée, red mustard, or spinach add tang to the dish and are a perfect foil to the mild eggplant.

Fresh from the garden: EGGPLANTS, BASIL, SALAD GREENS, SHALLOTS

6 servings | *910 calories, 76g fat, 700mg sodium*

FOR THE EGGPLANT SANDWICHES

2 medium globe eggplants, sliced into twelve 1-inch-thick pieces, ends discarded

¼ cup olive oil

Salt and freshly ground pepper

12 ounces mozzarella, preferably fresh

½ cup loosely packed fresh basil leaves

12 anchovy filets, rinsed and patted dry

1½ cups breadcrumbs

½ cup finely chopped walnuts

1 cup flour

3 large eggs, lightly beaten

Vegetable oil for frying

6 cups peppery salad greens

FOR THE SHERRY-SHALLOT VINAIGRETTE

2 tablespoons minced shallots

1 teaspoon Dijon mustard

1 teaspoon freshly squeezed lemon juice

2 tablespoons sherry vinegar

2 teaspoons dry sherry

Salt and freshly ground pepper

½ cup extra-virgin olive oil

MAKE THE SANDWICHES | Lightly brush the eggplant slices with oil and season with salt and pepper. Place them in a single layer on baking sheets and bake in a preheated 400°F oven until lightly brown and tender, about 20 minutes. Cut the cheese into ⅛-inch-thick slices and arrange on 6 of the eggplant slices. Chop the basil and anchovies together and sprinkle over the cheese. Top with an eggplant slice to form a sandwich. Stir the breadcrumbs and walnuts together. Dredge the sandwiches in flour and shake off the excess. Dip each sandwich in beaten egg and then in the breadcrumb mixture. The sandwiches can be prepared to this point and refrigerated, loosely covered, up to 8 hours before finishing.

In a frying pan, heat ½ inch of oil to 350°F. Cook the sandwiches in batches in a single layer, turning once, until they're golden brown on both sides. Drain on paper towels and keep warm while frying the rest. Sandwiches can be cooked ahead and reheated in a 300°F oven.

MAKE THE VINAIGRETTE | Using a whisk, combine all of the vinaigrette ingredients except the olive oil. In a steady stream, incorporate the olive oil into the mixture.

To serve, toss the greens with a little of the vinaigrette and arrange on plates. Place the eggplant sandwiches on top.

— *Recipe by John Ash*

Grilled Eggplant Bruschetta

Make this tasty appetizer when you've got the grill going. The roasted garlic can be made ahead, or use Oil-Simmered Garlic (p. 18).

....

Fresh from the garden: GARLIC, EGGPLANT, TOMATOES, BASIL
6 servings | *320 calories, 21g fat, 290mg sodium*

....

1 head garlic
6 tablespoons extra-virgin olive oil
Salt and freshly ground pepper
3 long slender eggplants, such as
    Thai Long Green or Waimanalo Long

6 Roma tomatoes
4 ounces soft melting cheese,
    like Teleme or Havarti

6 slices coarse Italian bread
2 tablespoons finely
    shredded fresh basil

....

Cut off the top quarter of the garlic head. Drizzle the garlic with 1 tablespoon of the olive oil and season with salt and pepper. Wrap securely in foil and bake in a 325°F oven until the garlic is soft, 30 to 40 minutes. Set aside to cool.

Remove the stems from the eggplant and slice lengthwise ¼ inch thick. Brush both sides with 2 tablespoons of the olive oil and season lightly with salt and pepper. Grill over hot coals (or medium-high on a gas grill) until just softened and lightly browned. Set aside.

Remove the stems from the tomatoes, cut them in half, and remove the seeds. Coat the halves with 1 tablespoon of the olive oil, season with salt and pepper,

and grill until just cooked through, about 5 minutes. Set aside.

Slice the cheese ¼ inch thick. Brush the slices of bread lightly with the remaining 2 tablespoons of the olive oil and grill or broil them until lightly toasted.

Squeeze the garlic purée from the cloves and spread it evenly on the bread. Next, layer the bread and garlic with the eggplant, tomato, basil, and cheese. The layers should completely cover the bread.

Place the bruschetta on a covered grill (or under a hot broiler) until the cheese just melts, 3 to 5 minutes. Top each one with a few grindings of pepper and serve them immediately.

— *Recipe by John Ash*

Okra Tempura with Soy Dipping Sauce

With okra, the challenge is how to bring its wonderful flavor to the table without any of the gooeyness most people dislike. Deep frying in a light tempura batter puts this characteristic to good use—okra's thick juices enhance the crispy fried batter.

....

Fresh from the garden: OKRA

4 appetizer servings | *210 calories, 11g fat, 1,040mg sodium*

....

FOR THE SOY DIPPING SAUCE

¼ cup soy sauce

¼ cup rice vinegar

3 tablespoons brown sugar

1 tablespoon freshly chopped ginger

FOR THE OKRA TEMPURA

16 ounces canola or vegetable oil

2 egg yolks

1⅔ cups ice water

1⅔ cups sifted flour

2 cups okra, cut in ¼-inch slices

....

MAKE THE DIPPING SAUCE | Mix all sauce ingredients together. Set aside.

MAKE THE TEMPURA | Heat the oil to 350°F in a deep fryer or a tempura fryer. If you have neither, use a heavy pot, 12 inches deep and wide.

Combine the egg yolks and the ice water in a bowl and mix gently. Add the flour and stir briefly; the batter should appear rough and only partially mixed.

Dip the okra in the batter to coat loosely. Deep fry in small batches until the okra is golden brown, 2 to 3 minutes. Serve with the dipping sauce.

— *Recipe by Clark Frasier*

Crispy Okra with Basil Pesto & Bacon

The flavors and textures of this dish—crunchy okra, rich pesto, and salty, smoky bacon—combine well with sliced yellow and red tomatoes or a small salad of garden-fresh greens, drizzled with a light vinaigrette.

Fresh from the garden: BASIL, GARLIC, OKRA

4 appetizer servings | *420 calories, 27g fat, 930mg sodium*

FOR THE PESTO

1 cup fresh basil leaves
¼ cup freshly grated
   Parmigiano-Reggiano
1 teaspoon salt
2 tablespoons olive oil
Juice of 1 lemon
1 teaspoon chopped garlic
¼ cup toasted pine nuts

FOR THE OKRA

2 pounds okra, cut into
   ¼-inch rounds
½ cup cornmeal
2 tablespoons olive oil
Salt and freshly ground pepper
8 strips crispy bacon
8 fresh basil sprigs

MAKE THE PESTO | Process all the pesto ingredients in a blender or food processor. Set aside.

FRY THE OKRA | Toss the okra with the cornmeal and place in a sieve to shake off any excess cornmeal. Heat the olive oil in a nonstick sauté pan until it's hot. Test by putting one piece of okra into the pan. If the oil sizzles right away, it's ready. Add the rest of the okra.

Sprinkle with salt and pepper and slowly sauté over medium heat until the okra is golden brown, about 4 minutes.

Arrange the okra and bacon on four plates, drizzle with pesto, garnish with basil sprigs, and serve at once.

— *Recipe by Clark Frasier*

Bagna Cauda

Bagna Cauda means "hot bath" in Italian. It is best when made with moist, recently cured garlic. You will need a flameproof bowl with a stand and a votive candle to keep the sauce warm. Or rig a stand from two bricks placed on their sides. Rest the dish atop the bricks and put the votive underneath the dish. For accompanying vegetables, choose whatever is in season. If cardoons (an artichoke relative) aren't available in your area, substitute fennel, celery hearts, small whole roasted beets, or blanched cauliflower.

Fresh from the garden: GARLIC; A SELECTION OF SEASONAL VEGETABLES—CARDOONS, NEW POTATOES, ARTICHOKES, SPRING ONIONS, RADISHES, SALAD GREENS, FENNEL, CELERY, BEETS, CAULIFLOWER
4 to 6 servings | *810 calories, 54g fat, 1,070mg sodium; based on 6 servings (2 ounces bread per serving)*

FOR THE BAGNA CAUDA

4 heads garlic, cloves peeled
¾ cup dry white wine
½ cup butter
2 ounces anchovy fillets, coarsely chopped
1 cup extra-virgin olive oil

SERVE WITH

6 to 8 cardoons, parboiled (see Note)
12 to 18 small new potatoes, roasted
3 large artichokes, boiled, leaves and hearts separated, choke discarded
6 spring onions, grilled
12 to 18 small radishes, trimmed
4 cups large leafy greens (such as endive, radicchio, or arugula)
1 loaf country-style bread

MAKE THE BAGNA CAUDA | Cut each garlic clove into 5 or 6 thin, lengthwise slices. Place the garlic in a medium saucepan, add the wine, and set over low heat. Simmer until the garlic begins to soften, 10 to 15 minutes. Meanwhile, melt the butter in a small saucepan, then stir in the anchovies. Simmer until the anchovies begin to break up, 2 or 3 minutes. Add the olive oil, heat through, and stir the mixture into the garlic and wine. Simmer the sauce for 3 or 4 minutes, remove from the heat, and set aside.

TO SERVE | Prepare the vegetables and arrange them on a large platter. Heat the bread, cut it into large chunks, and wrap it in a heavy cloth napkin to keep it warm.

Set the stand with a votive candle in the center of the platter, or alongside it.

Reheat the sauce, light the candle, and then pour the sauce into the flameproof bowl. Arrange all the elements in the center of the table. Guests use their fingers to dip the vegetables and bread into the sauce.

NOTE | To prepare cardoons, have a pot of boiling salted water ready. Select the tender, inner stalks and trim away any leaves. Cut them in half lengthwise, trim away the tough membrane on the inside of the stalk, and scrape off coarse fibers from the outside. Cut into 3-inch pieces and rinse. Simmer the cardoons in the water until just tender, 10 to 20 minutes, depending on size and variety. Drain, refresh briefly in ice water, and drain again.

— *Recipe by Michele Anna Jordan*

Shallots Braised in Sherry

This easy-to-make dish is ideal as an accompaniment to cheese or as an hors d'oeuvre with toast or crackers. It is most flavorful when served at room temperature a few hours after it is made.

Fresh from the garden: SHALLOTS
6 servings | *100 calories, 8g fat, 5mg sodium*

60 small white shallots (about ½ pound)	2½ tablespoons olive oil	¼ teaspoon freshly ground white pepper
1 tablespoon butter	5 tablespoons dry sherry	Salt
	1 teaspoon sugar	

Trim and peel the shallots and cut any large ones in half. Heat the butter and oil in a frying or sauté pan and add the shallots. Stir to coat the shallots evenly with the oil and butter mixture. Cover and sweat over medium-low heat for 15 minutes.

Add the sherry, sugar, and pepper. Cover and continue sweating until the shallots are soft and glazed, about 10 minutes. Season with salt to taste, and remove from the heat to cool. Serve at room temperature.

— *Recipe by William Woys Weaver*

Kale & Cheese Rolls

Frilly-edged dark green kale leaves give this healthful appetizer eye appeal. The rolls can be made a few hours ahead of time and left to sit at room temperature.

....

Fresh from the garden: KALE

Makes 24 rolls | *30 calories, 2g fat, 40mg sodium*

....

6 large kale leaves

6 ounces soft cheese, such as
   Teleme, Havarti, or Camembert,
   at room temperature

2 tablespoons rice vinegar

....

Wash the kale and shake off the excess water. Cut out the stems, leaving the two halves as long strips. Bring a small amount of water to a boil in a steamer. Steam the leaves until they are soft enough to roll but still bright green, about 3 minutes. Cut the pieces in half lengthwise to make long, narrow strips.

Dip each strip of kale in the rice vinegar and let the excess run off. Cut the cheese into 24 teaspoon-size cubes. Put one cube at the end of a kale strip and roll the leaf around the cheese. Insert a toothpick to hold each bite-size roll together. Serve as an hors d'oeuvre.

— *Recipe by Nan Wishner*

Green Olive Tapenade

This recipe can be varied in many ways. Made with green olives, it can be used on crostini (see Note) or whisked into a vinaigrette. With coarsely chopped black olives, it can be used as a stuffing for boned leg of lamb. Or spread it on a swordfish steak after you have turned it on the grill.

Fresh from the garden: GARLIC, SAVORY OR THYME
Makes 1 cup | *40 calories, 4g fat, 330mg sodium; per tablespoon*

½ pound (before pitting) cracked
  green olives
2 tablespoons capers
2 anchovies (preferably salt packed),
  torn into small pieces

1 clove garlic
Pinch of cayenne
Pinch of fresh savory or thyme

3 to 5 tablespoons mild
  extra-virgin olive oil

Pit the olives. Put all the ingredients and 3 tablespoons olive oil into a food processor. Pulse until tapenade is the desired texture, adding more oil to thin the mixture if necessary.

NOTE | To make crostini, heat the oven to 350°F. Cut a loaf of sourdough bread into slices ⅓ inch thick, brush both sides with olive oil, and toast until golden for about 5 to 7 minutes.

— Recipe by Maggie Blyth Klein

Baba Ghanoush

This roasted eggplant and thyme spread can be made with any type of eggplant but is prettiest when made with white-skinned ones. Instead of roasting the eggplant, try grilling it, which gives the vegetable a complex, smoky flavor. Angostura® bitters are a salt-free flavor enhancer made from gentian and vegetable extracts that give the dip depth. Look for it in the condiment aisle of your supermarket or at a liquor store, since it's often used in cocktails.

Fresh from the garden: EGGPLANT, GARLIC, THYME, PARSLEY
Makes about 2½ cups | *15 calories, 1g fat, 35mg sodium; per tablespoon*

- 1 medium eggplant (about 1 pound)
- ½ teaspoon salt
- 1 cup plain yogurt
- 3 tablespoons tahini
- 2 tablespoons freshly squeezed lemon juice
- 2 cloves garlic
- 1½ tablespoons minced fresh thyme leaves
- 2 tablespoons minced fresh flat-leaf parsley
- Few dashes of Angostura bitters
- ½ teaspoon Hungarian paprika

Pierce the eggplant with a long-pronged fork five or six times. Roast the eggplant on a baking sheet in a 400°F oven until it softens, 25 to 35 minutes. Let the eggplant sit until cool enough to handle, then cut the stem end off and halve the eggplant lengthwise. Scrape out the flesh and discard the skin.

Put the eggplant into a food processor and sprinkle it with the salt. Add the yogurt, tahini, lemon juice, garlic, and thyme; process until smooth. Blend in the parsley, bitters, and paprika.

The spread is best if allowed to stand for 30 minutes before serving.

— *Recipe by Susan Belsinger*

White Bean & Herb Spread

A generous portion of parsley adds punch to this spread. Scoop it up with pita triangles, spoon it into Belgian endive leaves, or spread it on top of grilled bread for a substantial—and healthy—bruschetta.

Fresh from the garden: GARLIC, PARSLEY, ROSEMARY, CELERY
Makes about 2 cups | *25 calories, 1g fat, 0mg sodium; per tablespoon*

2 cups cooked white beans or
   one 15-ounce can white beans,
   rinsed and drained
2 tablespoons olive oil
3 teaspoons balsamic vinegar

2 cloves garlic, minced
Generous ½ cup chopped
   fresh parsley
1 tablespoon minced fresh rosemary
⅓ cup finely chopped celery

Salt and freshly ground black pepper
Few pinches crushed red pepper
   flakes, optional

Put all of the beans in a bowl, and mash about half of them with a fork. Add the olive oil, vinegar, garlic, parsley, rosemary, and celery, and toss well. Season with salt, pepper, and red pepper flakes, if desired.

Let the spread stand, covered, for about 30 minutes before serving. Taste for seasoning, and adjust as necessary. If the spread has been refrigerated, allow it to come to cool room temperature before serving.

— *Recipe by Susan Belsinger*

Oil-Simmered Garlic

This technique produces a result similar to roasted garlic, but without the caramelizing that happens in the oven. A fringe benefit is the garlic-infused oil. With oil-simmered garlic on hand, you've got a shortcut to any recipe calling for roasted garlic. Quantities are flexible—simmer the cloves from as many heads as you wish. Using a small-diameter pan will keep the amount of oil you need to a minimum.

Fresh from the garden: GARLIC
70 calories, 7g fat, 0mg sodium; per tablespoon using equal parts garlic and olive oil

| 1 head garlic, or more | Olive oil to cover |

Peel the garlic and put the cloves in a small, heavy pan. Pour in olive oil to cover. Bring to a boil over medium heat. Then lower the heat to the lowest setting and simmer until the cloves are tender, 10 to 15 minutes. Store garlic and oil together in a covered container in the refrigerator.

NOTE | If you want, add herb sprigs to the pan with the garlic and oil.

— *Recipe by Yael Bernier*

Ten ways to use oil-simmered or roasted garlic

Oil-simmered or roasted garlic cloves have a creamy, pastelike consistency and a mild but rich flavor. Spread onto bread and topped with freshly ground sea salt and pepper, they are better than butter. Because it has a long molecular structure like an egg yolk and similar binding properties, garlic paste can replace egg yolk in many recipes, at the rate of one tablespoon of paste per yolk. Try it the next time you have a hankering for Caesar salad.

If you can stop yourself from eating the entire batch of roasted or simmered garlic in one sitting, there are lots of wonderful things to do with this staple.

- Mash a clove or two into a vinaigrette made with some of the garlic oil.

- Spread on bread when making sandwiches.

- Combine several cloves with mayonnaise.

- Mash and swirl into pan juices after sautéing to make a quick sauce for meat, fish, or vegetables.

- Add several cloves to a composed salad plate.

- Add cloves and oil to potatoes just before mashing or to baked potatoes instead of butter or sour cream.

- Add mashed cloves to a béchamel for lasagne.

- Use whole cloves and a little of the oil in an impromptu pasta sauce, with lots of minced parsley, grated cheese, and crushed red pepper flakes.

- Spread the garlic onto small pieces of lightly toasted bread, top with herbed goat cheese, and sprinkle a very few drops of garlic oil on top for an easy and quick appetizer.

- Mash garlic cloves with olive oil and a few drops of sherry vinegar or lemon juice to make a sauce for cooked vegetables or chickpeas.

Salt-Roasted Garlic

Packing garlic bulbs in salt insulates them and prevents burning. This method yields more than just delicious creamy cloves of roasted garlic. The skins can be used to flavor vegetable stock. The salt becomes garlic salt. You can reuse the salt two or three times to roast more garlic. After that, though, the garlic juices will burn and spoil the salt's flavor.

Fresh from the garden: GARLIC
Makes about 2 cups of paste | *10 calories, 0g fat, 20mg sodium; per teaspoon*

9 heads garlic	4 cups Kosher salt

Preheat the oven to 350°F. Place ⅛ inch salt in the bottom of an 8×8×2-inch baking dish. Put the garlic bulbs on top of the salt. Then fill the dish with salt until only the tips of the bulbs are showing.

Heat the dish in the oven for 45 minutes to 1 hour. When the garlic is done, the tips will ooze a little juice.

Remove the dish from the oven and let it cool for about 15 minutes. Remove the bulbs from the salt, cut them in half horizontally, and squeeze the paste from the cloves.

— Recipe by Jay McCarthy

Cool Sun Tea

If you can't harvest your own untreated hibiscus flowers and rose hips for this tangy, spicy refresher, buy dried ones at a natural-foods market.

Fresh from the garden: HIBISCUS FLOWERS, ROSE HIPS, LEMON VERBENA

3 parts fresh hibiscus flowers	1 part fresh lemon verbena leaves	1 small cinnamon stick
2 parts fresh rose hips	1 part orange slices	

Put ingredients in a jar or pitcher, add cold water to cover, and set in the sun for several hours. If you're putting it outdoors, cover with a lid or piece of plastic film to keep bugs out. Strain, sweeten with honey or maple syrup if desired, and serve iced. You can also add equal parts fresh apple and pineapple juice to the tea after it's brewed.

— *Recipe by Kathleen Brown*

Make your own herbal teas

Making an herbal tea (also called an infusion or a tisane) couldn't be easier. Simply put several leafy sprigs of clean herbs (rinse them if necessary) in your teapot, pour boiling water over, and let steep for anywhere from 5 to 15 minutes. Use about one ounce of fresh herbs to a quart of water.

Here's a list of herbs, fruits, flowers, and spices (and their flavor qualities) that make tasty teas.

HERBS
LEMON VERBENA, LEMON BALM, LEMONGRASS, CITRUS PEEL– citrus

BORAGE– cucumber

CHAMOMILE FLOWERS– applelike aroma and flavor

ROSEMARY– aromatic, piney

STEVIA– sweet

FRUITS
APPLE, CHERRY, PEACH, BLACKBERRY, RASPBERRY, ROSE HIPS (FOR TARTNESS), DRIED FRUIT

FLOWERS
ELDER, HIBISCUS, HAWTHORN, JASMINE, LAVENDER, LINDEN, RED CLOVER, ROSES

SPICES
ALLSPICE, CARDAMOM, CINNAMON, CLOVES, CORIANDER, AND GINGER

Melon Frost

Make this slushy drink with any type of cantaloupe or honeydew.
Just be sure to use a fully ripe and fragrant melon.

Fresh from the garden: CANTALOUPE OR HONEYDEW

4 servings | *190 calories, 1.5g fat, 55mg sodium*

2 cups puréed melon

1 cup plain low-fat yogurt

2 cups freshly squeezed
orange juice

1 tablespoon freshly squeezed lime juice

¼ cup sugar

¼ teaspoon powdered ginger or 2 dime-
size pieces of crystallized ginger

Fresh sprigs mint or
blueberries, for garnish

Place all ingredients in a food processor or blender and purée. Freeze the mixture in an uncovered bowl until it is the consistency of frozen slush, 2 to 4 hours. Return the mixture to the food processor or blender. Purée again. Spoon the mixture into chilled glasses. Garnish with fresh mint or blueberries.

— Recipe by Laurie Todd

Lively Lemony Punch

This herbal punch is refreshing on a hot summer day. For a pretty touch, use ice cubes with sprigs of lemony herbs frozen in them, and add a fresh sprig of lemon verbena or balm to the punch. For a spiked drink, add tequila or rum.

....

Fresh from the garden: LEMONGRASS, LEMON BALM, LEMON VERBENA

Makes 13 cups | *160 calories, 0g fat, 25mg sodium; per cup*

....

1 large pineapple

5 stalks fresh lemongrass

Two 46-ounce cans
   pineapple juice

½ cup freshly squeezed lemon juice

1 large bunch each fresh lemon balm
   and lemon verbena

3 lemons, cut into rounds

2 limes, cut into rounds

One 12-ounce bottle
   ginger ale

....

Peel and core the pineapple and cut it into bite-size chunks. Discard the rough outer leaves of 4 stalks of lemongrass. Gently mash the stalks and cut them into 2-inch segments. Save the fifth stalk for garnish.

Place the pineapple chunks, lemongrass, pineapple juice, lemon juice, and herbs (reserving some for garnish) in a glass pitcher and chill overnight.

Remove the herbs. Add the lemon and lime slices, the ginger ale, and fresh herb sprigs. Pour into tall glasses with a fresh piece of lemongrass in each glass.

— *Recipe by Lucinda Hutson*

Carrot Tomato Smoothie

If you always think of smoothies as fruit-based concoctions, give this savory vegetable version a try. It's a great way to drink up tomatoes from the summer garden.

....

Fresh from the garden: CARROTS, TOMATOES, PARSLEY, CELERY
1 serving | *160 calories, 1.5g fat, 250mg sodium*

....

1 cup carrot juice	¼ cup fresh parsley	Celery stalk and toasted
2 cups frozen tomato pieces	Dash of salt	sunflower seeds for garnish,
or cherry tomatoes	Hot sauce, optional	optional

....

If you can get fresh carrot juice, use it. And if you own a juicer, juice your own carrots. If not, you can use bottled juice.

Blend the carrot juice with the frozen tomatoes in the blender. Add the parsley at the last minute so that it retains some texture and color. Add salt to taste. You may wish to add a dash of hot sauce for additional kick. Garnish with a celery stick and toasted sunflower seeds.

— *Recipe by Lynn Alley*

Strawberry Smoothie

Any and all berries are welcome here. When berry season hits, freeze any you can't eat and you'll have plenty on hand for when the fresh berries are long gone. The banana shouldn't be very ripe or its flavor will dominate.

Fresh from the garden: BERRIES

1 serving | *410 calories, 1.5g fat, 200mg sodium*

1 cup plain nonfat yogurt

2 cups frozen strawberries (blackberries, raspberries, or any other berry can be substituted)

1 banana

1 to 2 tablespoons honey (according to the tartness of the berries)

1 scoop strawberry sorbet, optional

Begin by pulsing all ingredients in the blender to get any large pieces chopped up. Then blend until smooth.

— *Recipe by Lynn Alley*

Lemon Zinger

This classic combination of lemon, fruit, and ginger is packed with vitamin C. Made with perfectly ripe, juicy, and delicious peaches or nectarines, it's the perfect summer cooler.

Fresh from the garden: PEACHES OR NECTARINES
1 serving | *230 calories, 0g fat, 10mg sodium*

1½ cups lemonade, preferably made with freshly squeezed lemon juice

2 peaches or nectarines, cut up and frozen

¾-inch piece of fresh ginger, peeled and grated

Whir all the ingredients in a blender until smooth.

— Recipe by Lynn Alley

Watermelon Milkshake with Cardamom

The juicy fruit of the watermelon vine makes for a light milkshake. Cardamom adds a deliciously haunting, barely there perfume to this refreshing afternoon treat or playful dessert. For a thicker shake, be sure the ice cream is hard. Alternatively, you can make the shake ahead, freeze until not quite solid, then reblend and serve.

Fresh from the garden: WATERMELON
2 servings | *180 calories, 8g fat, 55mg sodium*

2 cups seedless watermelon chunks

1 cup vanilla ice cream
2 pinches cardamom

Combine the ingredients in a blender and purée.
Serve immediately.

— Recipe by Didi Emmons

BREAKFAST, BRUNCH & Egg Dishes

Fruits, herbs, and greens shine in these recipes. All of them are simple, delicious dishes you can make for the morning meal, whether it's breakfast or brunch, but they can be enjoyed at other times as well. The Blueberry Breakfast Popover and Blackberries in Pecan Crêpes are a great way to start the day, but they could also qualify as dessert. Serve the Baked Eggs with Sorrel atop a salad as a lunch or starter course to dinner. The rest make lovely lunches or light dinners.

A ll too often, breakfast is an afterthought, the orphan of meals, the one that doesn't get much attention or effort. We're in a hurry, so we eat a bowl of cereal or grab a bagel, and we're out the door. When the weekend comes, we're ready for a different approach.

That's the time to make a vegetable quiche or a savory omelet. Not everything has to wait for the weekend, however. The Breakfast Fruit Bowl mélange of poached fruits can be made ahead, reheated quickly, and added to hot cereal, or eaten with granola or just yogurt.

Blueberry Breakfast Popover

The fluffy texture of this breakfast dish makes it fun to eat, and since you add the sweetness separately, everyone can have it just to their liking. It's also excellent made with other soft fruits (try raspberries and raspberry jam). Just be sure not to open the oven door during the first 20 minutes of baking, or the popover might fall.

Fresh from the garden: BLUEBERRIES

2 servings | *500 calories, 19g fat, 300mg sodium*

1¼ cups milk	1 cup flour	1 tablespoon melted butter
3 eggs	Pinch of salt	½ cup blueberries

Preheat the oven to 450°F. Butter an 8-inch nonstick sauté pan with an ovenproof handle.

In a blender, combine the milk, eggs, flour, salt, and butter. Blend on high for 2 minutes until the batter is thoroughly mixed and well aerated.

Pour the batter into the pan and sprinkle the blueberries over the batter.

Bake 35 to 40 minutes, resisting the temptation to peek for at least the first 20 minutes. The popover is done when the top is slightly crispy and a knife inserted into the center comes out clean. The popover should slide out of the pan. Serve immediately with maple syrup or blueberry preserves.

—*Recipe by Elizabeth Holland*

Breakfast Fruit Bowl

Heavily spiced and sweetened with maple syrup, this poached breakfast compote is warm, homey, and versatile. Poach the fruit the night before, then reheat and serve atop hot oatmeal, buttermilk pancakes, or waffles. Or eat the fruit topped with a spoonful of yogurt.

Fresh from the garden: APPLES, PEARS, BLUEBERRIES
4 servings | *310 calories, 1g fat, 0mg sodium*

2 large Golden Delicious apples	½ cup sugar	1 teaspoon cinnamon
2 firm pears	½ cup unsweetened apple juice	½ teaspoon allspice
Juice of 1 lemon	¼ cup pure maple syrup	¾ cup blueberries

Peel and core the apples and pears and cut them into 1-inch pieces. Toss in a bowl with the lemon juice and sugar and allow to macerate for 30 minutes.

In a large saucepan or frying pan, bring the apple juice, maple syrup, cinnamon, and allspice to a boil. Stir in the apples and pears and their juices and lower heat to a simmer. Poach, spooning the liquid over the pieces if they are not submerged until the fruit is soft and glazed-looking, about 15 to 20 minutes. Stir in the blueberries.

Serve immediately or allow fruit to cool in the pan, then cover and refrigerate.

—*Recipe by Edon Waycott*

Blackberries in Pecan Crêpes

If you haven't made crêpes before, don't be intimidated—they're easy and quick. To turn the crêpe, you can use tongs (with a gentle touch) or simply pick up one edge with your fingertips and quickly flip it. If your crêpe pan is small and you're dexterous, you can even flip the crêpe over with a flick of the wrist. The crêpes themselves can be made ahead, even the day before. Reheat gently on a hot pan just before assembling the dish.

Fresh from the garden: BLACKBERRIES
4 to 6 servings (makes 12 crêpes) | *180 calories, 13g fat, 35mg sodium; per crêpe*

¼ cup sugar	2 eggs	4 tablespoons finely chopped, toasted
2 cups blackberries	2 teaspoons melted butter,	pecans, plus more for garnish
½ cup flour	plus additional for the pan	1 cup mascarpone or whipped
Pinch of salt	1 cup milk	cream cheese
Pinch of sugar		

Place ¼ cup of water and the sugar in a small, heavy saucepan and cook over medium heat until the sugar is completely dissolved, about 2 minutes. Add the berries, reduce the heat, partially cover, and simmer for 5 minutes. Keep warm.

Mix the flour, salt, sugar, eggs, and the 2 teaspoons melted butter until smooth. Add the milk and stir to mix well. Stir in the pecans.

Melt a little butter in a small, nonstick or heavy frying pan over medium heat. Spoon in about 3 tablespoons of the crêpe batter, tilt the pan to spread it evenly, and cook until golden brown, 2 to 3 minutes. Turn and brown the other side. Remove the crêpe to a plate and keep warm while you prepare the rest.

To assemble, place 2 to 3 crêpes on a warm serving plate. Spoon four or five berries and a little of the berry syrup over one half of each crepe, and fold the other half over the filling. Top each crêpe with a sprinkling of pecans and a small dollop of mascarpone or cream cheese.

NOTE | To toast pecans, spread them whole on a shallow pan and bake in a 350°F oven until lightly browned, about 8 minutes. Check often because the amount of oil in the nuts will vary, and they could burn easily. The nuts will become crisp as they cool. You can also toast them in a frying pan on top of the stove, tossing often.

—*Recipe by Jane Adams Finn*

Baked Eggs with Sorrel

Sorrel's sword-shaped leaves pack a citrus tang that is splendid with eggs. Thin ribbons of sorrel hide in the bottom of buttered ramekins in this dish, perfuming the eggs as they bake.

Fresh from the garden: SORREL

4 servings | *150 calories, 14g fat, 150mg sodium*

3 tablespoons butter, melted	12 to 15 sorrel leaves, washed and patted dry	4 eggs Salt and freshly ground pepper

Preheat the oven to 350°F. Brush four ramekins with some of the melted butter. If the sorrel leaves are large, destem them. Then cut the leaves into chiffonade. To do this, stack the leaves and cut them into very thin ribbons.

Divide the sorrel equally among the ramekins. Crack an egg into each ramekin and season with salt and pepper. Spoon melted butter over each egg. Set the ramekins on a baking sheet and place in the oven. Bake until the eggs are just set, about 15 minutes. Serve immediately.

—*Recipe by Fran Gage*

Cooking with sorrel

Sorrel's one unfortunate quality is that it turns dull gray green when it meets the heat. If I'm making a sorrel purée, I'll mix in some finely chopped raw sorrel at the end to perk up the color. A sorrel butter—finely chopped, uncooked sorrel beaten into soft butter—is delicious on grilled fish.

Sorrel can be used like spinach. I like the lemony tang that tender, young leaves add to a tossed salad. I also add a few handfuls of chopped sorrel leaves to leek and potato soup. And sorrel pizza is terrific, too—just thin strips of sorrel, tomato slices, salt and pepper.

— *Fran Gage*

Savory Corn Pancakes with Pepper Relish

In late summer, at the height of corn season, make these as a refreshing change from sweet pancakes. They are great for breakfast and perfect for brunch.

....

Fresh from the garden: TOMATO, BELL PEPPERS, SCALLIONS, PARSLEY, MARJORAM, CORN

Fifteen 5-inch pancakes | *Pancakes—150 calories, 6g fat, 240mg sodium; per pancake*
Pepper relish—15 calories, 0g fat, 5mg sodium; per tablespoon

....

FOR THE PEPPER RELISH

1 tomato, seeded and
  finely chopped

½ red bell pepper, finely diced

½ yellow bell pepper, finely diced

2 scallions, including half of the
  greens, sliced thin

3 tablespoons chopped
  fresh parsley

2 teaspoons chopped marjoram

Salt

Freshly ground pepper

Dash of vinegar

FOR THE PANCAKES

Kernels from 4 ears of corn

1½ cups buttermilk

2 tablespoons vegetable oil
  or melted butter

3 eggs

½ teaspoon salt

1 cup fine stone-ground
  cornmeal

1¼ cups flour

1 teaspoon baking powder

½ teaspoon baking soda

Butter for frying

Sour cream

....

MAKE THE PEPPER RELISH | Combine the tomato, peppers, scallions, and herbs in a small bowl. Season with a few pinches of salt, a little pepper, and a dash of vinegar. Taste and correct the seasonings, if needed. Set aside while you make the pancakes.

MAKE THE PANCAKES | Purée ½ cup of the kernels in a blender with the buttermilk for about 1 minute. Add the oil, eggs, and salt. Blend until smooth, then transfer to a bowl and whisk in the dry ingredients, stirring until just blended. Fold in the remaining corn kernels.

Preheat the oven to 200°F. Melt a little butter in a nonstick frying pan. When it bubbles, pour in some of the batter (¼ cup yields a 5-inch cake). Cook over medium-high heat until covered with holes, then turn and cook until the second side is set, about 1 minute. Hold in the oven while you finish cooking the batter.

Serve 2 or 3 pancakes to a plate with a dollop of sour cream and a spoonful of the relish on each.

—Recipe by Deborah Madison

Omelet with Sautéed Garlic Scapes

When garlic scapes reach about 12 inches in length with no flower heads, they are ready for cooking. Use only the stems.

....

Fresh from the garden: GARLIC SCAPES

Makes one omelet | *340 calories, 27g fat, 370mg sodium; with 2 eggs*

....

Olive oil

3 tablespoons chopped garlic scapes

2 tablespoons sliced or chopped
   mushrooms

Up to 1 tablespoon butter

2 or 3 eggs, lightly beaten

Salt

Scant ¼ cup grated cheese
   of your choice

....

Drizzle a little olive oil into a small frying pan and set over medium heat. Add the garlic scapes and mushrooms and sauté, stirring frequently, about 3 minutes. Sample a garlic scape. It should be still crisp but tender enough to eat. Remove the scapes and mushrooms from the pan and set aside.

Add the butter to the frying pan. Salt the eggs and pour them into the hot pan, tipping the pan to spread them. Lower the heat. After the omelet has cooked long enough to solidify on the bottom, arrange the scapes, the mushrooms, and the cheese on one half. Fold the omelet over the filling. Cook to desired doneness (about 1 to 2 minutes), flipping once.

—*Recipe by Yael Bernier*

What's a garlic scape?

Some garlic varieties form curling stems like a flower stalk. (Technically garlic doesn't form flowers, but tiny bulbils instead.) The graceful, curving scapes make good eating. Cut into short pieces and sauté briefly in butter or olive oil. They're delicious in salads, egg dishes, soups, pasta sauces, and risottos.

I love to lay raw scapes on the bottom of the pan under a chicken before roasting. When the chicken is roasted, the scapes are deliciously browned and tender, with a mildly garlic flavor.

—*Ruth Lively*

Fines herbes enliven springtime cuisine

Springtime brings many good things, among them fresh parsley, chervil, tarragon, and chives. In France, these four herbs are ready to pick in March and, as a result, are often used together in presolstice French cooking. Together, a mixture of finely chopped chervil, tarragon, chives, and parsley is called *fines herbes* (pronounced FEEN airb). It serves as the main source of flavor for some dishes and just a finishing touch for others.

Making *fines herbes* is all about proportions. You need equal quantities of chopped parsley leaves, chopped chervil leaves, chopped tarragon leaves, and sliced chives. But it's important not to measure the herbs or combine them before chopping. For one thing, the chives are easier to slice than to chop. Also, the parsley, tarragon, and chervil must be chopped separately because each herb has a different texture and leaf structure. If you tried to chop all three together, the chervil and tarragon would only bruise while the parsley, with the sturdiest leaf, would be chopped.

Don't expect *fines herbes* to keep long. Parsley, chervil, tarragon, and chives are delicate herbs and once cut, they begin to dry, and tarragon, to slowly blacken. Prepare the herbs right before you plan to use them and respect their delicacy when cooking. If you are using *fines herbes* in a cooked dish, add it when you're almost done cooking so the heat won't destroy the herbs' freshness.

Use *fines herbes* to enliven simple dishes. I sprinkle it on top of roasted chicken or broiled pork tenderloins. For an exceptional dish, mash potatoes with *fines herbes* and olive oil. Boil the potatoes in their skins. When they are cooked, drain off the water and mash them just until lightly crushed. Drizzle fruity olive oil on the potatoes, add a few large pinches of *fines herbes*, and season with coarse salt. The potatoes are light and heady with the aroma of herbs, and they take all of five minutes of actual work.

Sprinkle *fines herbes* on salad greens before dressing, or add to a standard vinaigrette and let the mixture sit for about 20 minutes before tossing with the salad. *Fines herbes* enliven plain egg salad, and the profusion of herbs is excellent stirred into homemade mayonnaise. Omelets, sautéed mushrooms, blanched asparagus, young carrots, and other tender vegetables all benefit from a dose of *fines herbes*.

— *Amanda Hesser*

Fines Herbes Omelet

Fines herbes are a classic of French cuisine. This blend of chives, tarragon, chervil, and parsley is delicious with eggs, as here in this pretty omelet, or sprinkled on a creamy cheese, or in a spring salad of butter lettuce. Chervil only grows in cool weather, so this is a spring and fall herb mélange.

Fresh from the garden: CHIVES, PARSLEY, CHERVIL, TARRAGON
1 serving | *270 calories, 23g fat, 250mg sodium; with 2 eggs*

2 to 3 eggs
1 to 2 teaspoons cream or water
1 tablespoon softened butter

Salt and freshly ground pepper
Vegetable oil for brushing pan

1 tablespoon or more chopped
fines herbes (equal parts chives,
parsley, chervil, tarragon)

Whisk the eggs with the cream, softened butter, salt, and pepper. Heat a 7- to 8-inch omelet pan over medium heat, brush with vegetable oil, and pour in the eggs.

As the omelet cooks, lift the edges to allow the uncooked egg to flow under the cooked portion. Turn the heat down to allow the surface to cook to the desired creaminess. Sprinkle with herbs, fold in half, and slide onto a plate. Eat at once.

—*Recipe by Frederique Lavoiepierre*

Crustless Vegetable Quiche

Kale is a nutritional powerhouse, and this recipe calls for lots of it, in addition to other vegetables. And no crust means this quiche comes together in a snap.

Fresh from the garden: KALE, RED ONION, CARROT, POTATO

6 servings | 320 calories, 26g fat, 150mg sodium

12 large kale leaves
1 to 2 tablespoons olive oil
½ medium red onion, peeled and chopped
1 medium carrot, peeled and diced

1 medium Yukon Gold potato (about 6 ounces), peeled and diced
2 eggs
1 cup heavy cream
Generous ¼ teaspoon Chinese five-spice powder

1 cup grated Gruyère
½ cup fresh breadcrumbs
¼ cup grated aged Asiago or Parmigiano-Reggiano

Preheat the oven to 350°F. Butter a 10-inch deep-dish pie plate.

Wash and drain the kale, remove the midrib, and chop or tear the leaves; you should have about 6 cups. Heat the olive oil in a large frying pan over medium heat and sauté the onion until it's translucent, about 5 minutes. Add the carrot and potato and cook on medium-low heat, stirring occasionally, until the carrot is just tender, 10 to 12 minutes. Add the kale. Cover and cook until the kale is just wilted, about 2 minutes.

In a large bowl, beat the eggs and whisk in the cream. Stir in the five-spice powder, vegetables, and Gruyère. Pour the custard into the pie plate and top with the breadcrumbs and Asiago or Parmigiano-Reggiano. Bake until the custard is set and golden brown, about 30 minutes.

—*Recipe by Nan Wishner*

Red Orach Frittata

Orach, sometimes called mountain spinach, is a heat-tolerant relative of spinach. It comes in both red and green varieties. The leaves are delicious steamed or raw. Of course, regular spinach is a fine substitute in this frittata.

Fresh from the garden: POTATOES, ORACH OR SPINACH, CHIVES, DILL

6 servings | *210 calories, 10g fat, 530mg sodium*

3 small baking potatoes (about 1 large round)	10 eggs	1 teaspoon salt
4 to 5 cups coarsely chopped red orach	½ cup minced fresh chives	1 teaspoon freshly ground pepper
	¼ cup minced fresh dill	1 tablespoon butter

Peel the potatoes and cut into ½-inch cubes. Put the potatoes in a pan, cover with cold water, bring to a boil, and cook until tender. Drain and set aside to cool.

Steam the orach until just wilted, 2 to 3 minutes. Cool, and then squeeze out as much water as possible with your hands. Set aside.

Preheat the broiler. Whisk the eggs in a bowl with the chives, dill, salt, and pepper. In a large, ovenproof frying pan, melt the butter over medium heat and swirl to coat the pan. Add the potatoes and orach. Stir briefly. Add the whisked eggs and stir again to distribute the ingredients evenly. Cook over medium heat until the bottom of the frittata is set and brown, and the eggs start to solidify at the top, about 5 minutes. Place the frying pan under the broiler until the frittata is brown and the eggs are set through. Let cool 10 minutes. Carefully slide or invert the frittata onto a large plate. Cut into wedges and serve.

—*Recipe by Jack Staub*

SAUCES,
Salsas &
VINAIGRETTES

This collection of recipes is to savory food what icing is to cake: Any one of the sauces, salsas, or vinaigrettes in the following pages will add pizzazz to your meals, lifting even the plainest foods out of the realm of the ordinary into Something Really Good. For that reason, these are some of the most exciting recipes in the book. A basic meal goes from good to memorable by having a bowl of Salsa Verde (or Tarragon & Hazelnut Pesto or perky Puttanesca Vinaigrette) on hand. Marinate fish in a little of the sauce before grilling, stir a ladleful into roasted vegetables just before serving, and put the rest on the table to drizzle wherever.

These recipes are a busy cook's best friends. They are quick to make, and they pay off in spades with big flavor. All can (and a few should) be made ahead, so you can do a little work when you have the time and reap the benefits all week long. When leftovers are on the menu, making up a fresh sauce or pesto to go along with it brings together a whole new meal.

Tomatillo Salsa Verde

Salsa verde is a staple of Mexican cuisine. It's an excellent all-purpose sauce that adds a south-of-the-border kick to many foods, from tacos to eggs to beans. Use it as is for a chip dip, or dress it up by stirring in chopped avocado and lime juice. It also goes wonderfully with meats. Brown pork chops, cover with salsa verde, and simmer everything in a tightly covered pan until the pork is tender. When you have leftover chicken, add salsa verde to make a quick enchilada dish—just pull the chicken apart into bite-size pieces, grate cheese, chop a mild onion, and combine. Fry corn tortillas in hot oil just until limp. Roll the chicken mixture in the tortillas and arrange in a casserole dish. Pour salsa verde over the tortillas and bake at 350°F for about 20 minutes.

....

Fresh from the garden: TOMATILLOS, ONION, GARLIC, CILANTRO, SERRANO CHILES
Makes 6 cups | *25 calories, 2.5g fat, 65mg sodium; per 2 tablespoons*

....

1 pound tomatillos (about 4 cups)	½ cup fresh cilantro	1½ teaspoons salt
1 cup chopped onion	2 serrano chile, seeds removed	½ cup oil
4 cloves garlic		

....

Husk the tomatillos and cut them in half. Place all the ingredients except 2 tablespoons of the oil in a blender or food processor with 1 cup of water and purée as smooth as you like.

Heat the remaining oil in a deep, heavy pan over medium heat. Pour in the purée and simmer for 10 to 12 minutes.

—*Recipe by Judy Barrett*

Parsley Salsa Verde

This piquant green sauce comes from Italy. It's a good match for grilled or roasted vegetables, meats, or fish. Spread it on a piece of crusty bread and top with a slice of ripe tomato for a simple summertime sandwich.

Fresh from the garden: PARSLEY, HERBS (BASIL, FENNEL, OR LOVAGE LEAVES), ARUGULA OR WATERCRESS, GARLIC | **Makes about 1^1/$_2$ cups** | *45 calories, 4.5g fat, 15mg sodium; per tablespoon*

One 1-inch slice stale country bread, crusts removed

2 cups packed fresh Italian parsley

½ cup packed fresh basil, fennel, or lovage leaves, or a mixture

½ cup packed arugula or watercress, optional

½ cup olive oil

2 or 3 cloves garlic, minced

2 teaspoons capers

2 tablespoons herb or wine vinegar

Salt and freshly ground pepper

Soak the bread in a little water for 10 minutes, and then squeeze out most of the liquid. Set the bread aside.

If you are using a mortar and pestle, pound the parsley, herbs, and arugula until they begin to break down and become pastelike. Use a little of the oil if necessary. Add the bread and garlic to the mortar and pound until well mashed; you should have a coarse green paste. Add the olive oil to the herbs as if making a mayonnaise, a few drops at a time, blending with the pestle to incorporate the oil. When all the olive oil has been added, pound in the capers and vinegar. Taste and season with salt and pepper as needed.

If you are using a food processor, combine the bread, parsley, herbs, arugula, garlic, capers, and vinegar in the work bowl. Pulse to chop coarsely, stopping to scrape down the sides. With the motor running, add the olive oil to the herbs in a thin stream, stopping to scrape down the sides if necessary. Taste and season with salt and pepper.

Let the sauce stand at least 30 minutes before using. Adjust the seasoning with salt, pepper, vinegar, or olive oil and serve at room temperature. The olive oil will not emulsify completely; a little will remain on top of the sauce. Leftover sauce will keep in a tightly covered glass container in the refrigerator up to 5 days.

—Recipe by Susan Belsinger

Basil Marinade

Soy sauce, ginger, and rice vinegar give this savory marinade an Asian profile. Marinate chicken or fish in it for several hours before grilling, or brush on vegetable kebabs, fish, or poultry shortly before cooking. This is a good place to use scented basils; try it with cinnamon or lime basil.

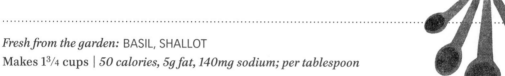

Fresh from the garden: BASIL, SHALLOT
Makes 1³/₄ cups | *50 calories, 5g fat, 140mg sodium; per tablespoon*

½ cup fresh basil leaves

⅓ cup freshly squeezed
   lemon juice

2 teaspoons honey

3 tablespoons soy sauce

¼ teaspoon powdered ginger

1 shallot, minced

2 tablespoons rice vinegar

½ cup olive oil

Stack 5 or 6 basil leaves together and, starting at the tips, roll the stack into a thin tube. Slice across the width of the tube into ¼-inch strips.

In a bowl, combine all of the ingredients. Stir until well blended.

—Recipe by Ellen Ogden

More great sauces, salsas, and vinaigrettes

In addition to the recipes in this chapter, you'll also find similar saucy accompaniments throughout the book. Sometimes the sauce was simply too critical to the success of the main recipe to be separated from it. (Of course, the Salads chapter, p.66, is full of vinaigrettes and dressings, too.) Here's a world of especially noteworthy sauces and dressings that'll keep your table well set.

Borrow the salsa from Spicy Carrot Fritters with Fresh Salsa (p. 6) anytime you need pico de gallo. This simple combo of tomato, onion, chile, and cilantro can be embellished with avocado—a little or a lot, depending on your taste and your menu.

Use the cilantro salsa from the Sweet Corn Soup recipe (p. 116) in tacos, on enchiladas, with grilled or sautéed vegetables, or drizzled over the filling of a quesadilla before folding it closed. Of course, cilantro doesn't always dance to a Latin beat. The pesto from Roasted Parsnips & Carrots with Cilantro Pesto (p. 135) makes a savory dressing for noodles and rice that is perfect for a meal with Asian flavors. Or toss it with boiled new potatoes while they're still hot for a warm potato salad. And speaking of pesto, you won't want to miss the Sorrel Pesto (p. 193) that appears in the Risotto with Celery recipe. Use it with other risottos, with fish and shellfish, or with chicken.

Another sauce with an Asian profile is the soy dipping sauce from the Okra Tempura dish (p. 10). This is fabulous with shellfish. Try it with fried calamari, boiled or grilled shrimp or lobster, and seared scallops. It's also an excellent dip for grilled eggplant and—of course—potstickers.

Two vinaigrettes with continental flavors are from the New Potatoes with Chervil Vinaigrette recipe (p. 162), and the Sherry-Shallot Vinaigrette that accompanies our Eggplant "Sandwiches" (p. 8). The chervil vinaigrette makes a great dressing for a green salad, grilled or poached chicken or fish, or steamed shellfish; the sherry-shallot vinaigrette is a deliciously vibrant dressing for all kinds of grilled or roasted vegetables, fish, and meats. And last but certainly not least, the Catalan romesco sauce from the Potato & Chickpea Stew (p. 208–209) is one of the best in the book. Use it on grilled, roasted, or steamed vegetables, roasted meats and fish, and polenta. *¡Buen provecho!*

—*Ruth Lively*

Cucumber & Yogurt Raita

This cool and refreshing sauce is welcome in the summer, when cucumbers and fresh herbs are abundant. Eat it with all kinds of fish, grilled meats (it's ideal with lamb), or roasted or grilled vegetables. It's a perfect foil to spicy Indian food; stir it into basmati rice, along with lots of freshly ground pepper and chopped scallions.

Fresh from the garden: CUCUMBER, A MIX OF DILL AND PARSLEY, OR CILANTRO AND MINT
4 servings | *35 calories, 1.5g fat, 25mg sodium*

1 cup peeled, coarsely grated cucumber	Salt ¾ cup plain yogurt	1½ tablespoons minced fresh dill and parsley, or cilantro and mint

Toss the grated cucumber with a large pinch of salt. Place in a colander set in the sink or over a bowl and let stand for 30 minutes or so. Squeeze the cucumbers to press out the juices. Much of the salt should wash away with the juices, but taste a bit of cucumber; if it seems too salty, rinse and press dry in a clean towel. Combine with yogurt and herbs, taste, and add more salt if necessary. Chill until ready to serve.

—*Recipe by Frederique Lavoipierre*

Sage & Roquefort Pesto

This pesto is great with grilled pork chops or roasted pork, or stirred into black bean soup, polenta, white beans, or pasta. Try adding some to stuffing. And it is superb on burgers.

Fresh from the garden: SAGE, PARSLEY, SPINACH, GARLIC
Makes about ²/₃ cup | *60 calories, 6g fat, 50mg sodium; per tablespoon*

⅓ cup fresh sage leaves

¾ cup fresh flat-leaf parsley leaves

¾ cup spinach

2 tablespoons toasted walnuts
   or pecans

2 large cloves garlic, smashed

3 tablespoons extra-virgin olive oil

1 to 2 ounces Roquefort or other
   strong blue cheese

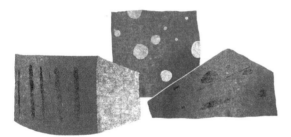

Blend the sage, parsley, spinach, nuts, and garlic in a food processor or blender until finely minced. Add the oil and cheese and process until blended.

—*Recipe by Steven van Yoder*

Thyme Mayonnaise

This mayonnaise is fabulous on sandwiches. The next time you have leftover roast chicken or turkey (or pork, beef, or lamb!), whip up of this mayonnaise and see if it doesn't make a good thing even better. It's also perfect for making deviled eggs.

Fresh from the garden: THYME
Makes 1¼ cups | *100 calories, 11g fat, 85mg sodium; per tablespoon*

1 egg

¾ teaspoon salt

2 tablespoons vinegar or Thyme Vinegar (see facing page)

½ teaspoon dry mustard

¼ teaspoon paprika

3 tablespoons fresh thyme (caraway thyme is especially good)

1 cup vegetable oil

An hour before making the mayonnaise, take the egg from the refrigerator. A cold egg won't take up oil as easily as a room-temperature egg.

Place the egg, salt, vinegar, spices, and thyme leaves in a blender or food processor and process until the egg is thoroughly blended. With the motor running, gradually add the oil in a thin stream. If the mayonnaise is too thick, thin it with a bit of water or more vinegar. Stored in the refrigerator, this mayonnaise will keep 3 to 4 days.

—*Recipe by Rex Talbert*

The best of thymes

Like many herbs, different types of thyme have different flavor nuances. My favorites include French thyme, lemon thyme, oregano-scented thyme, and caraway thyme. French thyme is the one most people know, and it's the most versatile. Lemon thyme goes well with vegetables and meats that aren't too strong in flavor, like chicken and pork, and is especially good with fish. I particularly like oregano-scented thyme in Italian and Middle Eastern dishes. I use caraway thyme in the same foods that call for caraway, especially sauerkraut and breads.

Thyme leaves release their essential oils most readily into fats, so butter and oil are good vehicles for thyme's flavor. An herb butter made by blending chopped leaves into softened butter is also a good way to preserve the harvest for use during winter. You can make it up and freeze it in a log shape or in small portions to rub on poultry before roasting, to thicken sauces, or simply to spread on bread and eat. I also like to make a blend of olive oil, oregano-scented thyme, and garlic. This concoction is delicious brushed on pita or bread and then grilled or heated in the oven.

Of course, you don't have to use fats to enjoy thyme's flavor. It works very well in a sherry and soy marinade for grilled tuna. I also like to infuse apple-cider vinegar with caraway thyme. I fill a clean bottle one third of the way full of thyme stems, add a clove of garlic, and then fill with vinegar. After a few weeks in a dark cupboard, the vinegar can be strained and rebottled. I use it on cooked greens and in homemade mayonnaise like the one on the facing page.

—*Rex Talbert*

Worth the effort

HOMEMADE MAYONNAISE

Homemade mayonnaise is a special treat, with a silky texture and a rich taste that store-bought just can't match. So while I always keep a jar of mayo on hand for everyday use, there are times when nothing but homemade will do. I especially love tweaking the seasonings. During tomato season, I make green garlic mayonnaise, which is flavored with garlic, basil, cilantro, and arugula, all ground to a paste in a mortar with a pinch of coarse sea salt. Post-Thanksgiving turkey sandwiches call for mayonnaise spiked with hot sauce. For composed salads that feature potatoes, cold vegetables, and leftover grilled fish or canned or poached tuna, I want a big dollop of golden lemon-saffron mayonnaise, made with lemon juice, a little grated zest, and a pinch of saffron. And I love to make garlicky aïoli for sandwiches, for dipping roasted or grilled vegetables, and for shellfish.

I'm not a traditionalist about method. I've made mayonnaise with a mortar and pestle and with a bowl and a whisk, but a blender is easier and quicker, which means I make mayonnaise more often.

If you're concerned about the safety of making mayonnaise with raw eggs, there's a USDA-sanctioned technique for pasteurizing the egg yolks by heating them gently in a small saucepan with vinegar or lemon juice and water, whisking all the while, until they reach a temperature of 160°F. Combining the yolks with acid and water while constantly stirring is key to preventing them from cooking. As soon as the mixture has reached the right temperature, take it off the heat, let sit for a few minutes, then scrape into the blender (or your bowl or mortar) and proceed with your recipe.

—*Ruth Lively*

Aïoli

This pungent olive oil and garlic mayonnaise from the south of France is a very robust, assertive sauce. Aïoli is best made summer through fall, when garlic is still fresh and juicy. You can make a tamer version by using less garlic. If an all-olive-oil mayonnaise is too powerful for your taste, substitute a neutral oil, such as canola or safflower, for some of the olive oil. You'll need a mortar to crush the garlic, salt, and yolks to a smooth paste, but if your mortar isn't large enough to make the full aïoli, transfer the egg yolk and garlic mixture to a medium mixing bowl and blend in the oil with a whisk.

....

Fresh from the garden: GARLIC

Makes about 1³/₄ cups | *110 calories, 12g fat, 140 mg sodium; per tablespoon*

....

5 to 15 cloves garlic	2 egg yolks	Juice of half a lemon
2 to 3 teaspoons Kosher salt	1½ cups extra-virgin olive oil	

....

Place 5 to 15 (depending on your personal preference) cloves of garlic in a large marble or porcelain mortar, add the salt, and pound with a wooden pestle until the garlic is reduced to a near-liquid paste. Add the egg yolks and, using the pestle, incorporate them into the garlic. Slowly pour in your best extra-virgin olive oil in a very thin stream and beat continuously with the pestle. As the mixture thickens, increase the flow of the olive oil slightly. Taste the sauce, add the lemon juice, and, if necessary, thin with 1 or 2 teaspoons warm water. Refrigerate the aïoli, covered, until ready to use.

—*Recipe by Michele Anna Jordan*

Chile Oil

Blended with lemon or lime juice, this chile oil makes a delightful warm dressing for fish or a chilled marinade for seafood, like seviche. Use one part chile oil to two parts lemon or lime juice. Add scallions and chopped parsley or cilantro.

Fresh from the garden: CORIANDER SEEDS, BELL PEPPER
Makes 2 cups | *120 calories, 14g fat, 5mg sodium; per tablespoon*

1 cup canola oil
1 cup olive oil
1 tablespoon chili powder
½ teaspoon dry mustard

½ teaspoon whole coriander seed
½ teaspoon ground cumin seed
½ teaspoon ground paprika

1 tablespoon dried chiles
   or ¼ of a chipotle
¼ red bell pepper, chopped

Place oils in a 4-quart saucepan. Add spices and peppers. Heat the oil briefly (do not boil), then remove from heat and allow to sit for one hour. Strain into glass jars and store, covered and refrigerated, for up to 10 days.

—*Recipe by Diane Forley*

Puttanesca Vinaigrette

This vinaigrette is a riff on traditional puttanesca, a spicy pasta sauce pungent with anchovies, capers, garlic, and black olives. Use it with pasta, grilled fish, and Mediterranean dishes, or chilled with antipasti.

Fresh from the garden: SHALLOTS, ONION, GARLIC, TOMATOES, PARSLEY
Makes 3½ cups | *25 calories, 2g fat, 0mg sodium; per tablespoon*

2 shallots, chopped fine
½ Spanish onion, chopped fine
½ cup olive oil
3 cloves garlic, chopped fine

5 large beefsteak tomatoes,
   4 coarsely chopped, 1 seeded
   and chopped fine
2 tablespoons capers, drained
3 anchovies, rinsed in cold water

2 tablespoons sugar
¼ cup balsamic vinegar
Salt and freshly ground pepper
¼ cup fresh flat-leaf parsley,
   leaves only, chopped

Gently sauté the shallots and onion in 2 tablespoons of the olive oil in a covered pan over low heat until translucent. When they're almost done, add the garlic. Then add the 4 coarsely chopped tomatoes. Cook the tomatoes, uncovered, over medium-low heat for 15 minutes.

Add the capers, anchovies, and sugar. Cook another 5 minutes, remove from heat, and cool. Place the sauce in a food processor and purée until thick.

Stir in the balsamic vinegar. Slowly whisk in the remaining olive oil. Season with salt and pepper. Fold in the finely chopped tomatoes and the parsley.

—*Recipe by Diane Forley*

Red-Wine Vinaigrette

This vinaigrette gains sweetness, complexity, and color thanks to the beet juice, so although it's listed as an optional ingredient, I urge you to use it. This dressing is good with chilled vegetables like leeks or tomatoes, mesclun greens, or even summer fruits.

Fresh from the garden: SHALLOTS
Makes 2 cups | *80 calories, 9g fat, 0mg sodium; per tablespoon*

¾ cup red-wine vinegar
2 shallots, minced
2 tablespoons sugar

1 tablespoon beet juice, optional
1¼ cups extra-virgin olive oil
Salt

1 teaspoon freshly ground pepper

Heat the red-wine vinegar with the shallots and sugar in a saucepan. Add the beet juice, which will liven up the color and turn the shallots a deep purple. Heat the liquid gently without boiling for at least 10 minutes.

Cool, and then whisk in the olive oil and season with salt and pepper.

—*Recipe by Diane Forley*

Invigorate your vinaigrettes by boosting your vinegars

There are several ways to put a spin on the classic vinaigrette. First, you can expand your choice of vinegars. Good ones include red-wine, white-wine, champagne, sherry, and balsamic. Each has distinctive properties.

RED-WINE VINEGAR– robust flavor, best with assertive foods

WHITE-WINE VINEGAR– lighter, good for delicate flavors

CHAMPAGNE VINEGAR– light, especially good for infusions and vegetable marinades

SHERRY VINEGAR– sweeter and more complex than other wine vinegars; good on substantial salads, especially those including meat; excellent with nut oils

BALSAMIC VINEGAR– dark, pungent, sweet, and tart; good in vinaigrettes or on its own

Take your vinegars a step further by infusing them with herbs and vegetables; good choices include onions, shallots, garlic, beets, or ginger. Put the vinegar and your additions of choice in a nonreactive pan and heat without boiling for 10 minutes. Let cool, then strain, and the vinegar is ready to use.

You can make an intense vinegar reduction by boiling vinegar until it is reduced by half or more. This softens the raw edges and results in a syrup with a sweet-sour taste, heightened flavor, and added viscosity. Sherry and balsamic vinegars are particularly good candidates for reduction.

— *Diane Forley*

Fast, Fresh, Piquant Tomato Sauce

This is a variation of the goes-with-everything Mexican table sauce, *salsa fresca*. The recipe calls for dried chiles, but if chile heat is not to your taste, use sweet pepper. In hot weather, this sauce is good over cold fare—one less thing to cook and one more interesting element.

Fresh from the garden: ONION, GARLIC, PLUM TOMATOES, CILANTRO
Makes 3½ cups | *45 calories, 0.5g fat, 10mg sodium; per ½ cup*

1 large yellow onion, chopped	8 large plum tomatoes (1 pound), chopped into ½-inch pieces	Juice of 2 oranges with pulp
4 large cloves garlic, chopped	Salt	⅔ cup coarsely chopped fresh cilantro
1 dried chile de arbol or other small dried chile, crumbled		

Warm a large, nonstick frying pan over high heat. Add the onion, garlic, and chile, and sauté, stirring, until the onions have softened and you feel the chile fumes in your throat, about 3 minutes.

Add the tomatoes; sprinkle the mixture with salt to taste, and stir until well blended. Cover and cook, stirring frequently and shaking the pan, until the tomatoes have slightly darkened and exuded some of their juice, about 5 minutes. Remove from the heat, blend in the orange juice and cilantro, taste for seasoning, and serve.

—*Recipe by Sylvia Thompson*

Apple Chipotle Salsa

The combo of chipotles, which are dried, smoked jalapeños, and apples results in a smoky-sweet salsa that is excellent for chips. Serve it with a generous dollop of sour cream that has been thinned slightly with milk. Try it also as a sweet surprise in a burrito. For this recipe, be sure to use dry chipotles, not those canned in adobo sauce.

Fresh from the garden: APPLE, ONION, BELL PEPPER, CILANTRO
Makes 1³/₄ cup | 90 calories, 7g fat, 45mg sodium; per ¹/₄ cup

2 dry chipotles

¹/₃ cup pumpkin seeds, lightly toasted

1 hard apple, such as Fuji or Cortland, diced large

¹/₂ small onion, coarsely chopped

1 small green bell pepper, coarsely chopped

2 tablespoons chopped fresh cilantro

Juice of 1 lime

1 tablespoon cider vinegar

2 tablespoons extra-virgin olive oil

Large pinch of salt

Pour 1 cup of boiling water over the chipotles, and let them soak until they soften, about 25 minutes. Remove them from the water, but save the water. Finely chop the chipotles.

Place the chipotles, pumpkin seeds, apple, onion, and bell pepper in a food processor. Pulse until the mixture is finely chopped and transfer the mixture to a bowl. Add ¹/₄ cup of the chipotle liquid, the cilantro, lime juice, vinegar, olive oil, and salt. Stir well and serve.

—*Recipe by Didi Emmons*

Grilled Tomato & Corn Salsa

This salsa pairs wonderfully with fish, particularly grilled swordfish. I also like adding cubed avocado and serving it as a guacamole-like appetizer with chips.

....

Fresh from the garden: TOMATOES, ONION, JALAPEÑO, CORN, GARLIC, CILANTRO
Makes 2 cups | *30 calories, 0g fat, 5mg sodium; per ¼ cup*

....

2 medium tomatoes	1 ear of corn, husked	1 tablespoon chopped fresh cilantro
½ red onion, thickly sliced	1 clove garlic, minced	Large pinch ground cumin
1 jalapeño	1 lime	Salt and freshly ground pepper

....

Place the tomatoes, onion, jalapeño, and corn over a low to medium fire on a grill. Move them around with tongs until each is well grilled, with visible dark spots.

Place the vegetables on a cutting board. Finely chop the tomato, onion, and jalapeño and strip the corn kernels from the cob. Place the vegetables in a bowl.

Add the garlic. Cut the lime in half and squeeze the juice into the salsa. Press one half of the lime hard onto the cutting board and cut away the flesh that sticks out from the inside. Add this to the salsa, and then do the same to the other lime half. Add the cilantro, cumin, and salt and pepper to taste.

—*Recipe by Didi Emmons*

Sweet & Savory Cherry Sauce

This tantalizing herb-infused wine sauce is delicious with duck, chicken, or roast pork. Make up extra during cherry season and stash jars in the freezer to bring out during the winter holidays. A pretty jar of this makes a welcome gift, too.

Fresh from the garden: BAY LEAVES, THYME, SWEET CHERRIES
Makes 2 cups | *70 calories, 0.5g fat, 25mg sodium; per ¼ cup*

2 cups dry red wine
1 tablespoon lightly packed
   brown sugar
3 whole bay leaves
4 sprigs fresh thyme
6 whole cloves

2 sticks cinnamon, about
   3 inches long
3 strips orange zest
10 whole black peppercorns
2 cups pitted dark sweet cherries
2 teaspoons cornstarch

2 tablespoons freshly squeezed
   orange juice
Pinch of salt
⅛ teaspoon coarsely ground
   black pepper

In a medium saucepan over high heat bring the wine, sugar, bay leaves, thyme, cloves, cinnamon, orange zest, and peppercorns to a boil. Reduce heat and simmer until the volume is reduced by half, about 20 minutes. Strain and return the liquid to the saucepan and add the cherries. Continue cooking over low heat until the cherries are softened, about 5 minutes. Bring to a boil again.

Dissolve the cornstarch in the orange juice and add to the saucepan. Stir constantly until the sauce thickens, about 3 minutes. Remove from the heat and stir in the salt and black pepper.

—*Recipe by Edon Waycott*

Chimichurri

Chimichurri is a zesty sauce from Argentina, where it is served on grilled meats or savory meat-filled empanadas. It makes a wonderful marinade for vegetables and fish, too. Stir some into plain boiled rice or oven-roasted vegetables. Unlike salsa verde (another garlicky, parsley-based sauce), chimichurri is spicy with red pepper, but has no capers.

Fresh from the garden: GARLIC, PARSLEY, CILANTRO, ROSEMARY
Makes 1¼ cups | 50 calories, 5g fat, 30mg sodium; per tablespoon

2 to 4 cloves garlic, minced
1 cup coarsely chopped fresh parsley
¼ cup coarsely chopped fresh cilantro
1½ teaspoons dried oregano

1 teaspoon dried thyme
1 teaspoon chopped fresh rosemary
¾ teaspoon freshly ground pepper
½ teaspoon crushed red pepper flakes

⅓ cup red-wine vinegar
½ cup olive oil
¼ teaspoon salt

Combine the ingredients in a blender or food processor
until they are finely chopped but not pulverized.

—*Recipe by Deborah Madison*

Ketchup

If this looks like a lot of ketchup, you can easily cut the recipe in half. It's so good, though, you might not want to.

....

Fresh from the garden: ONIONS, CORIANDER SEEDS, GARLIC, PASTE TOMATOES
Makes 3 quarts | 5 calories, 0g fat, 15mg sodium; per tablespoon

....

2 tablespoons olive oil

2 large onions, sliced ⅔ inch thick

1 teaspoon coriander seeds

1 teaspoon cumin seeds

1 teaspoon mustard seeds

1 cup red-wine vinegar

⅓ cup plus 1 tablespoon packed brown sugar

1 head garlic, cloves separated and peeled

¼ cup capers with their brine

¼ cup hot sauce

¾ teaspoon paprika

¾ teaspoon cinnamon

¾ teaspoon allspice

¾ teaspoon powdered ginger

¾ teaspoon freshly ground black pepper

¾ teaspoon powdered cardamom

Salt

6 to 7 pounds paste tomatoes

....

Lightly oil the onion slices and grill or broil them until blackened, about 15 minutes per side.

In a small, heavy frying pan, toast the coriander, cumin, and mustard seeds over medium heat until fragrant, about 5 minutes. Grind the toasted spices in a mortar and pestle or a spice grinder.

Put all the ingredients in a deep, heavy, nonreactive pot. Simmer the ketchup, uncovered, over low heat for about 3 hours, stirring it every 15 minutes to break up the tomatoes and to keep the ketchup from sticking to the bottom of the pot. The mixture should thicken.

Purée the ketchup in batches in a blender or food processor or use an immersion blender. If the puréed ketchup seems too thin, put it back in the pot and continue cooking until it has reduced to a consistency you like.

—Recipe by David Page and Barbara Shinn

SALADS

Green salads, fruit salads, slaws, warm salads, and marinated salads—there's a salad here for every occasion and craving. Some are intended to be the main event; others can be enjoyed as a side salad, or easily become a light meal when accompanied by a few slices of rustic bread and your favorite cheese.

Just a handful of the salads here are lettuce based. The focus is on nonlettuce greens, plus a whole range of vegetables, roots, and even fruits, for a collection of salads that are vibrant and exciting. My goal is to broaden your salad repertoire. Never had kohlrabi? Try it in a delightful little salad with fennel. There are some wonderful slaws in here, and not one with a run-of-the-mill mayonnaise dressing. For a winter celebration meal, I urge you to try the Winter Slaw of Roots in its zesty rum-spiked dressing.

And when the cherry tomatoes start producing, try Bread Salad with Tomatoes, Onions, and Olives. Both comforting and exciting at the same time, it's a meal in itself.

Not that I've a bias against lettuce. The few lettuce salads in this chapter are ones that match a type of lettuce—butterhead, romaine, Batavian—to a dressing that works particularly well with the lettuce's texture and flavor. And finally, there are instructions for making savory croutons, which will transform any green salad from basic to terrific.

Mâche with Beets & Walnuts

Mâche, also called field salad or corn salad, is a gorgeous little green with a delicate, nutty flavor. It's harvested and sold—and sometimes served—with the whole petite plant left intact. In North America, mâche is a specialty green, but in Germany and France, it's well known, much loved, and widely available. It thrives in cool weather, which means it's a spring or fall crop. If you can't find it at your market, growing it from seed is a cinch.

Fresh from the garden: BEETS, MÂCHE
8 servings | *140 calories, 13g fat, 30mg sodium*

½ pound beets, skins on
2 teaspoons caraway seeds, optional
5 tablespoons walnut oil

1 tablespoon red-wine vinegar
1 tablespoon balsamic vinegar
Salt

Freshly ground white pepper
½ pound mâche, washed and dried
½ cup chopped walnuts

Put the beets and caraway seeds in a small saucepan and add enough water to cover the beets. Bring the water to a boil, reduce the heat, and simmer the beets until tender, 30 to 40 minutes. Run the beets under cold water, and then remove their skin. (Alternatively, the beets may be wrapped in foil, baked whole in the oven, and then peeled.) When they're cool, chop the beets into ½-inch cubes and set aside in a bowl. The beets can be prepared in advance, but the rest of the recipe should be done just before serving.

Make the vinaigrette by combining the oil, vinegars, salt, and pepper. Pour half the mixture over the beets and allow them to marinate for about 30 minutes.

Arrange the mâche in a large bowl or on separate plates. Add the marinated beets and the walnuts, and mix gently. Drizzle the remaining vinaigrette over the salad. Serve immediately.

—*Recipe by Ingrid Bauer*

Curly Endive Salad with Bacon Dressing

This dish is so easy, so elegant, and so delicious. A hot dressing poured on at the last minute wilts the greens just slightly. With a couple of toasted slices of baguette spread with goat cheese, you've got a light lunch. Even better, set a poached egg atop the greens. Then put some French café music on and enjoy a classic bistro lunch. *Bon appétit!*

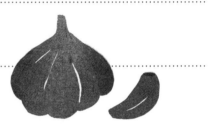

Fresh from the garden: CURLY ENDIVE (FRISÉE), GARLIC

4 servings | *200 calories, 14g fat, 180mg sodium*

2 heads curly endive	1 clove garlic, chopped
¼ pound bacon, diced	½ cup white wine

Separate the endive leaves, wash well, and spin dry. Place on serving plates.

Slowly fry the bacon pieces until brown. Remove the bacon from the pan. Pour off all but 3 tablespoons fat.

Sauté the garlic in the remaining bacon fat until lightly browned, and add the wine. Reduce the liquid by one-third, and then return the bacon to the pan. Pour the dressing over the endive on the serving plates.

— Recipe by Ed Miller

Kohlrabi & Fennel Salad

Kohlrabi has a delightful, delicate flavor—like a very mild cabbage with a touch of sweetness. Raw, it is crisp and crunchy with an applelike texture. When cooked Kohlrabi's fine-grained interior retains its integrity or makes a velvety purée. Kohlrabi is delectable sliced, steamed until barely tender, and served in a silky egg-lemon avgolemono sauce. Or try it cut into wedges and sautéed in a little butter with a sprinkling of fresh dill. Cooking diced kohlrabi in a *mirepoix* (equal amounts of finely chopped sautéed carrots, celery, and onion) with such herbs as parsley, thyme, marjoram, or dill is an excellent way to bring out its subtle sweetness. Diced, it makes a great soup or stew ingredient or a marvelous addition to stir-fries.

....

Fresh from the garden: KOHLRABI, FENNEL, PARSLEY
6 servings | *150 calories, 14g fat, 150mg sodium*

....

6 to 8 small kohlrabies (1½ cups)
1 medium bulb fennel with leaves
¼ cup chopped fresh parsley
5 tablespoons olive oil

1 tablespoon freshly squeezed lemon juice
1 tablespoon white-wine vinegar
½ teaspoon sugar

¼ teaspoon salt
⅛ teaspoon freshly ground pepper

....

Prepare kohlrabies by peeling them and cutting off the tops and bottoms. Cut the bulbs into julienne until there is enough for 1½ cups.

Remove the outer layer of the fennel bulb if it is tough. Reserve the leaves. With the fennel lying on a cutting surface, slice it down the middle and, with a paring knife, remove the core from each half. Slice the fennel thin; the pieces will be semicircular. Mix the kohlrabi and fennel in a bowl, and add the parsley and 1 tablespoon chopped fennel leaves.

Whisk together the remaining ingredients, and toss the dressing with the kohlrabi and fennel. Allow the salad to marinate for 1 hour before serving.

— *Recipe by Ashley Miller*

Coleslaw with Ginger-Mustard Vinaigrette

Traditional coleslaw is creamy, tangy, and usually a little bit sweet. This version, too, includes tart and sweet elements. The vinaigrette spiked with chile, cilantro, and ginger replaces the usual mayonnaise dressing.

....

Fresh from the garden: CABBAGE, CARROTS, RED ONION, GARLIC, SERRANO CHILES, CILANTRO
8 servings | 230 calories, 19g fat, 130mg sodium

....

2½ pounds shredded cabbage
    (1 medium head of red or green
    cabbage, or ½ of each)
4 carrots, peeled and grated
1 small red onion, diced
2 tablespoons apple-cider vinegar
4 tablespoons freshly squeezed
    lemon juice

2 tablespoons Dijon mustard
2 cloves garlic, crushed and minced
1 or 2 serrano chiles, minced
2 teaspoons peeled and finely grated
    fresh ginger
1 tablespoon sugar

⅔ cup olive oil
3 tablespoons minced fresh cilantro
Kosher salt
Freshly ground pepper

....

In a medium bowl, toss together the shredded cabbage, carrots, and onion, and set aside.

Make the dressing by whisking together the vinegar, lemon juice, mustard, garlic, chile, ginger, and sugar. Slowly whisk in the oil and then add the cilantro. Taste the dressing, season with salt and pepper, and pour over the cabbage mixture. Toss until all vegetables are well coated.

Let rest 10 minutes before serving, or cover and chill until ready to serve.

— *Recipe by Michele Anna Jordan*

Spring Coleslaw

This slaw is especially nice made with Savoy cabbage, with its corrugated texture and yellow-green color. For the best flavor, try to make it early enough that it can chill for several hours.

Fresh from the garden: CABBAGE, RADISHES, CHIVES, DILL, PARSLEY, LOVAGE

6 servings | *210 calories, 19g fat, 390mg sodium*

3 tablespoons whole-grain mustard
3 tablespoons balsamic vinegar
1 tablespoon sugar
½ cup vegetable oil

2 tablespoons milk or half-and-half
6 cups shredded cabbage
3 cups thinly sliced spring radishes
¼ cup minced fresh chives

¼ cup minced fresh herbs, a mixture
   of dill, parsley, and lovage
½ teaspoon salt
¼ teaspoon freshly ground pepper

In a food processor or a bowl, combine the mustard, vinegar, and sugar and pulse or whisk to combine. Add the oil, a little at a time until it thickens. Add the milk and pulse or whisk again. Set aside.

In a large bowl, toss the cabbage and radishes. Add the dressing, fresh herbs, salt, and pepper, and mix well. Chill the slaw for at least 2 hours. Taste, adjust the seasoning, and serve.

— *Recipe by Cynthia Hizer*

Winter Slaw of Roots

Who would think that these humble roots could make such a lovely and delicious slaw? The rum-spiked dressing is truly exceptional—walnut oil adds depth and complexity, and a mixture of citrus gives it a tart, bright flavor. This slaw is perfect for Thanksgiving or any special holiday meal. Consider making extra so you can send some home in pretty glass jars with your guests. Just be sure to save enough to tuck into the next day's turkey sandwich!

Fresh from the garden: CELERY ROOT, CARROTS, RUTABAGA, TURNIPS, WATERCRESS
6 servings | *240 calories, 18g fat, 75mg sodium*

¼ cup sherry vinegar

2 tablespoons orange blossom honey

2 tablespoons dark rum

Juice and zest of 1 lime

Juice and zest of 1 orange

1 tablespoon peeled and grated
  fresh ginger

½ cup walnut oil

1½ cups shredded celery root

1 cup shredded carrots

1½ cups shredded rutabaga

1¼ cups shredded turnips

1 cup chopped watercress

For the vinaigrette, combine the vinegar, honey, rum, fruit juice, zest, and ginger in a large serving bowl. Whisk in the walnut oil. Set aside.

As you finish shredding and measuring each root vegetable, add it to the vinaigrette bowl. Toss and combine. Add the watercress last. Let the juices meld for 30 minutes to 1 hour at room temperature, or store in the refrigerator for 24 hours.

— *Recipe by Dorette Snover*

Asian Slaw

Salads that can be dressed in advance and left to sit on the counter until time to serve mean one less thing to do at the last minute. The dressing in this slaw gets a little heat from ginger, a little pungency from grated onion, and zing from lime juice. Altogether, the flavors satisfy that irresistible craving for Japanese food.

Fresh from the garden: ONION, CHINESE CABBAGE, SCALLION
4 servings | 90 calories, 4g fat, 550mg sodium

1-inch knob fresh ginger
1 tablespoon grated onion
2 tablespoons soy sauce
Juice and zest of 1 lime

1 tablespoon vegetable oil
10 cups shredded Chinese
   or green cabbage

1 scallion, thinly sliced
   on the diagonal

Peel the ginger and grate it on a fine-holed grater. Discard any fibers that don't make it through the grating holes. Put the ginger, grated onion, soy sauce, and lime juice into a blender and blend until emulsified. Save the zest for garnish.

Put the cabbage into a large bowl and pour the dressing over the cabbage. Toss well. Let it sit about 20 minutes. Just before serving, toss again, and scatter the scallion and lime zest atop the cabbage.

— *Recipe by Ruth Lively*

Watermelon Salad with Habanero & Basil

Cool watermelon and a fiery habanero chile combine in this sweet and spicy fruit salad. Tossed with lime juice and basil, it's terrific with grilled fish or chicken.

Fresh from the garden: WATERMELON, ONION, GRAPES, BELL PEPPER, HABANERO, BASIL
Makes 4 cups | *45 calories, 2g fat, 0mg sodium; per ½ cup*

2 cups watermelon chunks
¾ cup minced onion
½ cup seedless grapes, quartered

1 green bell pepper, finely chopped
1 to 2 teaspoons minced habanero chile
3 tablespoons lime juice

1 tablespoon olive oil
3 tablespoons thinly sliced fresh basil
Salt and freshly ground pepper to taste

Combine all the ingredients in a bowl and toss well. Let sit at least 30 minutes to allow the flavors to meld before serving.

— Recipe by Didi Emmons

Alexander-the-Great Salad

Another Mediterranean salad, this is a challenger to the all-too-familiar Caesar salad. Greeks grow a lot of cabbage and hand-harvest oregano from the wild, which explains the flavor profiles of the dish.

Fresh from the garden: CABBAGE, BELL PEPPER, SCALLIONS, OREGANO
6 servings | *180 calories, 15g fat, 370mg sodium*

1 small green cabbage,
    sliced into thin strips
1 roasted red bell pepper,
    sliced into thin strips
4 ounces feta

⅓ cup pitted Kalamata olives
4 scallions, medium sliced
2 tablespoons fresh oregano,
    stripped off stem and crushed
    between fingers

2 tablespoons freshly squeezed
    lemon juice
4 tablespoons extra-virgin olive oil
Salt and freshly ground pepper

Place the cabbage, sweet pepper, feta, olives, and scallions in a large bowl. Sprinkle the oregano on top.

Mix the lemon juice and olive oil in a small bowl until thoroughly blended, then pour over the cabbage mixture and toss gently but thoroughly. Season the salad to taste with salt and pepper.

— Recipe by Jeanne Quan

Mediterranean Cucumber Salad

Served atop a bed of salad greens or alongside slices of vine-ripened tomatoes, this salad is a meal in itself. It's best if made a couple of hours ahead of eating, making it ideal for entertaining or picnicking.

Fresh from the garden: CUCUMBER, RED ONION, PARSLEY
4 servings | 420 calories, 40g fat, 530mg sodium

2 cups ¼-inch-diced cucumber

1 cup crumbled feta

½ cup thinly sliced red onion

2 tablespoons chopped Kalamata olives

1 tablespoon chopped fresh parsley

1 cup ½-inch cubes of stale bread

Juice of 1 lemon

¾ cup extra-virgin olive oil

Salt and freshly ground pepper

Combine the cucumber, feta, onion, olives, parsley, and bread. Mix the lemon juice with the olive oil, then pour three-quarters of it onto the salad and stir gently. Sprinkle with salt and pepper to taste. Add more dressing if necessary to moisten the bread. Chill for at least 2 hours before serving.

— Recipe by Frederique Lavoiepierre

Bread Salad with Tomatoes, Onions & Olives

If you are a stranger to bread salads, you will be delighted by this discovery. They lend themselves easily to whatever variation strikes your fancy. Use excellent, country-style bread that is at least a day old (so that it will absorb the dressing but still have some tooth to it), and add enough vinaigrette to moisten the bread evenly. Then let the season, your garden, and your pantry be your inspiration.

Fresh from the garden: GARLIC, CHERRY TOMATOES, RED ONION, PARSLEY, SALAD GREENS

4 servings | *540 calories, 47g fat, 670mg sodium*

2 tablespoons red-wine vinegar

Juice of 1 lemon

1 teaspoon Dijon mustard

2 cloves garlic, minced or pressed

⅔ cup best-quality extra-virgin olive oil

Kosher salt and freshly ground black pepper

4 cups day-old Italian bread, cut into 1-inch cubes

2 to 2½ cups cherry tomatoes

1 small red onion, diced

3 tablespoons minced fresh Italian parsley

½ cup pitted Kalamata olives, sliced

Salad greens

In a small mixing bowl, combine the vinegar, lemon juice, mustard, and garlic. Whisk in the olive oil. Taste the dressing and season it with salt and several turns of black pepper. If you prefer a little more bite, add another tablespoon of vinegar.

In a large mixing bowl, toss together the bread and most of the dressing, reserving 2 or 3 tablespoons. Let the bread sit for 30 minutes.

To serve, add the tomatoes, onion, Italian parsley, and olives to the bread and toss together lightly. Add the remaining dressing, toss, taste the mixture, and season with salt and pepper, if necessary. Spread the salad greens on a serving platter, top with the bread salad, and serve immediately.

VARIATION | For a tantalizing bread salad that evokes the BLT, fry 4 slices of bacon in a heavy frying pan until they are just crisp; transfer to absorbent paper to drain. In a small bowl, combine 2 tablespoons of the bacon fat and enough olive oil to make ⅔ cup, then add to the vinegar mixture, as described above. Crumble the bacon over the top of the salad just before serving.

— *Recipe by Michele Anna Jordan*

Warm Onion & Spinach Salad

The slight char of briefly broiled red onions, sautéed peppers, and toasted hazelnuts all lend complexity to this salad. The spinach is given a brief turn in the hot pan and then everything is spooned over slices of fresh mozzarella and drizzled with balsamic.

Fresh from the garden: RED ONIONS, BELL PEPPER, CHIVES, PARSLEY, SPINACH

4 servings | *360 calories, 27g fat, 420mg sodium*

3 large red onions

8 slices fresh mozzarella, ¼ inch thick

2 tablespoons olive oil

2 tablespoons butter

1 yellow bell pepper, chopped

2 tablespoons chopped fresh chives

2 tablespoons chopped fresh parsley

½ teaspoon salt

¼ teaspoon freshly ground white pepper

¼ cup toasted hazelnuts, halved

1½ cups spinach, coarsely torn

Balsamic vinegar

Cut the onions into half-moon slices about ½ inch thick and arrange the slices on a baking sheet. Broil about 5 minutes, or until the skins begin to char. Remove from the broiler and set aside to cool.

Arrange the cheese on a serving platter, cover with plastic wrap, and refrigerate.

In a large frying pan, heat the oil and butter over low heat until the butter melts. Increase the heat to medium, and then add the peppers and sauté until the peppers begin to turn translucent, 7 to 10 minutes. Peel the onions and add them to the pan along with the chives, parsley, salt, and white pepper, and mix with a spoon. Add the hazelnuts and spinach, mix briefly, and remove from heat.

Remove the cheese from the refrigerator, and spoon the mixture over the slices. Season with a drizzle of balsamic vinegar and serve immediately.

— *Recipe by Barbara Ciletti*

Spring Harvest Salad

The height of spring is a heady time in the market and garden. Ripe fruits and vegetables are plentiful. This salad's offerings shine in a simple lemon vinaigrette.

Fresh from the garden: PARSLEY, THYME, SPINACH, MESCLUN, BEET GREENS, ENDIVE, SCALLIONS, CUCUMBERS, RASPBERRIES | *6 servings* | *260 calories, 22g fat, 380mg sodium*

FOR THE LEMON VINAIGRETTE

½ teaspoon salt

1 tablespoon freshly ground green peppercorns

2 tablespoons white-wine vinegar

1 tablespoon fresh lemon zest

6 to 7 tablespoons extra-virgin olive oil

3 tablespoons chopped fresh parsley

1 teaspoon fresh lemon thyme

½ teaspoon Dijon mustard

FOR THE SALAD

2 cups young spinach

2 cups mesclun mix

1 cup young beet greens

1 cup young endive or chicory

4 scallions, chopped

1 cup seeded, chopped cucumbers

4 ounces mild goat cheese, crumbled

1½ cups red raspberries

3 hard-boiled eggs, chopped

MAKE THE VINAIGRETTE | Put all the vinaigrette ingredients in a bowl and whisk together. Set aside.

MAKE THE SALAD | Rinse, drain, and tear the spinach, mesclun, beet greens, and endive into pieces, discarding any large stems. Place the greens, scallions, and cucumbers in the salad bowl and toss. Gently toss in the goat cheese. Add 1 cup of the raspberries. Drizzle the vinaigrette over the salad and toss lightly. Add the eggs and toss lightly. Top the salad with the remaining ½ cup of raspberries and serve immediately.

— *Recipe by Barbara Ciletti*

Wilted Red & Green Chopped Salad

Orach, Aztec red (also called red Aztec or lamb's quarters), and New Zealand spinaches are all pseudospinaches, plants that taste similar to true spinach and that can be used like true spinach. They all have one important difference, though: they love heat, which means you can grow them right through summer. If you can't find these spinach imitators, don't despair; this salad is just as good made with the real thing.

Fresh from the garden: ORACH, AZTEC RED SPINACH, NEW ZEALAND SPINACH (OR TRUE SPINACH), BELGIAN ENDIVE, GARLIC | **6 servings** | *270 calories, 22g fat, 1,010mg sodium*

3 cups coarsely chopped orach or Aztec red spinach

3 cups coarsely chopped New Zealand spinach

3 heads Belgian endive

¼ pound pancetta

8 ounces Gorgonzola

1 clove garlic

Scant ¼ cup olive oil

⅛ cup balsamic vinegar

Freshly ground pepper

Salt, if needed

Rinse the spinaches well, spin dry, and toss them in a bowl. Halve the endives, slice into slivers, and throw in with the spinach. Cut the pancetta into medium dice and sauté in a little olive oil until crisp. Reserve the pan drippings. Sprinkle the pancetta on the salad. Crumble Gorgonzola on top of everything.

Add the garlic clove and enough olive oil to the pancetta pan drippings to make ¼ cup. Add the balsamic vinegar and a few twists of fresh pepper. Taste, and add salt if necessary. Bring to a boil, stirring. Remove the garlic clove and pour the dressing over the salad. Toss and serve.

— *Recipe by Jack Staub*

Butter Lettuce Salad with Merlot-Raspberry Dressing

Delicate, soft butterheads need a light touch. Don't overwhelm them with heavy or strong-flavored dressings—simple vinaigrettes or light creamy dressings are best. Butterheads pair nicely with fruits, fruity vinegars, and soft cheeses. In the fresh raspberry dressing in this dish, the blend of raspberry vinegar, honey, sour cream, and the rich flavor of Merlot wine all enhance the flavor of the luxuriant, buttery leaves.

Fresh from the garden: GARLIC, SHALLOT, RASPBERRIES, BUTTER LETTUCE, CHIVES, PARSLEY

4 servings | *230 calories, 19g fat, 95mg sodium*

FOR THE DRESSING

1 large clove garlic, minced
1 shallot, minced
1 teaspoon Dijon mustard
1 tablespoon honey
2 tablespoons raspberry vinegar
½ cup Merlot wine
¼ teaspoon salt
¼ teaspoon fresh ground pepper
2 tablespoons olive oil
3 tablespoons vegetable oil
1 cup raspberries
3 tablespoons low-fat sour cream

FOR THE SALAD

1 large head butter lettuce
1 to 2 tablespoons chopped fresh chives
2 tablespoons chopped fresh parsley
½ cup raspberries
½ cup toasted pecans

MAKE THE DRESSING | Combine all the dressing ingredients in a food processor or blender and mix until smooth. Working over a bowl, tear the lettuce into pieces.

MAKE THE SALAD | Add the chopped herbs and about half of the dressing. Toss gently to coat, adding more dressing if necessary. Garnish with whole raspberries and pecans and serve.

— *Recipe by Renee Shepherd*

Warm Shrimp Salad with Ginger-Tarragon Dressing

Batavian lettuces are a type of crisphead, but they bear no resemblance to iceberg lettuce. Batavians are full and elongated, like a chubby romaine, and their leaves have curled edges. They are gorgeous, taste great, and are heat tolerant, so they don't bolt at the first sign of warm weather. Their bright, full flavors really shine in this warm shrimp salad with a tarragon and ginger dressing. If you can't find Batavian lettuce, use romaine or a combination of romaine and escarole.

Fresh from the garden: GARLIC, SHALLOTS, TARRAGON, LETTUCE, ARUGULA, BELL PEPPER

4 servings | 440 calories, 33g fat, 460 mg sodium

FOR THE DRESSING

2 large cloves garlic, minced

2 shallots, minced

2 tablespoons chopped
    fresh tarragon

2 tablespoons chopped
    fresh ginger

¼ cup freshly squeezed lime juice

3 tablespoons white-wine vinegar

1 tablespoon soy sauce

½ cup olive oil

1 tablespoon sesame oil

Freshly ground pepper

FOR THE SALAD

1 pound large shrimp, peeled
    and deveined

2 heads crisp lettuce like Batavian,
    preferably one green and one red

1 bunch arugula

½ each, red and yellow bell pepper,
    sliced into thin strips

MAKE THE DRESSING | Combine the dressing ingredients in a blender or food processor and mix until well blended.

MAKE THE SALAD | Marinate the shrimp in 3 tablespoons of the dressing for 30 minutes. Arrange the greens in a large salad bowl. In a frying pan, heat 1 tablespoon of the remaining dressing. Add the shrimp and stir-fry quickly over medium-high heat until no longer translucent, 1 to 2 minutes. Scatter the hot shrimp on the greens and garnish with pepper strips. Pour the remaining dressing over the salad. Toss well and serve.

— *Recipe by Renee Shepherd*

Classic croutons

Not only should a salad be dressed for success, it should be accessorized in style. And nothing in the salad realm has such enduring style as croutons, a triumph of texture. Their appeal can be summed up in a single word: crunchy.

A case for homemade croutons could be built on frugality grounds alone, but I think the edible evidence is more persuasive. Homemade croutons have more character and better texture than the packaged kind, which are more fragile and heavy-handed with weird seasonings.

Your choice of bread, then, is the key issue. The rule of thumb is, the sturdier the bread, the crunchier the croutons. Soft white breads aren't firm enough to make croutons of any substance. The higher-end white breads, like Arnold® or Pepperidge Farm®, yield fine results. And chewy sourdough breads make the crunchiest croutons of all, sometimes too crunchy if the crust is very chewy; consider trimming it off. Whole-grain breads make less tender croutons than white breads do. Steer clear of sweet breads. Slightly old, dry bread is fine, but not if it's moldy.

Finishing Touch Croutons

4 cups ¾-inch bread cubes
½ teaspoon dried oregano
½ teaspoon dried basil
2 tablespoons olive oil
Salt and freshly ground pepper

Preheat oven to 325°F. Put the bread cubes, oregano, and basil in a large bowl and drizzle the olive oil over the bread, tossing gently.

Spread the bread cubes on a large baking sheet; salt and pepper lightly. Toast until golden brown, about 13 to 18 minutes. Cool thoroughly on the sheet. Store the croutons in a zip-top plastic bag and use within a few days.

— *Ken Haedrich*

SALADS | 83

Garden Chef's Salad with Creamy Caper Dressing

Since romaine can stand up to heavier dressings and big flavors, indulge with capers in a creamy dressing that combines these savory little spice buds with anchovies, fresh lemon, garlic, and parsley, all bound together with a little mayonnaise and fruity olive oil.

Fresh from the garden: SHALLOT, GARLIC, PARSLEY, ROMAINE LETTUCE, RED ONION, TOMATOES, JICAMA OR FENNEL, RADISHES | 4 *generous servings* | *230 calories, 16g fat, 630mg sodium*

FOR THE DRESSING

3 anchovies, minced

1 large shallot, minced

1 large clove garlic, minced

2 tablespoons freshly squeezed
   lemon juice

1 teaspoon Dijon mustard

3 tablespoons chicken stock

1 tablespoon low-fat mayonnaise

3 tablespoons olive oil

2 tablespoons capers, drained

3 tablespoons chopped fresh parsley

FOR THE SALAD

1 large head romaine

½ small red onion, sliced very thin

2 small tomatoes, quartered

½ cup julienne strips of jicama
   or fennel

½ cup thinly sliced radishes

2 ounces Parmigiano-Reggiano
   or Asiago

½ cup croutons (see p. 83)

MAKE THE DRESSING | Mash the anchovies, shallot, and garlic together and put them into a large salad bowl. Add the remaining dressing ingredients and mix well.

MAKE THE SALAD | Tear the romaine into pieces and add it along with the vegetables to the bowl. Toss gently until thoroughly mixed. Using a vegetable peeler, shave the cheese into thin slices over the salad and scatter the croutons on top. Toss again briefly and serve immediately.

— *Recipe by Renee Shepherd*

Hearts of Romaine with Chopped Fennel

Romaine and fennel are cool-season crops, which makes this salad perfect for early summer or fall. Use any leftover dressing on a salad of shaved fennel or roasted beets.

Fresh from the garden: ROMAINE LETTUCE, FENNEL LEAVES

6 servings | *190 calories, 18g fat, 250mg sodium; using ½ cup dressing*

2 heads romaine
¾ cup crumbled feta
¾ cup finely chopped fennel

¼ cup rice-wine vinegar
¾ cup olive oil

Pinch of salt
Freshly ground pepper

Place the lettuce in a large bowl, using mainly hearts or torn large leaves. Sprinkle the feta over the lettuce, and the chopped fennel over the cheese.

Whisk the vinegar, olive oil, and salt until emulsified. Pour some of the dressing over the salad and toss. Refrigerate the rest of the dressing for use on future salads (it will keep a week or longer in the fridge). Grind some pepper on the salad and serve.

— Recipe by Noel Richardson

Caring for a wooden salad bowl

The sight of a fetching green salad piled high in a wooden bowl speaks to our souls. To keep your bowl in good shape, it needs simple care.

The most common way to make a wooden salad bowl is to turn it on a lathe, either from a single piece of wood or from pieces of wood joined in butcher block fashion. A bowl turned from a single piece of wood is beautiful and impressive, but it might be more liable to develop cracks.

Improper washing will shorten the life of a wooden bowl. Never put the bowl in a dishwasher, which can cause irreparable harm, and never let it soak in water. Soap and water washing probably isn't even necessary so long as you limit the use of your wooden bowl to salads. Just wipe the inside dry with a paper towel. Any residual oil will be rubbed into the surface and help preserve the wood. If you do wash the bowl, fine. Use hot sudsy water but no abrasive scouring pads. Dry it immediately.

Finally, to keep your wooden bowl in tiptop condition, once or twice a month rub it with food-grade mineral oil.

— Ken Haedrich

Salad of Bitter Greens & Persimmon

This salad is beautiful, a little fancy, and outrageously good. Toast the seasoned pecans ahead of time for convenience and be sure to use the squatty, flat-bottomed, nonastringent Fuyu persimmons.

Fresh from the garden: ESCAROLE OR ENDIVE, FUYU PERSIMMONS, RED ONION

6 servings | 360 calories, 34g fat, 700mg sodium

1 cup pecan halves	2 medium Fuyu persimmons, trimmed	4 tablespoons freshly squeezed lemon juice
1½ teaspoon Kosher salt	2 small blood oranges	1 tablespoon finely grated fresh ginger
⅛ to ¼ teaspoon cayenne	½ small red onion	Freshly ground black pepper
¼ teaspoon powdered ginger	½ cup crumbled Gorgonzola	
8 cups escarole, endive, or frisée leaves	½ cup olive oil	

Position a rack in the center of the oven and preheat the oven to 325°F. Combine the pecans, ½ teaspoon salt, cayenne, and powdered ginger in a small bowl and mix thoroughly. Spread the nuts on a cookie sheet and toast in the oven for about 8 minutes. Set aside to cool.

Wash and dry the greens, rip them into small pieces, and put them in a large mixing bowl. With a sharp knife, cut the persimmons into quarters, then slice each quarter thinly. Add the pieces to the bowl.

Cut away the rind from the blood oranges, carefully trimming off all the white pith. Cut each orange into slices horizontally, then each slice in half, removing the white core. Add to the mixing bowl.

Slice the red onion very thin and put in the bowl. Add the Gorgonzola and pecans.

In a small bowl, whisk together the olive oil, lemon juice, grated ginger, remaining teaspoon salt, and a few grinds of pepper. Pour over the salad, mix thoroughly, and serve immediately.

— *Recipe by Kathleen Stewart*

Insalatone

This marinated multivegetable salad is most flavorful if made the day before it is served. The upside to all this prep is that on the day you eat it a major part of the meal will be ready to serve with no work on your part.

Fresh from the garden: ROSEMARY, GARLIC, BELL PEPPERS, ASIAN EGGPLANTS, ZUCCHINI, CELERY, CARROTS, RED ONION, PARSLEY, BASIL | 6 servings | *110 calories, 6g fat, 100mg sodium*

FOR THE ROSEMARY-INFUSED OIL
½ cup olive oil
3 or 4 sprigs fresh rosemary
2 or 3 cloves garlic, sliced

FOR THE MARINADE
½ cup red-wine vinegar
2 to 4 tablespoons olive oil
½ teaspoon salt

FOR THE SALAD
2 or 3 red bell peppers
3 or 4 Asian eggplants
½ pound zucchini, sliced lengthwise, ¼ inch thick
2 cups celery hearts and stalks, sliced ¼ inch thick
1½ cups carrots (3 to 4), sliced ¼ inch thick

2 red onions, quartered and sliced thin
3 to 4 tablespoons chopped fresh parsley
3 to 4 tablespoons chopped fresh basil
Kosher salt
Freshly ground black pepper
2 tablespoons Rosemary-Infused Oil
Freshly squeezed lemon juice
Lemon slices for garnish

MAKE THE ROSEMARY–INFUSED OIL | Heat the ingredients in a small, heavy pan slowly to a low simmer. Remove from the heat and let stand 1 hour. Strain.

MAKE THE MARINADE | Combine the ingredients with 1 cup of water in a medium, nonreactive saucepan. Set aside.

MAKE THE SALAD | Broil the peppers and eggplants until the skin is blackened on all sides. Remove them from the oven and cover the peppers with a kitchen towel to facilitate peeling. When cool, peel and slice the peppers and the eggplant.

Put the sliced zucchini in the saucepan with the marinade. Bring to boil, and then reduce the heat and simmer, covered, for 5 minutes. Remove the zucchini with a slotted spoon, drain, and chill.

Cook the remaining vegetables individually in the marinade the same way: the celery, 7 to 8 minutes; the carrots, 3 to 4 minutes; the onions, 2 to 3 minutes. Refrigerate the vegetables until needed.

Put the chilled vegetables in a large bowl. Add the parsley, basil, salt, and pepper. Before serving, dress with the rosemary olive oil and a squeeze of lemon juice. Serve chilled or at room temperature, with additional lemon slices.

— *Recipe by Louise Langsner*

Celery Root & Apple Salad

Celery root's hints of celery and parsley go well with the tart sweetness of apples. Made with Thyme Mayonnaise (p. 52), this salad is perfect for a special springtime meal.

Fresh from the garden: CELERY ROOT, APPLES, PARSLEY
6 servings | *330 calories, 21g fat, 190mg sodium*

1 medium to large celery root	2 large crisp apples	½ cup chopped walnuts
¾ cup freshly squeezed orange juice	½ cup mayonnaise	½ cup raisins
	3 tablespoons chopped fresh parsley	Salt and freshly ground pepper

Peel and grate the celery root to make 3 cups. Place ½ cup of the orange juice in a medium bowl and add the grated celery root.

Peel and core the apples, chop into ½-inch chunks, and add to the celery root and orange juice. Marinate for 10 minutes, stirring occasionally.

In a small bowl, whisk together the mayonnaise and the remaining ¼ cup orange juice until smooth. Pour over the celery root and apples. Add the parsley, walnuts, raisins, and salt and pepper to taste; mix well. Chill for at least 2 hours before serving.

— Recipe by Ashley Miller

Pea, Feta & Tomato Salad

Fresh English peas are the star ingredient in this colorful salad, and feta adds piquancy. Most of the ingredients are combined ahead of time, but the peas are added at the last minute.

Fresh from the garden: CHERRY TOMATOES, SCALLIONS, MINT, GARLIC, PEAS
6 to 8 servings | *250 calories, 18g fat, 320mg sodium*

6 ounces feta
1 cup yellow cherry tomatoes
1 cup red cherry tomatoes
3 to 4 scallions
½ cup loosely packed fresh
    mint leaves

¼ cup freshly squeezed
    lemon juice
2 cloves garlic
½ cup extra-virgin olive oil
¼ teaspoon salt
Freshly ground pepper

2 tablespoons rice vinegar
1 to 2 tablespoons honey
3 cups peas

Cube the feta. Halve the tomatoes. Cut the scallions into thin rounds and place them, along with the tomatoes and feta, in a large bowl.

Chop the mint coarsely and put it and the lemon juice in a small mixing bowl. Mince the garlic and add it to the lemon juice and mint. Whisk in the oil. Add the salt and pepper, rice vinegar, and honey. Taste and correct the seasoning with salt, pepper, vinegar, or honey, depending on your taste.

Add the dressing to the cheese, tomatoes, and scallions. Allow it to sit several hours or overnight in the refrigerator.

Blanch the peas in boiling water for 2 minutes, drain, and refresh by plunging into cold water. Toss the peas into the salad no more than a half hour before serving.

— *Recipe by Sheri Sullivan*

BREADS & SANDWICHES

For easy meals at any time of the day, nothing satisfies quite like a delicious, bready treat. From scones, biscuits, and yeasted breads to savory Escarole-Filled Calzones (the dough can be used for making pizzas, too), recipes in this chapter will hit the spot. And then there are the sandwiches— open-face Grilled Cheese with Fennel; anchovy-studded Mediterranean Toasts; rolls stuffed with roasted chiles, cheese, and avocado; and a fabulous, gussied-up version of the classic BLT.

But there's more here, too. Tucked among the baker's dozen of bread and sandwich recipes, you'll find extra gems, all of which can stand alone. For example, vanilla-scented Rhubarb Conserve, used in the Strawberry Rhubarb Muffins (as well as on them), is a delicious spread for hot biscuits, scones, or toast. It can also be used as a filling for tiny jam tarts. The sautéed escarole in the calzones makes a wonderful fall side dish all on its own. And I predict the slow-roasted tomatoes used in the Open-Face Cornbread Sandwiches will become a staple in your late-summer kitchen.

Strawberry Rhubarb Muffins

Years ago, rhubarb used to be known as pie plant, and that's probably still the use that comes most quickly to mind. For sure, it does make a great pie, but rhubarb combined with ripe, juicy strawberries is scrumptious in muffins, too.

....

Fresh from the garden: RHUBARB, STRAWBERRIES

2 dozen muffins | *200 calories, 8g fat, 105mg sodium; per muffin*

....

3½ cups flour

1 cup rolled oats or oat bran

4½ teaspoons baking powder

¾ cup brown sugar, tightly packed

1½ teaspoon cinnamon

½ teaspoon powdered ginger

¼ teaspoon freshly grated nutmeg

2 large eggs

¾ cup canola oil

1¼ cups milk

1 teaspoon pure vanilla extract

½ teaspoon balsamic vinegar

1 cup Rhubarb Conserve
  (see the facing page)

3 cups coarsely chopped strawberries

....

Position 2 racks near the center and lower third of the oven, and preheat the oven to 400°F. Grease muffin tins.

In a large bowl, mix all dry ingredients. In a separate bowl, whisk together the eggs, oil, milk, vanilla, and balsamic vinegar. Add the Rhubarb Conserve, chopped strawberries, and wet ingredients to the dry ingredients, and gently mix until just combined.

Scoop the batter evenly into the muffin tins using an ice cream scoop. Bake until the center of a muffin springs back when pressed, about 20 to 25 minutes, switching the pans from rack to rack and rotating 180 degrees halfway through baking.

— *Recipe by Elizabeth Holland*

Preserving rhubarb

One of my favorite uses for rhubarb is in a conserve, which is fast, easy, and versatile. It can be incorporated into our Strawberry Rhubarb Muffins (see facing page), but it's also great spread on them, as well as on croissants, popovers, or even toast. Fold it into whipped cream and layer between baked squares of puff pastry, brush the top layer with more conserve or sprinkle it with powdered sugar, and you have a quick, elegant rhubarb napoleon. Or you can use it to fill tiny tart shells, to go between the layers of a cake, or to top ice cream.

Rhubarb Conserve

4 cups diced rhubarb
1¼ cups sugar
Splash of freshly squeezed orange juice
1 teaspoon pure vanilla extract

Bring the rhubarb, sugar, and orange juice to a simmer in a medium, nonaluminum saucepan over medium-low heat. Cook the mixture until it thickens considerably and coats the back of a spoon, about 20 minutes. Stir occasionally. Add the vanilla at the end of the cooking time. Cool. The conserve can be refrigerated for up to 2 weeks.

— *Recipe by Elizabeth Holland*

Carrot & Cranberry Muffins

Grated carrots add sweetness and a little bit of texture to these colorful harvest muffins, while fresh cranberries add zing. If you like, sprinkle with your favorite streusel topping before baking.

....

Fresh from the garden: CARROTS

Makes 12 muffins | *210 calories, 8g fat, 260mg sodium; per muffin*

....

Butter, for the pan

1½ cups grated carrots

1 cup fresh cranberries, chopped

⅔ cup packed light brown sugar

Finely grated zest of 1 orange

1¼ cups milk

1 egg, lightly beaten

⅓ cup vegetable oil

1½ cups flour

¾ cup whole-wheat flour

2 teaspoons baking powder

½ teaspoon baking soda

½ teaspoon salt

½ teaspoon cinnamon

½ teaspoon allspice

....

Position a rack in the center of the oven and preheat the oven to 400°F. Butter a muffin tin. Mix the carrots, cranberries, brown sugar, and orange zest in a small bowl; set aside. In a separate bowl, whisk the milk, egg, and oil. In a large mixing bowl, combine the remaining ingredients.

Stir the carrot mixture into the liquid ingredients. Make a well in the center of the dry ingredients; add the wet mixture and stir until the batter is blended.

Divide the batter evenly in the muffin tin. Bake until the muffins are golden brown and the tops feel springy to the touch, about 22 to 23 minutes. Cool the muffins in the tin for 10 minutes, then transfer to a cloth-lined basket and serve.

— *Recipe by Ken Haedrich*

Buttermilk Cream Scones with Lemon Basil

These delicious scones can be prepared for breakfast, brunch, a tea party, or even served as dessert. If you don't have lemon basil, try substituting a combination of sweet green basil and lemon balm. The candied ginger is a nice counterpoint here; however, if you don't have it on hand, try using minced dried apricots. The scones are excellent eaten plain. Or, for an extra treat, serve them with lightly sweetened whipped cream and lemon marmalade or a peach or ginger preserve.

Fresh from the garden: LEMON BASIL

Makes 8 large or 12 medium scones | *170 calories, 5g fat, 270mg sodium; per large scone*

2½ cups plus 2 tablespoons flour

3 tablespoons sugar

¾ teaspoon salt

3 teaspoons baking powder

½ teaspoon baking soda

4 tablespoons butter

¼ cup finely chopped crystallized ginger

½ cup buttermilk

½ cup cream or milk

¼ cup chopped fresh lemon basil

1 heaping tablespoon lemon zest

2 tablespoons freshly squeezed lemon juice

About 1 tablespoon melted butter, optional

About 2 teaspoons sugar, optional

Put a rack in the center of the oven and preheat the oven to 400°F. Combine the flour, sugar, salt, baking powder, and baking soda in a large bowl and blend thoroughly. With a pastry cutter or 2 kitchen knives, cut the butter into the dry ingredients until the butter is about the size of small peas. Stir in the candied ginger.

Stir the buttermilk and cream together with the lemon basil, zest, and lemon juice. Add the liquid to the dry ingredients and stir to form a soft dough.

Turn the dough onto a floured pastry marble or board, and knead gently until it just comes together. Shape into a ball. Press the dough with your hands to flatten the ball. Using a rolling pin, roll the dough into a round about 1 inch thick. Cut the dough with a sharp knife or pizza cutter into 8 or 12 wedges.

Place the scones about 1 inch apart on an ungreased baking sheet. Brush the tops with melted butter and sprinkle with sugar, if desired. Bake the scones until golden brown, about 18 minutes. Transfer them to a baking rack to cool slightly.

Scones are best served warm right after baking.

— *Recipe by Susan Belsinger*

Scorched Corn Biscuits

There's something compelling about the taste of lightly browned corn. These biscuits are superb made with corn kernels cut fresh from the cob, but they're still very good made with frozen kernels, so don't let a lack of fresh corn deter you.

Fresh from the garden: CORN, SAGE, OREGANO, THYME

Makes 12 to 14 biscuits | *140 calories, 6g fat, 190mg sodium; per biscuit, based on 14 biscuits*

2 cups corn kernels	1 tablespoon baking powder	1 teaspoon fresh oregano
1 cup flour	½ teaspoon salt	½ teaspoon fresh thyme
1 cup cornmeal	1 teaspoon fresh sage, minced	1 cup cream
¼ teaspoon sugar		

Position a rack near the center of the oven and preheat the oven to 425°F.

Cook the corn in a dry sauté pan over medium-high heat, stirring constantly until the kernels turn brown, about 5 to 10 minutes. Cool completely.

Stir together the flour, cornmeal, sugar, baking powder, salt, herbs, and corn kernels in a large mixing bowl. Add cream. Stir with a fork until a soft dough forms. Work quickly and do not overmix.

With a tablespoon, drop the biscuit batter 2 inches apart onto a buttered baking sheet. Bake until the tops are golden brown, about 12 to 15 minutes.

— *Recipe by Mimi Luebbermann*

Dill Biscuits

A cup of dill folded into an easy biscuit recipe gives the day an elegant start or a little something delightfully different for a mid–day snack. The biscuits are a nice accompaniment to a subtle soup like cucumber, asparagus, leek, or celery. Or serve them with a mesclun salad and slices of smoked salmon.

Fresh from the garden: DILL LEAVES AND SEEDS

Makes 12 biscuits | *130 calories, 5g fat, 170mg sodium; per biscuit*

2 cups flour

1 tablespoon baking powder

½ teaspoon salt

4 tablespoons cold butter

1 cup finely chopped fresh dill

1 cup whole milk

2 tablespoons dill seeds

Position a rack near the center of the oven and preheat the oven to 450°F. Combine the flour, baking powder, and salt in a medium bowl. Cut in the butter until you have a coarse meal texture. Stir in the chopped dill. Add the milk and stir just until the mixture clings together.

Drop spoonfuls of the mixture onto an ungreased cookie sheet, leaving about an inch between each biscuit. Sprinkle lightly with dill seeds.

Bake until the biscuits are tinged brown, about 15 minutes. Serve immediately.

— Recipe by Peter Garnham

Open-Face Cornbread Sandwiches with Goat Cheese & Slow-Roasted Tomatoes

The cornbread and slow-roasted tomatoes are delicious recipes on their own. The tomatoes have a long cooking time but are worth waiting for.

Fresh from the garden: TOMATOES, ARUGULA

Sandwiches—4 servings; cornbread—one 9-inch loaf; tomatoes—3 to 4 cups | *Sandwiches—630 calories, 45g fat, 600mg sodium; with ½ teaspoon vinegar and ½ teaspoon oil | Cornbread—210 calories, 7g fat, 280mg sodium; per slice | Tomatoes—280 calories, 28g fat, 15mg sodium; per ½ cup*

FOR THE CORNBREAD

2½ cups flour

1½ cups yellow cornmeal

1 tablespoon baking powder

1 teaspoon salt

½ cup sugar

2 large eggs

1¾ cups buttermilk

¼ pound melted butter

FOR THE SLOW-ROASTED TOMATOES

12 medium tomatoes

1 cup olive oil

Kosher salt and freshly ground pepper

FOR THE SANDWICHES

8 slices cornbread

2 bunches baby arugula

1 pound goat cheese, sliced into 8 rounds

Freshly ground pepper

16 halves Slow-Roasted Tomatoes

Aged balsamic vinegar

Extra-virgin olive oil

MAKE THE CORNBREAD | Position a rack near the center of the oven and preheat the oven to 350°F. Butter a 9-inch loaf pan and line it with parchment or waxed paper.

In a medium bowl, combine all the dry ingredients. Break the eggs into a small bowl and beat lightly. Stir the buttermilk and melted butter into the eggs. Pour the liquid ingredients into the dry ingredients and stir to form a smooth batter. Pour into the prepared pan. Bake for 30 minutes. Check to see if it is done by inserting a toothpick into the bread. If the toothpick comes out dry, the bread is done. Cool in the pan before turning out.

ROAST THE TOMATOES | Lower the oven temperature to 200°F. Core the tomatoes and cut them in half. Cut plum tomatoes end to end; with regular tomatoes, cut through the middle. Remove the seeds and juice and reserve for a sauce or soup.

On a baking sheet or in a shallow casserole pour half the olive oil and spread evenly. Arrange the tomatoes cut side down and brush with the remaining olive oil. This cooking method intensifies the wonderful flavor of fresh tomatoes, so salt and pepper are optional. Place in the oven and roast for 4½ hours.

ASSEMBLE THE SANDWICHES | Place a slice of cornbread on a plate, cover with a few arugula leaves, a slice of cheese, a twist of pepper, and 2 tomato halves. Finish with a sprinkle of balsamic vinegar and olive oil.

— Recipe by Carole Peck

Sweet Potato Sugar Bread

With its topping of brown sugar, cinnamon, and nuts, this is a delicious bread to feature at a brunch, paired with fresh fruit. It's also a wonderful break-time treat with coffee, tea, or mulled cider.

Fresh from the garden: SWEET POTATOES

12 servings | *320 calories, 13g fat, 220mg sodium*

FOR THE BREAD

1 package (about 2 teaspoons) active dry yeast

1 cup baked sweet potato flesh (from 2 good-size potatoes)

½ cup milk at room temperature

¼ cup packed light brown sugar

1 egg at room temperature

1 teaspoon salt

3 tablespoons vegetable oil

½ cup whole-wheat flour

2¾ cups flour

FOR THE TOPPING

¾ cup packed light brown sugar

½ cup walnuts

1 teaspoon cinnamon

5 tablespoons butter, melted and slightly cooled

MAKE THE BREAD | In a small bowl, sprinkle yeast over ¼ cup warm water; set aside 5 minutes. Meanwhile, purée the sweet potato, milk, brown sugar, egg, salt, and vegetable oil in a food processor.

Transfer to a large mixing bowl and stir in the dissolved yeast and whole-wheat flour. Stir in 1½ cups of the flour. Using a wooden spoon, beat vigorously for 100 strokes. Cover the bowl with plastic wrap and set aside at room temperature for 15 minutes. Beat in enough of the remaining flour, ¼ cup at a time, to make a very soft but kneadable dough. (I use a large rubber spatula at this point, paddling the dough in the bowl as I add the flour.)

Turn the dough out onto a well-floured surface and knead until the dough is smooth and bouncy, about 5 or 6 minutes; use enough of the remaining flour to keep the dough from sticking. Don't knead too roughly or the dough will stick to your hands. Return the dough to the bowl, cover with plastic wrap, and set aside in a warm, draft-free spot until doubled in bulk, 1 to 1½ hours.

Butter a 9x13-inch shallow baking dish and set aside.

When the dough has doubled, deflate it by tapping it down gently, but don't knead it. Turn the dough into the center of the buttered dish, cover loosely with plastic wrap, let rest for 10 minutes, and then pat it evenly into the pan. Cover loosely again and set aside in a warm spot for 15 minutes. Position a rack in the center of the oven and preheat the oven to 350°F.

MAKE THE TOPPING | Put the brown sugar, walnuts, and cinnamon in a food processor and process until the nuts are chopped fine. Spread the topping evenly over the dough. Poke 12 deep indentations in the dough with your finger, making three evenly spaced rows of four. Spoon the melted butter over the surface, and a little into the holes. Let the dough rise, uncovered, for 10 minutes.

Bake 35 minutes. The top will become dark brown and crusty. Cool in the pan, on a rack, for 10 minutes.

— *Recipe by Ken Haedrich*

Potato & Onion Focaccia

This focaccia is fantastic for sandwiches and pairs beautifully with soups, stews, and other saucy dishes. Using pie pans for the final rise helps contain the dough, resulting in a little more height.

Fresh from the garden: POTATO, ROSEMARY, ONION

Three 10-inch round loaves; 24 servings | *120 calories, 2.5g fat, 200mg sodium*

- 1 cup peeled and diced potato
- 1 package (about 2 teaspoons) active dry yeast
- 5½ cups flour

- 2 teaspoons salt
- 2 teaspoons chopped fresh rosemary or 1 teaspoon crushed dried

- 4 to 5 tablespoons olive oil
- 1 large onion, chopped fine

Put the potato and 3 cups lightly salted water in a small saucepan. Bring to a boil and cook gently until very tender, about 10 minutes. Drain, reserving 2 cups of the potato water in a large mixing bowl. Finely mash or rice the potato; stir into the potato water. Cool to lukewarm, and then sprinkle the yeast on top. Set aside for 5 minutes.

Using a wooden spoon, stir 3½ cups of the flour into the potato water. Beat vigorously for 100 strokes. Cover the bowl with plastic wrap and set aside for 15 minutes.

Stir the salt and rosemary into the dough. Beat in 1½ cups more flour, ¼ cup at a time, to make a soft dough. Turn the dough out onto a well-floured surface and knead, gently at first, for 8 minutes. Place the dough in an oiled bowl. Cover the bowl with plastic wrap and set aside in a warm, draft-free spot until doubled in bulk, 1 to 1½ hours. Lightly oil 3 deep-dish 9-inch pie or cake pans.

While the dough rises, heat 2 tablespoons of the oil in a large frying pan. Add the onion and sauté over medium heat until golden, about 8 to 9 minutes. Remove from heat and cool.

Once the dough has doubled, deflate it by tapping it down; turn it onto a well-floured surface. Spread the onions over the dough, pull up the sides of the dough, and knead in the onions for 1 minute. Divide the dough into equal thirds, and knead each piece into a ball. Place a piece seam down in each pan, cover loosely with plastic wrap, and let rest for 10 minutes. Press the dough into the pans, up to the edges. Brush the top of the dough with some of the remaining olive oil. Set the pans aside in a warm spot, loosely covered, and let rise for 20 minutes. Position two racks in the center and lower third of the oven, and preheat the oven to 425°F.

After 20 minutes, make 10 to 12 deep indentations in each focaccia with outstretched fingers. Drizzle 1 teaspoon olive oil over the top of each focaccia; let rest 10 minutes. Bake the breads until dark golden brown, 25 to 30 minutes, switching the pans from rack to rack halfway through baking. Cool in the pans for 1 minute, then slip them onto a cooling rack. Cool 10 to 15 minutes before slicing.

— Recipe by Ken Haedrich

Escarole-Filled Calzones

Sautéed escarole makes a savory side dish for four all on its own or a tasty stuffing for calzones. The dough can be used for making pizza, too. Try making it on the grill, topped with garden-fresh vegetables.

Fresh from the garden: ONION, ESCAROLE

16 appetizer or 4 main-dish servings | *160 calories, 6g fat, 230mg sodium; per appetizer serving*

FOR THE DOUGH

3 cups bread flour

1 teaspoon salt

1 teaspoon active dry yeast

2 tablespoons olive oil, plus additional
    for brushing the tops

FOR THE FILLING

1 large onion, sliced

4 tablespoons olive oil

2 heads escarole, ¾ to 1 pound each,
    cut into 1-inch strips

4 tablespoons mellow olives, such
    as Niçoise, pitted and quartered

2 tablespoons capers, rinsed

Salt

MAKE THE DOUGH | Place the flour, salt, and yeast in a food processor and mix briefly. With the food processor running, slowly add 1 cup warm water and the 2 tablespoons oil until the dough forms a sticky ball. Remove to a floured surface and knead well until silky, adding more flour if necessary. This process can also be done by hand. Let the dough rise until doubled, 2 or more hours.

MAKE THE FILLING | In a large pan, sauté the onion in oil until lightly browned. Add the escarole with the moisture clinging to it. Cover and cook, stirring occasionally, until the escarole is tender, 10 to 15 minutes.

Remove the cover and raise the heat under the pan. Add the olives and capers and cook until the liquid is completely gone, about 5 minutes. Salt to taste.

Position a rack near the center of the oven and preheat the oven to 400°F.

To make the pies, divide the dough in half. Roll out each piece into a 10-inch circle. Place half the escarole filling over half of each circle of dough, leaving a ½-inch margin clean at the edges. Fold the dough over the escarole, moisten the edges with a little water, and pinch the edges together firmly to seal. Lightly brush the tops with olive oil. Bake until nicely browned, about 20 minutes.

VARIATION | Add small pieces of cooked Italian sausage to the chopped onion.

— *Recipe by Ed Miller*

BLT Extraordinaire

The bacon-lettuce-and-tomato sandwich is, to my palate anyway, one of America's finest culinary contributions, far better than the ubiquitous hamburger for which we are known the world around. Is anything more mouthwatering than the silky texture of a summer tomato against the salty crunch of bacon, the crisp refreshing snap of the lettuce, and the juicy mingling of mayonnaise and tomato drippings? It's sheer delight. Although you can get a BLT in almost any American coffee shop year-round, my advice is to wait until tomato season and make your own with real summer tomatoes. This version takes the concept beyond the classic BLT, adding the rustic elegance of pancetta, the pleasant spiciness of arugula, and the garlicky richness of freshly made aïoli.

Fresh from the garden: TOMATOES, ARUGULA

4 servings | *350 calories, 7g fat, 1,330mg sodium; with 3 ounces bread, no aïoli*

⅓ pound thinly sliced pancetta	Aïoli (p. 55)	Kosher salt
1 loaf sourdough bread	4 tomatoes, sliced	2 cups arugula, lightly packed

Sauté the pancetta until it is just crisp. While it is cooking, cut the bread into eight ½-inch slices, and grill or toast them lightly until they are just golden brown. Spread aïoli over the surface of each slice of bread. Arrange the tomato slices on 4 of the pieces of bread and add a sprinkling of salt. Divide the slices of pancetta among the sandwiches, placing them on top of the tomatoes. Add a handful of arugula on top of the pancetta and cap with the remaining slices of bread, aïoli side down, of course. Cut in half and serve immediately.

— *Recipe by Michele Anna Jordan*

Evie's Szentesi Sandwich

Szentesi is a large, thick-fleshed Hungarian wax chile. Although any chile plant can put out an uncharacteristically hot pepper when you least expect it, you can count on szentesis to be mild to medium, and they have a flavor that is more like a sweet pepper than a hot chile. They are terrific in salsas or grilled for sandwiches. In place of szentesi chiles, you can use a pimento-type pepper or even a standard red bell pepper, although the flavor will be less complex.

Fresh from the garden: SZENTESI CHILES, LETTUCE, TOMATOES

4 servings | *540 calories, 34g fat, 590mg sodium*

4 szentesi chiles	8 ounces Monterey Jack, sliced	2 tomatoes, sliced
4 sourdough rolls	8 large lettuce leaves	2 avocados, peeled and sliced

Roast and peel the chiles (see p. 123). Remove the stems and seeds.

Split the rolls, top them with cheese, and toast under a broiler until the cheese is melted. Put a chile, some lettuce, and a slice of tomato and avocado on each roll. Serve immediately.

— *Recipe by Lee James and Wayne James*

Mediterranean Toasts

If you've been throwing out the oil from canned anchovies, this recipe will change that habit. The open-face toasted sandwiches are reminiscent of pizza, but with a composed approach.

....

Fresh from the garden: TOMATOES, RED ONION, GARLIC, OREGANO, PARSLEY
4 servings | *240 calories, 12g fat, 840mg sodium*

....

2 large tomatoes, about 1 pound each, sliced 3/8-inch thick	4 large slices white or rye bread, crusts removed	Heaping 3 tablespoons fresh oregano
1 medium red onion, sliced thin	2 tablespoons extra-virgin olive oil	1/2-ounce Parmigiano-Reggiano, sliced paper thin
1 clove garlic, sliced in half lengthwise	One 3/4-ounce tin anchovy fillets	Freshly ground black pepper
	8 large black olives, pitted and halved	Sprigs of fresh parsley to garnish

....

Reserve the 4 largest tomato rounds, and then cut the 4 next-largest in half. Warm a large, nonstick frying pan over medium-high heat. Add the onion and sauté, without fat, until softened, about 5 minutes. Remove from the heat.

Gently rub the garlic over both sides of the bread. Brush one side of the bread with olive oil and the other with oil from the anchovy tin. Set the bread on a baking sheet, anchovy-oil sides up.

To construct the toasts, arrange a portion of onions over each piece of bread. Set half a tomato slice at each end of the toast, then center a tomato round on top of them. Cross 2 anchovy strips over the tomatoes, and set an olive half in each corner of the cross.

Tear 2 tablespoons of the oregano leaves over the tops of the slices. Neatly lay on the cheese, grind on some pepper, and sprinkle with the remaining olive oil.

Heat the oven to 425°F. If you have a baking stone, set it on a rack in the middle of the oven. Bake the toasts uncovered until you can smell them, and their edges are browned, about 10 minutes. Arrange the toasts on a heated platter, tear the reserved oregano leaves over them, and serve at once with sprigs of parsley on one side.

All elements can be prepared a few hours in advance. Assemble the toasts up to an hour before baking.

— *Recipe by Sylvia Thompson*

Grilled Cheese with Fennel

The cool, fragrant taste of fennel is an unexpected counterpoint to savory Cheddar in this update on a classic toasted cheese sandwich. Using the fennel seeds intensifies the flavor.

Fresh from the garden: FENNEL LEAVES AND SEEDS
1 serving | *410 calories, 21g fat, 690mg sodium*

4 tablespoons chopped fennel	2 slices of good sandwich bread (rye, sourdough, or whole-grain)	2 slices sharp Cheddar Fennel seeds

Sprinkle the chopped fennel on the bread. Cover the bread with the cheese slices and sprinkle a few fennel seeds on top of the cheese. Broil until the cheese bubbles. Serve hot.

— *Recipe by Noel Richardson*

Comforting or elegant, brothy or thick, light or hearty, smooth or rustic—the possibilities inherent in soup are positively endless. There are recipes here for every taste and every season, starting with spring and going right through winter. A good number of them are vegetarian as written; most of the rest can be made so simply by using vegetable stock.

Good soup starts with good stock, and homemade is the best. If you think you don't have time to make stock, let me reassure you. Our classic chicken stock, which takes longest to prepare of the three stock recipes you'll find, requires only about three hours, but you can make an express version in about an hour. Vegetable stock also takes only about an hour, with the actual work completed in just minutes; while the pot is simmering, you can be doing other things.

If you have a slow cooker, you are well on your way to making stock. Get the liquid simmering on the high setting, then lower the heat and let it bubble gently all day or all night. Making stock is also a great way to use bones left from a roast. I routinely make chicken stock from the carcasses of roast chicken, sometimes (but not always) with the addition of some uncooked wings or necks or a package of chicken feet (which give the stock lots of body).

However, if making your own stock simply isn't in the cards, just buy the best-tasting stock you can, opting for low-salt versions that will give you more control over the final seasoning of your dish. You can always improve store-bought stock by simmering it with a few herbs and vegetables (even scraps such as leek tops, mushroom stems, celery leaves), bones, or—for fish soups—shrimp peels or fish heads.

Leek & Potato Soup

One of the simplest soups in the world, leek and potato soup is also one of the best. The leeks lend elegance and subtlety, and the potatoes add substance. It's wonderful at its plainest, but you can also dress it up in any number of ways besides the recommended cream and thyme or chives. Try thinly sliced dark green leek tops that have been fried until crisp, a dollop of sour cream, crumbled fried bacon, a drizzle of basil oil, a spoonful of salsa verde, or a sprinkling of pale green chopped celery leaves. If you have a bone from a grilled steak or chop stashed in the freezer, simmer it along with the soup, then retrieve it just before pureeing; it gives marvelous flavor.

Fresh from the garden: LEEKS, POTATOES

4 servings | *190 calories, 7g fat, 65mg sodium*

2 tablespoons butter	3 medium round white potatoes,	Salt
3 medium leeks, halved	peeled and cut into 1-inch cubes	
5 cups chicken broth		

In a large saucepan, melt the butter over low heat. Cut the leeks into 1-inch pieces. Add to the pan and stir to coat with butter. Cover the pan and cook the leeks until softened but not brown, 8 to 10 minutes. Meanwhile, in a medium saucepan, bring the broth to a simmer over moderate heat. Keep the broth hot, but don't let it boil.

Add the potatoes to the leeks and pour the hot broth over the vegetables. Bring to a boil, then reduce the heat and simmer until the potatoes are tender, 15 to 20 minutes.

Take the pan from the heat and let cool slightly. Transfer to a food processor (you may want to do this in batches) and purée until very smooth. Return the purée to the pot and place over moderately low heat. The soup should be smooth but not thick.

If necessary, add water to loosen the consistency. Season to taste with salt.

Serve hot or let cool before serving. Garnish as desired.

NOTE | During the last minute of cooking, you may swirl some cream into the soup for added richness or stir in a sprinkling of thyme, chives, or dill.

— Recipe by Amanda Hesser

Chicken stock

Chicken stock is so valuable in the kitchen that professional chefs call it liquid gold. With a quart or so of stock on hand you can easily transform garden vegetables into a quick and satisfying soup or stew. It's also good to use instead of water to add flavor and depth to a dish. Because chicken stock has a neutral flavor, you can use it in most recipes calling for beef, vegetable, or even fish stock.

START WITH CHICKEN PARTS AND A FEW VEGETABLES

Just put several pounds of inexpensive chicken parts—thighs, legs, wings—in a large pot and cover with cold water. Bring the water to a boil and then reduce the heat until the water is barely bubbling.

A lot of foam will rise to the surface at first. If you spend a few minutes skimming it off, you'll have a clearer stock. Then add coarsely chopped carrots, celery, and onions, as well as a large handful of herbs, such as parsley and thyme. You can also toss in a bay leaf and a few peppercorns. I suggest that you leave the stock unsalted and season the dish you eventually use it in.

At this point, you may want to personalize the stock by adding your favorite vegetables and herbs. I tend to add leeks, garlic, and a pinch of fresh rosemary because I often use stock in Italian dishes. Simmer the stock gently over low heat, uncovered, until all the flavor is out of the chicken, about two hours. During this time, add water if necessary to keep the chicken covered.

WHEN IT'S DONE, STRAIN AND STORE

Lift out the meat, vegetables, and herbs. They'll be nearly flavorless, so just discard them (or feed them to your cat or dog). Pour the stock through a strainer into containers. Refrigerate until it is cold; the fat will form a hard layer on top, making it a snap to remove. If you're not going to use the stock for a couple of days, freeze it.

When using the stock with garden vegetables, it should have a good but light flavor to let your vegetables take center stage. But if you want a more intensely flavored stock, after the fat is removed, let it simmer on the stove to reduce it a little.

If you are in a hurry, you can make an express stock, lighter in flavor but still quite useful. It's also economical because you can save the chicken to serve in other dishes. Cook express stock as you would regular stock, but chop the vegetables very fine by hand or in a food processor so that they release their flavor quickly. When the chicken is cooked, after about 45 minutes, strain the stock and reserve the meat. The resulting poached chicken, moist and flavorful, is lovely in salads of tossed greens or steamed vegetables, or shredded and added to soups.

—*Amy Cotler*

Vegetable soup stocks are swell
NO BONES ABOUT IT

If you're serious about vegetarian fare, good vegetable stocks are a necessity. Start with a basic foundation of flavor-enriching vegetables and herbs: onions or leeks or both, garlic, celery, carrots, parsley, and bay leaves.

Gently sautéing onions and leeks in a little butter or oil brings out their natural sweetness. The object is to soften the vegetables slowly over relatively low heat, so they release their moisture gradually. Avoid browning, which will make the stock dark and give it a pronounced caramelized flavor that would overpower a delicately flavored soup.

....

1½ tablespoons oil or butter

1 onion, peeled and sliced

2 leeks, cleaned and sliced

3 to 4 cloves garlic

2 stalks celery, chopped

2 carrots, peeled and chopped

Large handful of fresh parsley

2 bay leaves

Salt

Optional: potato peelings or a waxy-fleshed potato, corn cobs, tomatoes, summer squash, sautéed eggplant, herbs

....

Heat the oil or butter in a heavy-bottomed soup pot. Stir in the onion and leeks and sauté over gentle heat, stirring occasionally, for about 10 minutes. Stir in 3 to 4 bruised cloves of garlic; sauté another minute or so.

Add 10 cups cold water, the celery, carrots, parsley (stems and all), and bay leaves. These and all other ingredients you use in your stocks should be carefully scrubbed. No stock in my book would be complete without the addition of potato peels—or just plain potatoes, peels and all. Whole potato chunks will break down, release their starch, and make the stock somewhat cloudy. But how often does it really matter? In most cases, the extra flavor and body are welcome and wonderful.

Other ingredients can also be added to stock as it starts to simmer—scraped corn cobs, summer squash, ripe tomatoes, the stringy seeds of winter squashes (but not the flesh, which falls apart and dominates the broth). Eggplant adds body and distinctive flavor; add cubes of it just before you add the garlic and sauté covered 3 to 4 minutes, before adding water. Stay away from cabbage, cauliflower, and Brussels sprouts, as they give an off-flavor and aroma.

When it comes to herbs, fresh ones are best, but as with everything that goes into stock, no one flavor should dominate. It's hard to use too much parsley, though. A little chervil, oregano, thyme, and basil are excellent. Dried herbs can also be used, though in moderation.

Simmer stock uncovered, about 45 minutes; it should reduce quite a bit—by half isn't too much. I salt as I go, so I can tell how the stock is maturing, but I always undersalt and adjust the seasoning at the end. Strain, cool, and refrigerate. The stock will keep for 2 days in the fridge or several months in the freezer.

— *Ken Haedrich*

Cream of Lovage Soup

Lovage's stems, leaves, and aroma will remind you of celery, but its flavor is deeper, richer, more complex, and more robust. Its outer leaves can have a strong taste, so I favor the small, pale inner leaves, especially for salads. If you prefer, you can use the same technique for making celery soup; see the note at the end of the recipe.

Fresh from the garden: LOVAGE, POTATO

4 servings | *250 calories, 22g fat, 80mg sodium*

4 cups vegetable stock	1 medium potato, peeled and minced	1 cup heavy cream
1 cup chopped lovage leaves and stems	2 tablespoons freshly squeezed lemon juice	Salt and freshly ground pepper
		Chopped lovage leaves for garnish

Combine the stock, lovage, and potato in a large pan and bring to a boil. Lower the heat and let the mixture simmer for 15 to 20 minutes. Stir in the lemon juice, and then pour the mixture through a strainer into a container to remove the solids, pressing gently to extract the flavored liquid.

Whisk in the cream and add salt and pepper to taste. To serve, heat gently, ladle into small bowls, and garnish with chopped lovage leaves.

NOTE | If you don't have lovage, or if you prefer a milder flavor, you can make cream of celery soup by using a whole head of chopped celery, with leaves, in place of the lovage. When the vegetables are tender, put them through a food processor with enough of the liquid to purée them, return the mixture to the pan, and proceed with the recipe.

— *Recipe by Noel Richardson*

Fresh Pea Soup with Mint

This fresh, simple soup is easy and quick to prepare. It is wonderful when new peas are in season, but it also works well with frozen peas.

Fresh from the garden: PEAS, SPEARMINT, SHALLOTS OR LEEK

6 servings | *170 calories, 6g fat, 40mg sodium*

1½ pounds fresh peas, shelled, or about 1 pound frozen	2 shallots or 1 leek, finely diced (about ⅓ cup)	1½ cups milk or half-and-half
¼ cup chopped spearmint	2 tablespoons butter	Salt
		Freshly ground white pepper

Put the peas and chopped mint in a pan and barely cover them with water. Cover the pan and bring to a boil. Lower the heat and simmer until the peas are just tender, about 5 minutes; frozen peas will take a little less time.

Sauté the shallots in the butter in a small pan over moderate heat until they are soft and golden, 3 to 4 minutes.

Purée the peas and shallots together. Return them to the pan and add the milk or half-and-half, and salt and pepper to taste. If you want a completely smooth soup, pour it through a strainer. Heat over low heat until the soup is very hot, but do not allow it to boil.

NOTE | The original recipe appears in *Herbs in the Kitchen* by Susan Belsinger and Carolyn Dille (Interweave Press, 1991).

— Recipe by Susan Belsinger and Carolyn Dille

Japanese Soup with Shiitakes

If snap peas—the kind with edible pods—aren't available, you can substitute snow peas. This quick, brothy soup is extremely pretty and very savory, a perfect spring tonic.

Fresh from the garden: ASIAN GREENS, SNAP PEAS, SCALLIONS
4 servings | *170 calories, 3g fat, 410mg sodium*

5 dried shiitake mushrooms

4 cups vegetable or chicken stock
   (low-salt if canned)

1 tablespoon grated fresh ginger

¼ cup mirin (sweet rice wine)
   or sweet sherry

4 cups shredded greens (bok choy,
   Asian mustard, mizuna, chard,
   spinach, or a combination)

¼ pound medium shrimp, peeled and
   deveined, or diced, seasoned tofu

2 cups snap peas, stringed
   and cut in half

1 to 3 tablespoons soy sauce

½ tablespoon rice
   or apple-cider vinegar

2 tablespoons toasted sesame seeds

3 tablespoons chopped scallions

Cover the mushrooms with hot water and soak for 20 minutes. Drain the mushrooms, and add the soaking liquid to the soup pot. Slice the mushrooms thin, discarding any tough stems. Bring the stock to a boil, and add the ginger root and mirin. Simmer for 2 minutes, and then add the mushrooms, greens, and shrimp or tofu. Simmer an additional 3 to 4 minutes. Add the peas, 1 tablespoon of the soy sauce, and the vinegar. Simmer briefly, about 2 minutes. Add more soy sauce to taste. Serve immediately, topped with sesame seeds and scallions.

— *Recipe by David Hirsch*

Fresh Asparagus Soup

While I'm getting this recipe started, I like to simmer the tough asparagus ends—the parts usually discarded—in the broth to extract every bit of asparagus flavor.

Fresh from the garden: ASPARAGUS, ONION

4 servings | *210 calories, 15g fat, 910mg sodium*

1 pound asparagus	2 tablespoons butter or margarine	1 cup milk
½ cup chopped onion	2 tablespoons flour	½ cup sour cream
1 pint homemade or low-salt chicken broth	1 teaspoon salt	1 teaspoon freshly squeezed lemon juice
	Pinch of freshly ground pepper	

Cut asparagus into ½- to 1-inch pieces. Put the asparagus, chopped onion, and ½ cup chicken broth in a saucepan, cover, and bring to a boil over high heat. Reduce heat and simmer uncovered until asparagus is tender, about 12 minutes. Process the mixture in a blender to purée the vegetables. Set aside.

In the same pan, melt the butter over medium-low heat. Blend in the flour, salt, and pepper. Cook, stirring constantly for 2 minutes. Don't let the mixture brown. Whisk in the remaining chicken broth. Raise the heat to medium and cook, stirring constantly until the mixture boils. Stir in the asparagus purée and the milk.

Put the sour cream in a small bowl, ladle a little of the hot mixture into the sour cream to warm it, and stir to blend. Add the sour cream mixture and the lemon juice to the soup and stir well. Continue stirring while heating the soup to serving temperature, but don't allow it to boil. Serve immediately.

— *Recipe by Karen Pendleton*

Carrot-Top Soup

If you grow carrots or buy them with tops on, don't just toss the greens; they're full of flavor and nutrients and make for a delicious soup.

Fresh from the garden: CARROTS WITH TOPS, GARLIC, RED ONION, POTATOES, CELERY
6 servings | *260 calories, 16g fat, 390mg sodium*

½ cup butter
1½ cups chopped carrot tops, firmly packed
6 cloves garlic, minced

1 large red onion, diced
4 large potatoes, peeled and cut into ¾-inch chunks
½ teaspoon salt

½ teaspoon freshly ground pepper
1 stalk of celery, diced
2 carrots, diced
4 cups chicken stock or water

Melt the butter in a large saucepot over medium heat. Add the chopped carrot tops, garlic, onion, potatoes, salt, and pepper. Sauté over medium heat for 10 minutes, stirring frequently to avoid sticking. Add the celery and carrots and continue cooking for an additional 1 minute. Pour in the stock and bring the mixture to a boil. Immediately reduce the heat to a simmer and continue cooking until the vegetables are tender. Add more salt and pepper to taste, and serve immediately.

— *Recipe by Rosemary Campiformio*

Sweet Corn Soup with Cilantro Salsa

To get all of the meat and sweet juices but none of the fibrous skins from corn, shave off only the top halves of the kernels as you cut down the ear. When you've worked your way all around the ear, turn your knife over and, with the dull side of the blade, scrape down the cob, extracting the remaining solids and creamy juices. The cilantro salsa topping the soup makes a brightly flavored condiment that can also be used for tacos and enchiladas, or a dipping or drizzling sauce for grilled or sautéed vegetables.

Fresh from the garden: CORN, ONION, POTATO, JALAPEÑO, CILANTRO, BASIL, MINT, GARLIC, CORIANDER SEEDS, SCALLIONS | 6 servings | Soup—*110 calories, 3g fat, 400mg sodium; without garnishes* | Salsa—*110 calories, 12g fat, 5mg sodium; based on 12 portions*

FOR THE SOUP

6 ears of corn
1 tablespoon butter or corn oil
1 small onion, sliced thin
½ cup grated waxy potato
7 cups Quick Corn Stock (see p.118) or water
1 teaspoon salt
½ cup cream or half-and-half, optional

FOR THE SALSA

1 jalapeño, seeded
1 large bunch fresh cilantro, stems removed, about 2 cups
½ cup fresh basil
2 tablespoons fresh mint
1 clove garlic
½ cup plus 2 tablespoons extra-virgin olive oil
¼ teaspoon ground cumin
½ teaspoon ground coriander
2 scallions, sliced thin
Juice of 1 to 2 limes
Salt and freshly ground pepper

MAKE THE SOUP | Shuck the corn, remove the silk, and slice off the kernels. You should have about 4 cups. (Use the flavor-filled cobs in the stock if you're making one.)

In a wide soup pot, melt the butter, and then add the onion, potato, and 1 cup of the stock or water. Cover the pot and stew over medium heat until the onion is soft, about 10 minutes. Add the corn, salt, and remaining stock or water and bring to a boil. Then simmer, partially covered, for 10 minutes. Allow the soup to cool a bit. Working in

batches, purée the soup in a blender until smooth. Pass through a food mill or fine strainer, then return the soup to the stove; stir in the cream, if desired. Season with more salt and a little pepper, if necessary.

MAKE THE SALSA | Chop the jalapeño, herbs, and garlic very fine, and then combine with ¼ cup water, the oil, spices, and scallions. Add the juice of 1 lime and ¼ teaspoon salt, or more to taste. Adjust the balance of lime juice to oil if needed. Alternatively, chop everything coarse, then purée in a blender or food processor until smooth.

Ladle the soup into bowls and make a swirl of the salsa in each.

— Recipe by Deborah Madison

A bouquet of flavor

The bouquet garni (boo-kay gar-nee) is the backbone of soups, stocks, and sauces. This little bundle of herbs and spices adds a fuller flavor to these liquids while tying together all of the ingredients. In the past, the bouquet garni was a prescribed mixture of thyme, bay leaf, and parsley. But thankfully the traditional formula has changed as cooking methods have become less regimented. Choose the contents based on the fragrance you would like to permeate your dish as well as the season in which you are cooking.

I generally tie together 5 or 6 herb sprigs or leaves per quart of cooking liquid. A very economical approach to the bouquet garni is to use only the stems of herbs, saving the leaves to add to another dish.

Not all herbs work well. Mint and basil, which you might think would add the perfect flavor, turn black and slimy when they simmer in hot liquid.

A bouquet garni does not have to be wedded solely to herbs either. For example, you can tie in lemon peel or celery stalks. The most important rule is to use what's in season and what works with the dish you are making. In winter, bay leaves and winter savory may play a big part in your bouquet; in spring, perhaps new chives, tarragon, and young leek greens. In summer, bay leaves, fennel, and orange peel make a refreshing stock. In the fall, when I like to roast poultry, a chicken stock made with a bouquet garni filled with lots of thyme appeals to me.

Some cookbooks will tell you to wrap the herbs in cheesecloth, but who has tons of cheesecloth lying around? I suggest using kitchen string to tie them up like a bundle of wood. What I often use to hold the herbs together is the green part from a leek. I take one blade and lay it flat. On top of it, I stack the herbs, and then top them with another green leek blade and tie this sandwich together with kitchen string. If the leek blade is very large, you can fold it in half and stuff the herbs in the center. The leek holds in the herbs and contributes its own flavor to the cooking liquid.

For stock, add the bouquet garni at the beginning and leave it in until the stock is finished simmering. Then strain it out with the rest of the ingredients. For stews, soups, sauces, and even grains, leave it in for the duration of the cooking, and then remove it before serving.

—Amanda Hesser

Quick Corn Stock

This stock is worth making for the additional depth of flavor it gives corn soup. You could also use it for corn or seafood chowders or for making polenta. If you're using commercial stock, simmer the corn cobs in it to boost its flavor.

Fresh from the garden: ONION, CELERY, CARROT, BOUQUET GARNI (LEEK LEAF, BAY LEAF, THYME, PARSLEY, GARLIC), CORN COBS, TOMATO | **About 7 cups** | *30 calories, 1.5g fat, 290mg sodium; per cup*

1 tablespoon vegetable oil or butter
1 onion, sliced thin
1 celery stalk, sliced
1 carrot, sliced

Bouquet garni (see p.117), including
    plenty of fresh parsley stems
Corn cobs

Tomato trimmings or a whole tomato
1 teaspoon salt

Heat the oil in a saucepan, add the onion, celery, and carrot and cook over medium-high heat, stirring occasionally, until the onion begins to color. Add the rest of the ingredients and 2 quarts water and bring to a boil.

Simmer for 25 minutes, then strain, pushing as much liquid as you can from the vegetables.

— *Recipe by Deborah Madison*

Fresh Tomato & Walnut Soup with Rosemary

Pan-roasting the tomatoes until they're lightly browned in places adds depth of flavor, and fresh orange juice adds unexpected brilliance to this delicious and unusual soup.

Fresh from the garden: TOMATOES, ROSEMARY

4 servings | *410 calories, 33g fat, 70mg sodium*

6 large tomatoes (3 pounds), quartered
Salt and freshly ground black pepper
3 tablespoons olive oil

2 cups good-quality beef broth (you can use one 14½-ounce can of ready-to-serve broth plus 1½ ounces water to make up the difference)

1 cup walnuts, broken into ½-inch pieces
Juice of 1 orange with pulp
½ cup sour cream
2 tablespoons finely chopped fresh rosemary

In a large saucepan, mix the tomatoes with salt and pepper, and drizzle with 1 tablespoon of the oil. Use your hands to mix so that each piece is coated with oil.

Cook the tomatoes over high heat until bits here and there have browned, about 5 minutes. Turn the tomatoes into a food processor (don't rinse the saucepan) and process until they've reached a fairly smooth purée. Pour the purée back into the saucepan, and stir in the beef broth and the remaining 2 tablespoons of olive oil.

Warm a large nonstick frying pan over medium heat. Add the walnuts and toast them, stirring frequently and shaking the pan, until they're richly colored, 2 to 3 minutes. Slide the walnuts into a bowl and set aside.

To serve, bring the soup just to a simmer over medium heat. When it bubbles, turn off the heat, blend in the orange juice, taste, and season as needed with salt and pepper. Ladle into hot soup plates, strew walnuts over each, then add a dollop of sour cream in the center and sprinkle the sour cream with rosemary.

— *Recipe by Sylvia Thompson*

Red Gazpacho

The ancestors of this soup can be found in Andalusia, where fragments of bread and other leftover ingredients were combined with vinegar, water, oil, garlic, and other seasonings and served at room temperature. Today, gazpacho remains true to its spiritual, if not culinary, roots in that it is one of the finest uses for an abundance of vegetables that might otherwise go to waste. And the original ingredients, especially vinegar, olive oil, and garlic, remain essential to a successful gazpacho. This full-bodied version of contemporary gazpacho is best at the peak of harvest, when all of the vegetables are dazzlingly ripe.

Fresh from the garden: TOMATOES, SERRANO CHILE, GARLIC, CUCUMBERS, BELL PEPPER, RED ONION, BASIL, PARSLEY, CILANTRO | 8 servings | *220 calories, 19g fat, 35mg sodium*

4 or 5 large tomatoes, peeled, seeded, and chopped

1 serrano chile, seeded and minced

5 cloves garlic, minced

2 lemon cucumbers, peeled, seeded, and diced

1 red bell pepper, seeded and diced

1 red onion, peeled and diced

1 slightly firm avocado, peeled and diced

4 cups light beef stock or chicken stock

2 tablespoons freshly squeezed lemon juice

2 tablespoons red-wine vinegar

2 tablespoons chopped fresh basil

2 tablespoons chopped fresh Italian parsley

4 tablespoons chopped fresh cilantro

Kosher salt

Freshly ground black pepper

½ cup best-quality extra-virgin olive oil

Combine the tomatoes, serrano chile, garlic, cucumbers, bell pepper, onion, and avocado in a large bowl.

Add the stock, lemon juice, and vinegar, and stir briefly. Stir in the fresh basil, parsley, and cilantro, and season with salt and pepper to taste. Chill the soup for at least an hour before serving. Remove it from the refrigerator, stir, and let rest for 15 minutes before serving. Ladle into bowls, drizzle each bowl with about a tablespoon of olive oil, and serve.

— *Recipe by Michele Anna Jordan*

Cold Cucumber Dill Soup

This soup is lovely and refreshing on a hot summer day. You can use any type of cucumber for it: English, slicers, picklers, or best of all, the juicy, mild Persian types.

Fresh from the garden: CUCUMBERS, CHIVES, DILL
6 servings | *50 calories, 1.5g fat, 35mg sodium*

2 medium cucumbers
3 cups vegetable stock
2 tablespoons flour

1 cup plain yogurt
1 tablespoon chopped fresh chives

2 tablespoons chopped fresh dill plus
   dill fronds for garnish

Peel, seed, and chop the cucumbers. In a large saucepan, combine the cucumbers and 1 cup of stock. Cook over medium heat just until the cucumbers are soft.

Mix the flour with 2 tablespoons of stock to make a smooth paste, then combine with the rest of the stock and add to the cucumbers. Stir over low heat until heated through, and then simmer for 5 minutes. Allow the mixture to cool, then purée. Refrigerate.

When ready to serve the soup, thoroughly whisk the yogurt, chives, and dill into the refrigerated mixture.

— *Recipe by Peter Garnham*

Golden Squash Blossom Crema

This classic, classy, pale yellow wonder is the squash blossom dish of dreams. Make it at the height of summer, when squash blossoms are available at the market or from your garden.

Fresh from the garden: WHITE ONION, POTATO, SQUASH BLOSSOMS, POBLANO CHILES, ZUCCHINI, CORN, EPAZOTE OR PARSLEY | 6 servings | *180 calories, 12g fat, 660mg sodium*

1½ tablespoons butter

1 large white onion, chopped into
   ¼-inch dice

3 cups chicken broth

1 small boiling potato, peeled
   and coarsely chopped

25 large, fresh squash blossoms
   (3- to 4-inch male blossoms)

2 poblano chiles

1 cup milk

1 medium zucchini, cut into
   ¼-inch pieces

Kernels from 1 large ear of corn

½ cup heavy cream or crème fraîche

1½ teaspoons salt

Epazote or fresh parsley for garnish

In a 4-quart soup pot, melt the butter over medium heat. Add the onion and cook, stirring frequently, until lightly brown, about 5 minutes. Scoop out half of the onion and set aside. Add the broth and potato, partially cover, and simmer over medium-low heat for 20 minutes.

While the broth is simmering, prepare the squash blossoms. Peel off the sepals that come out from the base of the blossoms. Break off the stems. Remove the stamen in the center of each flower and discard. Cut the blossoms crosswise into ¼-inch strips, including the bulbous base.

Add half the blossoms to the broth and simmer 3 minutes. In a food processor or in batches in a blender, purée the mixture and return it to the pot.

Roast the chiles directly over a gas flame, or on a medium-hot gas grill, or 4 inches below a very hot broiler. Turn occasionally until blistered and blackened on all sides, 4 to 6 minutes for the flame or grill, about 10 minutes for the broiler. Cover with a kitchen towel and let stand about 5 minutes. Peel off the charred skin, cut out the seed pod, and scrape away any straggling bits of skin and seeds. Cut into ¼-inch dice.

Add the chiles to the soup along with the milk and reserved onion; bring to a simmer and cook for 10 minutes. Add the zucchini and corn, simmer a couple of minutes, then add the remaining squash blossoms. Simmer a couple of minutes longer (the strips of blossom will soften into a deep golden color). Remove from heat, stir in the cream, taste, and season with salt. Serve in warm bowls garnished with epazote or parsley.

— *Recipe by Rick Bayless*

Fire in the kitchen!
COOKING WITH CHILES

Cooking chile peppers enhances their sweet and savory flavor components and makes for a more robust taste. But while the flesh softens in cooking, the skin becomes tough, so you'll want to remove it. Cooking a chile makes it easier to peel off the tough skin. It also tames its sharp heat, and the pod develops a smoky, rounded flavor.

There's more than one way to skin a chile. One of the easiest methods to cook larger varieties is to set them over an open gas flame. The flame chars the skin quickly while letting the flesh develop richer flavor. Setting a rack from a small grill (like a Weber Smokey Joe®) over the flame lets you roast several chiles at once over one burner. Use tongs to turn the chile frequently (you don't want to puncture the skin), letting the flame caress the chile until it blisters evenly. The idea is to char the skin, but not burn the flesh.

For even better flavor, roast chiles on an outdoor wood-burning grill, stoked until it is red hot. The coals add a nice, smoky edge to a chile's flavor. You can char the chiles while waiting for the coals to be ready for whatever else you're grilling.

An oven broiler works like a grill but has a tendency to steam the chile, so for broiling, I recommend splitting chiles in half lengthwise and broiling them skin side up.

The heat in chile peppers is due to capsaicin, a compound found in the chile's pulpy membrane. Capsaicin is insoluble in water, which makes it tough to douse when you've bitten into too much heat. (That's why drinking water doesn't help a mouth that's burning with chile heat. Try sucking on a lime or lemon wedge instead.)

The capsaicin-containing oils can go far beyond your hands to anything else you touch—your forehead, your nose, your eyes. So treat chiles with respect. I highly recommend gloves if you have sensitive skin or if you are working with peppers for the first time, especially when handling habaneros. After peeling chiles, wash your hands with soap and water. Lemon juice also helps break down the oils that cause the burning sensation.

Once your roasted chiles have cooled, rub the skins with a terry cloth or coarse paper towel, or peel them with your fingers. Do not peel under running water, or most of the flavorful oils will be washed away. When the skin is removed, slit the chile, cut out the core, and scrape away the seeds. A few char spots won't hurt; in fact, they'll enhance the flavor.

To store roasted chiles, put them in zip-top bags and freeze them. Or freeze them individually in ice cube trays, and later transfer them to freezer bags. They'll last a year in the freezer.

— *Jay McCarthy*

Garlic Lime Soup

Tomatillos and greens add body, flavor, and nutrition to this soup, while cilantro, garlic, lime, and jalapeño add zing. Packed full of Vitamin A, C, and K, this is a great antidote to the common cold.

Fresh from the garden: GARLIC, TOMATILLOS, ONION, CILANTRO; COLLARDS, SPINACH, OR OTHER GREENS; JALAPEÑO | 4 servings | *150 calories, 5g fat, 55mg sodium*

10 cloves garlic, peeled and chopped fine

1 tablespoon oil

16 tomatillos, husks removed

½ onion, cut into ¼-inch-thick crescents

4 cups stock

½ cup packed, finely chopped fresh cilantro

1 pound collards, spinach, or other greens, stemmed (about 10 cups roughly chopped)

1 jalapeño, seeded

Juice of 1 lime

Salt and freshly ground pepper

In a large soup pot, stir the garlic and oil over medium-low heat until the garlic is toasted and soft, 4 to 6 minutes. Be careful not to burn the garlic.

Add the tomatillos whole and stir for 3 to 5 minutes. Then add half the onions and continue stirring until they are translucent.

Add the stock and bring to a simmer. Now add the cilantro, the collards, spinach or other greens, and the jalapeño. Simmer until the greens wilt, about 5 minutes. Remove from the heat and let cool.

Purée the soup in a food processor or blender, or run it through a food mill. Return the purée to the pot and reheat. Add the lime juice a little at a time until the soup reaches the desired piquancy. Add salt and pepper to taste. Serve immediately to preserve the vibrant color. Garnish with the remaining onion.

— Recipe by Jay McCarthy

Italian Cannellini Soup

Rustic and hearty bean soups are true comfort food. This soup gets its thick, creamy texture when you mash half the beans right in the pot.

Fresh from the garden: GARLIC, ROSEMARY, GREENS
6 servings | *320 calories, 4.5g fat, 310mg sodium*

1 pound dried cannellini beans (white kidney beans)
1 tablespoon olive oil
¼ pound pancetta or Canadian bacon, cut in ½-inch pieces

1 large head garlic, cloves separated and peeled
1 teaspoon dried rosemary, crumbled, or 4 teaspoons chopped fresh
Salt and freshly ground pepper

2 tightly packed cups coarsely chopped greens (such as kale, chard, or beet greens)
1 tablespoon red-wine vinegar

Pick over the beans, removing any small pebbles or debris. Rinse, put in a large bowl with 6 to 8 cups cold water, and let soak at least six hours or overnight. Drain.

In a medium soup pot, heat the oil over medium heat. Fry the pancetta or Canadian bacon, stirring frequently, just until it starts to release its fat but does not brown, about 3 minutes.

Add the beans, 9 cups water, the garlic, and the rosemary. Bring to a boil, cover, and reduce heat to a simmer. Cook until the beans are tender, about 2 hours.

Turn off the heat and use a potato masher to mash half the beans and garlic cloves. Season generously with salt and freshly ground pepper.

Bring the soup to a simmer and add the greens and vinegar. Heat until the greens are wilted but still bright, 2 to 5 minutes. Ladle into warm bowls.

— *Recipe by Amy Cotler*

Beef & Radish Soup

The all-white daikon is the best-known of the winter radishes. Look for red- or green-fleshed varieties at Asian markets. If you can't find them, use turnips instead. And if you can't get your hands on fresh egg noodles, then substitute fresh linguini.

Fresh from the garden: ONION, GARLIC, ROSEMARY, RUTABAGA, WINTER RADISHES, BLACK RADISHES

8 servings | *230 calories, 11g fat, 440mg sodium*

3 to 4 tablespoons olive oil
1 pound stewing beef cubes
1 large onion, peeled and diced
3 large cloves garlic, minced
6 ounces sliced mushrooms
½ cup red wine

3 to 4 teaspoons fresh rosemary, chopped
1 medium rutabaga, peeled and cut into 1-inch cubes
1 teaspoon salt

½ teaspoon freshly ground pepper
Two medium red- or green-fleshed winter radishes
Two medium black radishes
8 ounces fresh egg noodles

Heat 3 tablespoons of the oil in a large Dutch oven. Add the beef cubes and brown over medium-high heat, about 10 minutes. Remove the beef to a platter. In the same pan, brown the onions slowly over medium heat, about 10 minutes. Add another tablespoon of oil if necessary. Add the garlic and mushrooms and finish the browning, about 5 minutes.

Add the beef, 2 quarts water, the wine, rosemary, rutabaga, salt, and pepper. Bring to a boil, then cover and simmer over low heat for about 30 minutes. Add more water if needed.

Meanwhile, scrub the radishes. Slice them ½-inch thick, and then cut the slices into quarters. Add the radishes to the soup and simmer with the lid ajar until they are tender, about 20 minutes. With 7 to 10 minutes to go, add the noodles and cook until al dente.

— *Recipe by Cynthia Hizer*

Fall Harvest Soup

This soup is especially good with spicy Mexican chorizo, but you can use any flavorful sausage. Try mild Portuguese lunguiça, a smoked chicken sausage, or duck or lamb sausage.

Fresh from the garden: ONION, GARLIC, WINTER SQUASH, RUSSET POTATOES, CABBAGE, CILANTRO
8 servings | 460 calories, 28g fat, 740mg sodium

3 tablespoons olive oil
1 yellow onion, diced
3 cloves garlic, minced
1 pound Mexican chorizo,
   casings removed

3 cups diced winter squash
2 medium russet potatoes, diced
½ head white cabbage, cored
   and shredded
3 cups beef or duck stock

2 cups cooked white beans
Salt and freshly ground pepper
¼ cup fresh cilantro leaves

Heat the olive oil in a large, heavy pot. Add the diced onion and sauté until it is soft and fragrant, about 8 minutes. Add the garlic and sauté for 2 minutes. Add the chorizo, breaking it up with a fork while it cooks. When the chorizo appears to have released its fat, drain off the excess fat and return the pot to the heat.

Add the squash and potatoes and sauté 3 to 4 minutes, stirring frequently. Add the cabbage, stirring until it wilts. Add the stock, 3 cups water, and the beans.

Bring the liquid to a boil, reduce the heat, and simmer partially covered until the squash and potatoes are just tender, about 15 to 20 minutes.

Taste the soup and season with salt and pepper. Ladle into warmed soup bowls, top each serving with a sprinkling of cilantro leaves, and serve immediately.

— *Recipe by Michele Anna Jordan*

Cabbage Paprikash Soup

To stretch this soup, add up to ½ cup chopped tomatoes. Chopped fresh dill and a dot of sour cream make the perfect garnish.

Fresh from the garden: ONION, CABBAGE, GARLIC, CARROT

6 servings | 90 calories, 4g fat, 45mg sodium

2 tablespoons butter

1 large onion, quartered
    and thinly sliced

4 cups thinly sliced cabbage

Salt

2 cloves garlic, minced

1 tablespoon paprika

5½ to 6 cups vegetable stock

1 large carrot, peeled and grated

2 tablespoons tomato paste

Juice of 1 lemon

2 to 3 teaspoons sugar

Freshly ground pepper

Melt the butter in a medium soup pot. Stir in the onion and sauté over medium heat until translucent, about 8 to 9 minutes. Add the cabbage, salt lightly, and sauté until all the cabbage is wilted, about 10 minutes more. Stir in the garlic and paprika and cook, stirring often, for 1 minute.

Add the vegetable stock, carrot, tomato paste, and more salt to taste, and bring to a boil. Reduce the heat and simmer gently for 10 minutes, stirring occasionally.

Add about half each of the lemon juice and sugar; simmer briefly, then taste, adding more sugar and lemon juice to get a mellow but distinctly sweet-tart broth. Add pepper to taste. Serve hot.

— *Recipe by Ken Haedrich*

Pompa Sisters' Fall Soup with Scarola

This is the kind of soup often served at holidays in Italian-American households, but you don't have to wait for a special occasion to enjoy it. It's a great dish for cool fall weather. If you can't find fresh shelling beans, try using small pasta.

....

Fresh from the garden: ONION, GARLIC, CARROTS, ESCAROLE, SHELLING BEANS

4 servings | *240 calories, 12g fat, 100mg sodium*

....

1 medium onion, sliced

3 tablespoons olive oil

4 cloves garlic, peeled and minced

1 cup chopped carrots

6 cups beef or chicken stock

1 medium head escarole, washed well and cut into 1-inch strips

2 cups fresh shelling beans, or ¼ pound small pasta, cooked and drained

Salt

Crushed red pepper flakes

....

In a soup pot, sauté the onion in olive oil until golden. Add the garlic and carrots, and cook for a few minutes. Add the stock and the escarole. Cover and cook until the escarole is tender, about 30 minutes.

Separately, boil the shelling beans until tender in enough water to cover them by at least 2 inches and drain. (Fresh beans will take only a few minutes.) Finish by adding the cooked beans to the soup. Salt to taste. Serve with red pepper flakes on the side.

— *Recipe by Ed Miller*

Kale & Sausage Soup

Kale is wonderful in soups because it becomes tender without losing all its chewy texture. Here, it is simmered with sausage to make a Portuguese-style soup. I like to pass cruets of olive oil and red wine vinegar for garnish, along with a bowl of grated Parmigiano-Reggiano.

Fresh from the garden: KALE, ONION, GARLIC, CARROTS, TOMATOES, BASIL
6 servings | *300 calories, 20g fat, 550mg sodium*

½ to ¾ pound linguiça or chorizo	6 to 7 cups chicken or vegetable stock	1 tablespoon fresh basil, chopped,
1 large bunch kale (about ¾ pound)	2 large carrots, peeled and diced	or 1 teaspoon dried
2 tablespoons olive oil	Salt and freshly ground pepper	2 to 3 teaspoons red-wine vinegar
2 cups chopped onion	1½ cups diced fresh or chopped	
2 cloves garlic, minced	canned tomatoes	

Bring a medium saucepan of water to a boil. Prick the sausage 8 or 10 times with a fork, add to the boiling water, and boil for 8 minutes to cook out some of the fat. Transfer the sausage to a plate. While the sausage cools, strip the kale leaves from the stems, tearing the leaves into bite-size pieces. Put the leaves in a large bowl, cover with cool water, and agitate the leaves to loosen dirt and grit. Transfer the leaves to a colander and set aside. When the sausage is cool enough to handle, cut it into ¼-inch slices.

Heat the olive oil in a large, nonreactive soup pot. Add the chopped onion and sauté over medium heat until translucent, for 8 to 9 minutes. Stir in the garlic, sauté several more seconds, and then add the stock and carrots. Bring the stock to a boil, reduce the heat, cover partially, and simmer for 5 minutes. Stir in the kale, sliced sausage, and salt and pepper to taste; simmer for 10 minutes. Stir in the tomato and basil and simmer another 8 to 10 minutes, adding more salt if necessary. Turn the heat off and let the soup sit for 30 minutes. Reheat, stirring in the vinegar, to taste, just before serving.

— Recipe by Ken Haedrich

Curried Winter Vegetable Soup

Coconut milk, curry powder, and cilantro give winter vegetables an Indian twist. This warming soup is wonderfully fragrant and filling.

Fresh from the garden: LEEK, POTATO, SWEET POTATO, TURNIP, PARSNIP, CARROT, CILANTRO

4 servings | 270 calories, 7g fat, 95mg sodium

1½ teaspoons butter

1 tablespoon curry powder

1 large leek, chopped

4 cups chicken or vegetable stock

½ cup dried red lentils

1 waxy potato, peeled and diced

1 sweet potato, peeled and diced

1 medium turnip, diced

1 parsnip, sliced on the diagonal

1 carrot, sliced on the diagonal

¼ cup coconut milk

2 tablespoons chopped fresh cilantro

Salt

⅛ to ¼ teaspoon cayenne

In a medium soup pot, melt the butter. Add the curry powder and leek, and cook over low heat for 1 minute, stirring frequently. Add the stock and lentils. Bring to a boil, reduce to a simmer, and cook, covered, over medium heat until the lentils are soft, about 10 minutes.

Add the potato, sweet potato, turnip, parsnip, and carrot. Simmer, covered, until the vegetables are soft but not mushy, about 25 minutes. Remove the soup from the heat. Stir in the coconut milk and cilantro. Season with salt and cayenne. Ladle into warm bowls.

— Recipe by Amy Cotler

SIDE
DISHES

Side dishes are where vegetables really shine. And when made with freshly harvested, primo ingredients— glossy eggplants, tender corn, juicy tomatoes, crisp greens, crunchy peppers, plump squash, and all manner of aromatic herbs—side dishes can steal the show. At one memorable summer Sunday dinner that I recently attended, there were no fewer than seven vegetable sides passed around the table. We all loved the roast lamb, but what we all really went crazy for were the vegetables: harvested at their peak, simply prepared—they distilled the essence of the season.

Whether your tastes run to the traditional or the new, you'll find recipes here that appeal, from Pole Beans with Country Ham to Eggplant and Roasted Chile Salad. There's a recipe here for nearly every type of vegetable. Work-horse vegetables like green beans, summer squash, and potatoes—ones that are prolific in the garden and ubiquitous in the markets—get a variety of treatments. For knock-your-socks-off flavor, try one of Rick Bayless's Mexican recipes featuring zucchini or Sam Gittings's wonderful Asian salad made inventively with squash "noodles." You may find yourself planting an extra hill of squash next summer.

The key to great sides is having recipes for every season. Celebrate spring's arrival with Creamed Spinach, Favas with Pancetta, Roasted Asparagus, and Braised Fennel with Garlic. Summer brings so many wonderful vegetables; that's the time to make Rapid-Roasted Tomatoes, Moroccan-Style Summer Vegetable Sauté, Chunky Ratatouille, Grilled Green Beans with Warm Gorgonzola Vinaigrette, and Deviled Tomato Slices. There are savory gratins and roasted vegetables for when the weather turns cool. And there are wonderful special-occasion dishes, as well. For your next holiday meal, try the Butternut Squash with Dried Cherry Compote, or Brussels Sprouts Braised in Red Wine and 40 Cloves of Garlic, or Bread Stuffing with Quinces. You might be inspired to create your own Sunday Supper with Seven Sides, then sit down with friends, enjoy the meal, and collect the accolades.

Steamed Carrots with Sesame Vinegar

Newly harvested carrots, available from late spring through fall, make for an exceptionally sweet, tender dish. Cilantro, ginger, orange juice, and brown sugar combine in a vibrant and sassy dressing that is perfect for carrots.

Fresh from the garden: CILANTRO, CARROTS
6 servings | *45 calories, 0g fat, 35mg sodium*

2 teaspoons finely chopped fresh cilantro

1 tablespoon finely chopped fresh ginger

½ teaspoon sesame seeds, toasted

½ cup rice vinegar

¼ cup freshly squeezed orange juice

2 tablespoons brown sugar

8 carrots

Combine all ingredients except the carrots and set aside.

Cut the carrots on the diagonal in ¼-inch slices. Steam them in a steamer basket over boiling water until just tender, approximately 10 minutes. Do not let the carrots get mushy. Remove them from the steamer and toss with the sweet vinegar mixture. Serve hot or chilled.

— *Recipe by Rosemary Campiformio*

Roasted Parsnips & Carrots with Cilantro Pesto

Carrots are sweet vegetables, and parsnips are especially so. Roasting caramelizes their sugars, deepening their flavors and adding complexity. Cilantro pesto enhances the earthiness of the roasted roots.

Fresh from the garden: PARSNIPS, CARROTS, ONIONS, GARLIC, CILANTRO
6 servings | 390 calories, 27g fat, 115mg sodium

5 large or 12 small parsnips
5 large or 12 small carrots
2 onions
½ cup plus 2 tablespoons olive oil
1½ tablespoons grated fresh ginger

FOR THE PESTO
3 cloves garlic
¼ cup unsalted, roasted peanuts
2 cups loosely packed fresh cilantro
   (1 large bunch)

¼ cup grated Parmigiano-Reggiano
Salt and freshly ground pepper
¼ teaspoon crushed red pepper flakes

Preheat oven to 450°F. Scrub the parsnips and carrots. If small, leave whole. Otherwise, trim the tops and root ends and cut the vegetables crosswise into ½-inch rounds. Peel the onions and cut them lengthwise into six wedges. Toss the vegetables with 2 tablespoons of the oil. Spread on a baking sheet and roast in the oven for 15 minutes. Toss the vegetables with the grated ginger and lower the heat to 375°F. Roast until tender, about 10 to 20 minutes more, stirring the vegetables or shaking the pan once or twice to prevent sticking.

MAKE THE PESTO | Meanwhile, in a food processor or blender, purée the garlic, peanuts, and cilantro with ¼ cup of the oil. Add the cheese and, with the motor running, slowly pour in the rest of the oil. Season with salt, pepper, and red pepper flakes. Let the pesto stand at room temperature for 15 minutes to let the flavors meld.

Toss the roasted vegetables with the pesto until they are lightly coated. Let stand for another 15 minutes and serve.

NOTE | Use the cilantro pesto to dress noodles for the Grilled Eggplant Stacks on p. 210. Instead of the red pepper flakes, add a chopped, seeded jalapeño and the juice of half a lime.

— *Recipe by Jesse Cool*

Braised Fennel with Garlic

You can adapt this recipe with any number of substitutions: butter instead of olive oil, white wine instead of water, and shallots or onion slices instead of garlic.

Fresh from the garden: FENNEL, GARLIC
4 servings | *100 calories, 7g fat, 200mg sodium*

2 large or 3 small bulbs fennel
2 tablespoons olive oil

4 or more cloves garlic, peeled
(if using freshly harvested garlic,
use 1 to 2 heads)

¼ teaspoon salt
Freshly ground pepper

Trim the fennel and slice vertically about ½ inch thick. Chop the leaves and set them aside.

Choose a large sauté or frying pan that can be covered. Add the oil and arrange the fennel slices so they don't overlap. (If necessary, brown the fennel in two batches or use an extra pan for this step.) Over medium-low heat, slowly brown the fennel on both sides, about 15 minutes. The more you brown it, the deeper and richer the flavor will be. After 10 minutes, add the garlic. If using new garlic, watch it carefully because it can burn easily.

Add ½ cup water and the salt, lower the heat, and cover; cook slowly until the fennel and garlic are very soft, another 20 to 30 minutes. Watch closely during the final stages of cooking to be sure there is still liquid in the pan, and add 1 to 2 tablespoons water, as needed, to keep the pan from going dry. During the last few minutes, add the chopped fennel leaves and season with freshly ground pepper to taste.

— *Recipe by Ed Miller*

Broccoli with Garlic & Hot Peppers

Have you been dropping your broccoli into a pot of already boiling water? Try this for perfect al dente broccoli: Place the head in a pot of cold, salted water and cover. Bring to a boil over high heat and remove immediately.

....

Fresh from the garden: BROCCOLI, GARLIC
4 servings | *190 calories, 14g fat, 350mg sodium*

....

2 large broccoli heads (about 2 pounds)	3 cloves garlic, pressed or minced	½ teaspoon salt
¼ teaspoon crushed red pepper flakes	¼ cup olive oil	1 lime, cut into 6 slices

....

Trim broccoli leaves and put the whole head into a large pot of cold, salted water. Place over high heat and cover. When the water comes to a boil, remove the head. Cut the top into small pieces of uniform size. Peel the stalk and cut it into pieces.

In a large frying pan, heat the pepper and garlic in the olive oil over high heat. When the garlic and olive oil begin to sizzle, add the broccoli. Stir-fry quickly to coat all surfaces.

Add the salt and 2 tablespoons of water, lower the heat, cover, and cook over low heat until the broccoli reaches desired tenderness, 10 to 12 minutes.

Serve with lime wedges for squeezing liberally over the broccoli.

— *Recipe by John Okas*

Favas with Pancetta

This quick sauté exemplifies the best of Italian cooking.
The ingredients are few and the technique is simple,
allowing the flavor of garden-fresh favas to shine.

Fresh from the garden: FAVAS, ONION

4 servings | *390 calories, 7g fat, 430mg sodium*

4 pounds unshelled favas	1 tablespoon olive oil	Salt and freshly ground pepper
2 ounces pancetta, cut into small pieces	1 small onion, coarsely chopped	

Shell the favas and blanch for 1 minute in boiling water. Drain and let cool. Slip the skins from the beans.

Brown the pancetta in a large, heavy frying pan over medium-low heat. Remove the pancetta and set aside, but leave the fat in the pan.

Using the same frying pan, add the olive oil and sauté the onion until soft. Add the favas and just enough water to slightly moisten everything. Reduce heat, and cook for another 2 to 5 minutes, depending on the maturity of the beans. Add salt and pepper to taste and stir in the pancetta. Serve.

— *Recipe by Ed Miller*

Green Beans Sautéed with Radishes & Rosemary

Sautéing radishes with the beans adds a water-chestnut-like crunch and a little bite and heat to an otherwise mild dish. If you haven't tried rosemary with beans before, you'll find it's a nice flavor match.

Fresh from the garden: GREEN BEANS, RADISHES, ROSEMARY, SCALLIONS

4 servings | 100 calories, 7g fat, 150mg sodium

¾ pound green beans (about 4 cups), snapped in half

5 large red radishes

1 tablespoon butter

1 tablespoon olive oil

1½ tablespoons chopped fresh rosemary

3 scallions, finely sliced

1 tablespoon balsamic vinegar

¼ teaspoon salt

¼ teaspoon freshly ground pepper

In a medium saucepan, bring about 6 cups of lightly salted water to a boil. Add the beans and blanch them for 4 minutes. Drain the beans in a colander and immediately immerse them in an ice-water bath to stop them from cooking.

Cut the radishes into matchsticks. To do this, first trim the roots and tops evenly. Next, slice the radishes, from top to bottom, into ⅛-inch pieces. Then slice the pieces lengthwise to form matchstick shapes.

In a nonstick pan, melt the butter on low heat and add the olive oil. Increase the heat to medium and add the rosemary. When the rosemary becomes aromatic, in about 3 minutes, add the beans, radishes, scallions, balsamic vinegar, salt, and pepper. Sauté an additional 4 minutes and serve immediately.

— *Recipe by All Kovalencik*

Grilled Green Beans
with Warm Gorgonzola Vinaigrette

Grilling green beans gives them a slight nutty flavor. The warm Gorgonzola vinaigrette is delicious with other vegetables, too; try it with asparagus in spring, ripe summer tomatoes, or bitter fall greens like endive and radicchio.

Fresh from the garden: GREEN BEANS, GARLIC, SHALLOTS, THYME, BASIL
6 servings | *80 calories, 4g fat, 110mg sodium*

1 pound green beans (about 6 cups)	¾ teaspoon chopped garlic	½ teaspoon chopped fresh basil
1 tablespoon olive oil	¾ teaspoon chopped shallots	or ¼ teaspoon dried
¼ cup balsamic vinegar	½ teaspoon chopped fresh thyme,	Salt and freshly ground pepper
¼ cup crumbled Gorgonzola	or ¼ teaspoon dried	
1 tablespoon brown sugar		

In a medium saucepan, bring about 6 cups of lightly salted water to a boil. Add the beans and blanch them for 4 minutes. Drain the beans in a colander and immediately immerse them in an ice-water bath to stop them from cooking.

In a small saucepan, combine 1½ teaspoons of the olive oil and all the remaining ingredients. Warm over medium heat until the ingredients start to combine, about 7 minutes.

Toss the green beans in the remaining olive oil and season lightly with salt and pepper. Quickly grill the beans on a hot charcoal or gas grill, about 30 seconds on each side. Toss the beans in the warm vinaigrette and serve immediately.

NOTE | Always blanch beans before grilling or sautéing them. Blanching keeps the beans bright green and ensures they won't be undercooked. Leaving a bean too raw keeps it from exuding its natural sweetness, just as surely as overcooking destroys its texture.

— *Recipe by All Kovalencik*

Versatile Green Bean Salad

At its most basic—beans, olive oil, sea salt—this is a simple and delicious side dish so using really good olive oil and sea salt is crucial. Dressed up with extras, it's fit for a party, especially if you use the slender, tender French-style filet beans. The dish is good warm or at room temperature. Quantities are flexible, too—just eyeball how much you think you'll need. Because there's no acid in the dressing, leftovers keep well.

....

Fresh from the garden: GREEN BEANS, PLUS OTHER OPTIONAL INGREDIENTS (SCALLIONS, RED ONION, CHERRY TOMATOES, CORN, HERBS) 4 **servings** | *60 calories, 3.5g fat, 290mg sodium; ¹/4-pound serving with 1 tablespoon oil*

....

| 1 pound green beans | 1 tablespoon best-quality extra-virgin olive oil | Sea salt |

....

Put a pot of water on to boil. Trim the stems from the beans, and boil until just tender, about 4 minutes. Drain well. Spread the hot beans on a shallow serving dish or platter, and immediately drizzle with the olive oil to coat. Using your hands or two serving forks, turn the beans gently until they are thoroughly coated with oil. Sprinkle with sea salt. At this point, the beans are ready to eat. If you want, add some extra ingredients noted at right, toss gently to mix, and adjust seasoning.

NOTE | The list of optional extra ingredients for this dish is almost limitless. Some good ones include toasted nuts of almost any kind; toasted sesame seeds; cherry tomatoes; sun-dried tomato strips; roasted pepper strips; thinly sliced red or sweet onion; sliced scallions; grilled or boiled corn, cut from the cob; currants; diced dried apricots; and minced herbs.

— *Recipe by Ruth Lively*

Garlicky Pole Beans with Dill

The pole bean is a vegetable of substance and needs a longer cooking time than its more delicate relative, the regular green bean. For that reason, it stands up well to cooking in a pot with a few new potatoes or topped with quartered ears of corn. If you're using regular green beans, shorten the cooking time accordingly. If you can't find pole beans, flat-podded Italian beans make a good substitute.

Fresh from the garden: POLE OR GREEN BEANS, GARLIC, DILL
4 servings | *80 calories, 4g fat, 10mg sodium*

1 pound pole beans	1 tablespoon chopped fresh dill	Salt
1½ tablespoons butter	¼ teaspoon crushed red pepper	
6 cloves garlic, peeled and halved	flakes, optional	

Trim, string, and rinse the beans. Cut them into 1-inch lengths on the diagonal and steam until just tender, 10 to 15 minutes. Drain the beans and, if preparing in advance of serving, rinse under cool water to stop the cooking.

When ready to serve, melt the butter in a heavy frying pan, add the garlic, and cook over low heat, stirring occasionally, until the garlic is soft and brown, about 5 minutes. Mash or remove the garlic, according to your preference. Add the dill and stir. Add the beans and red pepper flakes, cover, and cook over low heat until heated through, about 5 minutes. Salt to taste and serve.

— *Recipe by Jane Adams Finn*

Pole Beans with Country Ham

If you don't yield to the temptation to cut the cooking time in this recipe, you'll be rewarded with succulent texture and flavor that just won't quit.

Fresh from the garden: SHALLOTS, POLE OR GREEN BEANS
4 servings | *130 calories, 3.5g fat, 1,160mg sodium*

2 medium shallots, peeled and left whole 1 teaspoon sugar	4 ounces country ham, plus 2 ounces for garnish 1 pound pole beans	Salt and freshly ground pepper

Bring 3 cups of water to a boil and add the shallots, sugar, and 4 ounces ham, cut into large strips. Return the water to a boil, then reduce the heat, cover, and simmer for about 20 minutes.

Meanwhile, trim and string the beans and break them into halves or thirds. Add the beans to the pot, return to a boil, then reduce the heat, cover, and simmer for another 20 minutes or until the beans are as tender as you like them.

While the beans are simmering, cut the remaining ham into julienne and sauté in a heavy frying pan until the ham is lightly browned.

Remove the ham and shallots from the pot and drain the beans. You may reserve the broth from the beans to use in soup stock or for cooking other vegetables. Season the beans with salt and pepper to taste. Top with sautéed ham and serve.

— *Recipe by Jane Adams Finn*

Grilled Radicchio with Anchovy Butter

Salty, pungent anchovy sauce is a perfect foil to slightly bitter radicchio. This dish is well paired with a main course of mild-flavored veal or pork. You can also make this with Belgian endive.

Fresh from the garden: RADICCHIO, GARLIC
4 servings | *140 calories, 13g fat, 230mg sodium*

3 large radicchio heads	4 anchovy fillets	1 clove garlic, pressed
2 tablespoons olive oil	½ tablespoon freshly ground	2 tablespoons softened butter
Salt	black pepper	

Clean and oil the grill grates. Light a charcoal fire on one side of the grill or fire up one burner on a gas grill.

Cut the radicchio lengthwise into quarters. Pour the olive oil on a plate, and roll the radicchio pieces in the oil until they are thoroughly coated.

Lightly salt the radicchio. When the charcoal is covered with light gray ash, grill the radicchio away from the heat, with a cut side down. Cover the grill, and cook the radicchio until tender, 15 to 20 minutes.

Meanwhile, in a small bowl, mash the anchovies with a fork. Stir in the pepper, garlic, and butter, and continue mashing until it is thoroughly mixed and creamy.

Transfer the radicchio to a warm platter and slather with the anchovy butter. Serve immediately.

— *Recipe from Cort Sinnes, developed by food writer Janet Fletcher*

Creamed Spinach

Boursin® adds both flavor and creaminess to this easy spinach dish. If you can't get Boursin, you can make something similar from two parts cream cheese, one part butter, a finely minced clove of garlic, chopped chives and thyme leaves, salt, and pepper.

Fresh from the garden: SPINACH, SCALLIONS
6 servings | *160 calories, 11g fat, 330mg sodium*

3 pounds spinach
1½ tablespoons butter
6 scallions, trimmed and minced

1 package garlic and herb Boursin cheese
2 tablespoons light cream

¼ teaspoon freshly grated nutmeg
Salt and freshly ground pepper

Wash and stem the spinach. In a medium frying pan melt the butter over medium heat. Add the scallions and sauté until softened, 2 to 3 minutes. Crumble the Boursin into small chunks and add to the frying pan. Reduce heat, and stir constantly until the cheese is melted and smooth. Keep warm over low heat.

Place a steamer in a large, dry pot, and add the spinach. Steam the spinach over medium-high heat until it has collapsed, 3 to 4 minutes (the water clinging to the leaves provides ample moisture for steaming). Remove the spinach and chop it fine, or use a food processor to create a coarse purée. Add the spinach to the melted cheese in the skillet, stirring to combine well. Raise the heat to warm the mixture, and add the cream to thin it slightly. Season the spinach with nutmeg, salt, and pepper to taste.

— *Recipe by Sarah Leah Chase*

Slow-Cooked Southern Greens

Ben Barker, chef and owner of Magnolia Grill in Durham, North Carolina, has particular feelings about preparing his Southern-style cooked greens: They should be braised slowly until tender, always cooked with a piece of pork and hot peppers, and finished with vinegar. Cornbread is only nominally optional. This recipe can be made with a mix of young turnip greens and curly mustard greens; just cook them a little less. Collards picked after the first heavy frost are righteous, but demand a powerful exhaust fan and a tolerance for that cabbagy aroma.

Fresh from the garden: ONIONS, GARLIC, COOKING GREENS (COLLARD, MUSTARD, OR TURNIP)
8 servings | 310 calories, 21g fat, 100mg sodium

6 ounces side meat (or fatty bacon), cut into ¼-inch dice	½ teaspoon crushed red pepper flakes, or 2 small hot chiles, diced	Salt and freshly ground black pepper
2 onions, cut into ¼-inch dice (about 1¼ cups)	7 pounds collard greens, stems and ribs removed	Cider vinegar
4 cloves garlic, minced	About 3 cups chicken stock or water	

In a heavy-bottomed, 4-quart pot, cook the side meat over medium heat until rendered and golden brown. Add the onions and cook until translucent but not colored. Stir in the garlic and red pepper flakes and cook for 1 minute.

Working in batches, add large handfuls of collards to the pot, stirring to wilt. When all the greens have wilted, add the chicken stock or water to come to the level of the greens. Bring to a boil, and then reduce to simmer. Cook 40 to 90 minutes (20 to 40 minutes for mustard or turnip greens), adding more stock or water if necessary. The age of the greens determines the cooking time. When done, the greens should be tender but still somewhat resilient.

Season with salt, pepper, and a liberal lacing of cider vinegar. Serve immediately, or cool, then refrigerate. Rewarm over low heat.

NOTE | This recipe is from *Not Afraid of Flavor: Recipes from Magnolia Grill* by Ben and Karen Barker. Photographs by Ann Parks Hawthorne. Copyright © 2000 by Ben and Karen Barker. Used by permission of the University of North Carolina Press, www.uncpress.edu.

— *Recipe by Ben Barker*

Asian Squash-Noodle Salad

If overly prolific zucchini has worn out its welcome in your kitchen, this is a delicious and pretty salad that will make it easy to use up some of the surplus.

Fresh from the garden: ZUCCHINI, SCALLIONS
4 servings | 70 calories, 3.5g fat, 640mg sodium

4 zucchini, each about 10 inches long
2 tablespoons minced scallions
3 tablespoons soy sauce
2½ teaspoons sugar
2 tablespoons dry sherry or Scotch
1 tablespoon rice vinegar
1 tablespoon toasted sesame oil
¼ teaspoon freshly ground black pepper
1 tablespoon finely chopped fresh ginger

If you have a mandolin, use it to cut the zucchini lengthwise into shoestring "noodles." Otherwise, with a knife, cut the zucchini lengthwise into ⅛-inch-thick slices. Stack the slices and cut them lengthwise into ¼-inch strips.

Steam the zucchini noodles for 5 minutes or until just tender. Rinse them under cold water to stop the cooking, drain them well, and put them in a large bowl.

In a separate bowl, whisk together 1 tablespoon of the minced scallions and all the other ingredients until the sugar is dissolved. Pour the dressing over the zucchini noodles and toss well. Garnish with the remaining minced scallions.

— *Recipe by Sam Gittings*

Quick-Fried Zucchini with Toasted Garlic & Lime (*Calabacitas al Mojo de Ajo*)

Chicago chef Rick Bayless learned this simple technique from a taco-stand cook. Try spooning the concoction into steaming corn tortillas and sprinkling them with crumbled, tangy, fresh cheese. Or serve the zucchini alongside spicy grilled fish.

Fresh from the garden: ZUCCHINI, GARLIC, PARSLEY
4 servings | *110 calories, 9g fat, 780mg sodium*

1 pound zucchini (4 small),
   cut into ½-inch pieces
1 scant teaspoon salt
1 tablespoon butter
1 tablespoon vegetable oil

5 cloves garlic, thinly sliced
1 tablespoon freshly squeezed lime juice
Generous ¼ teaspoon freshly
   ground pepper

½ teaspoon dried oregano
2 tablespoons chopped fresh parsley

In a colander, toss the cut zucchini with the salt; let stand over a plate or in the sink for 30 minutes. Rinse and dry the zucchini.

About 15 minutes before serving, heat the butter and oil over low heat in a frying pan large enough to hold the zucchini in a single layer. Add the garlic and stir until light brown, about 3 minutes. Do not burn. Scoop the garlic into a fine-mesh sieve set over a small bowl, then scrape the strained butter mixture back into the pan; set the garlic aside. Raise the heat to medium-high.

Add the zucchini to the pan and fry, stirring frequently, until browned and tender but still a little crunchy, 8 to 10 minutes. Remove from the heat. Add the lime juice and toasted garlic and toss thoroughly. Sprinkle with pepper, oregano, and parsley, then mix. Taste for salt, and season if necessary. Serve in a warmed dish.

— *Recipe by Rick Bayless*

Zucchini with Roasted Peppers, Corn & Cream (*Calabacitas con Crema*)

Roasted poblano chiles and cream—one of the showstoppers of Mexican cuisine—welcomes zucchini and corn into the classic mix. As is, it's an unbeatable taco filling; with grilled or broiled chicken, the combination becomes an unforgettable main dish.

Fresh from the garden: ZUCCHINI, POBLANO CHILE, CORN, WHITE ONION

4 servings | *260 calories, 22g fat, 610mg sodium*

1 pound zucchini (4 small), cut into
 ½-inch pieces
1 scant teaspoon salt
1 poblano chile
1 tablespoon butter

1 tablespoon vegetable oil
Kernels cut from 2 ears fresh sweet
 corn (about 1 cup), or 1 cup
 frozen corn, defrosted

½ medium white onion, thinly sliced
⅔ cup heavy cream or crème fraîche

In a colander, toss the cut zucchini with the salt; let stand over a plate or in the sink for half an hour. Rinse and dry the zucchini.

Roast the poblano directly over a gas flame, on a medium-hot gas grill, or 4 inches below a very hot broiler. Turn occasionally until blistered and blackened on all sides, 4 to 6 minutes for the flame or grill; about 10 minutes for the broiler. Cover with a kitchen towel and let stand about 5 minutes. Peel off the charred skin, cut out the seed pod, and then scrape away any straggling bits of skin and seeds. Cut into thin strips.

Heat the butter and oil over medium-high heat in a frying pan large enough to hold the zucchini in one layer. Fry the zucchini, stirring frequently, until it's browned and just tender, 8 to 10 minutes. Remove the zucchini, draining as much butter and oil as possible back into the pan. Reduce the heat to medium.

Add the corn kernels, poblano, and onion to the frying pan. Stir regularly until the onion is lightly browned, 8 to 10 minutes.

A few minutes before serving, stir in the zucchini and cream, and simmer until the cream is reduced to a thick glaze. Add a little salt, if necessary.

Serve warm.

— *Recipe by Rick Bayless*

Eggplant & Roasted Chile Salad

Roasted poblanos add complexity and just a hint of pungency to mild, creamy eggplant. Add fresh goat cheese and crusty country bread alongside this salad and it becomes a meal.

Fresh from the garden: EGGPLANTS, ONION, GARLIC, POBLANO CHILES, TOMATOES, DILL, PARSLEY

6 servings | *190 calories, 14g fat, 15mg sodium*

1¾ pounds globe eggplants, sliced into ⅓-inch-thick rounds, ends discarded

6 tablespoons olive oil

Kosher salt and freshly ground pepper

1 large white onion, diced

2 tablespoons finely slivered garlic

1 teaspoon crushed red pepper flakes

3 poblano chiles (or bell peppers), roasted, peeled, and diced

¾ pound tomatoes, seeded and chopped, or 2 cups canned tomatoes, drained and diced

½ teaspoon sugar

1 tablespoon red-wine vinegar

1 tablespoon balsamic vinegar

2 tablespoons chopped fresh dill

2 tablespoons chopped fresh parsley

Fresh lemon juice

Fresh dill and parsley sprigs

Lightly brush both sides of the eggplant with 4 tablespoons of the olive oil. Place the eggplant slices in a single layer on a baking sheet. Season the slices with salt and pepper. Roast the eggplant in a preheated 400°F oven until the slices are lightly browned and soft, about 25 minutes.

Meanwhile, in a medium sauté pan, heat the remaining 2 tablespoons of olive oil. Add the onion, garlic, and pepper flakes and sauté until just softened but not brown. Remove from the heat and transfer the mixture to a large bowl. Add the poblanos, tomatoes, sugar, vinegars, and fresh herbs.

Cut the roasted eggplant slices into 1-inch pieces and add to the mixture. Season with salt, pepper, and several drops of lemon juice. Garnish with herb sprigs. Serve warm or at room temperature.

— Recipe by John Ash

Leeks Braised in Red Wine

This French classic is good served hot, cold, or at room temperature. That means you can make it ahead, a real bonus. You also can use a dry white wine, such as white Burgundy or Picpoul de Pinet, instead of the red.

Fresh from the garden: LEEKS
4 servings | 140 calories, 7g fat, 25mg sodium

2 tablespoons olive oil	Salt
4 medium leeks, halved, with 1 to 2 inches of green top	1 cup red wine
	½ cup vegetable broth or water

In a large sauté pan, heat the olive oil over medium-high heat until hot. Add the leek halves, cut side down, season lightly with salt, and sauté until brown on the edges. Turn and brown the other side. Turn the leeks once more so they are cut side down, and pour the wine and vegetable broth over them. Reduce the heat to a simmer, and cook until the leeks are very tender, 10 to 12 minutes.

Remove the leeks to a serving dish. Increase the heat to high and reduce the sauce to a glaze. Pour over the leeks.

— *Recipe by Amanda Hesser*

About leeks

In America, leeks are considered a specialty item and priced accordingly. But in Europe, leeks are a day-in, day-out vegetable and inexpensive. They're available at every store or market vendor that sells produce, and you see them in every shopper's basket. And what leeks! The shanks are straight, pearly white, and long—sometimes as long as 12 inches. They are a leek-lover's dream.

SAVE THE LEEK TOPS!

I often see instructions for discarding the dark green leek tops, but in truth the whole plant is edible. I routinely throw away only the entire outer layer, root to leaf tip, and the top couple of inches of greens. I use the lighter green portions along with the white bases of the leek in whatever I'm making. The dark green tops can be used in soups, stocks, and risottos; cut into pieces and tucked inside or under a roast (yielding delicious caramelized tidbits to serve with the meat and a wonderful flavor base for a pan sauce); tied in a bundle with herbs for a bouquet garni; or

sliced very thinly (⅛ inch or less), and shallow-fried until crisp and just barely beginning to color (just a few minutes in shimmery-hot olive oil), then salted for a crunchy garnish.

THOROUGH CLEANING IS IMPORTANT

To blanch the leek shank to the desired whiteness, soil is piled around it as it grows, offering plenty of opportunity for grit to get lodged into the notches where the leaves start to flare outwards. The easiest way to clean a leek is to cut it in half lengthwise. If you want to retain the appearance of whole leeks in your dish, you can just cut about two-thirds of the way through the shank vertically, and then hold the cut leek root-end-up under a strong stream of cold water and, using your thumbs, fan open the layers as if they were a deck of cards. Do this a couple of times and your leek should be clean.

— *Ruth Lively*

Caramelized Onions

The secret to caramelized onions lies in slow cooking over low heat. They are delicious served alone on pizza, focaccia, or pasta, but they are wonderful when complemented by the tang of Kalamata olives and crumbled Gorgonzola or other blue cheese.

Fresh from the garden: YELLOW ONIONS, THYME

Makes about 3 cups | *70 calories, 4.5g fat, 5mg sodium; per ¼ cup*

2 to 2½ pounds yellow onions
2 tablespoons extra-virgin olive oil
2 tablespoons butter

5 fresh thyme sprigs,
   about 3 inches long
Salt

Freshly ground black pepper
1 to 2 tablespoons balsamic
   or red-wine vinegar

Peel and halve the onions lengthwise; if they are large, quarter them lengthwise. Then cut the onions crosswise into slices ¼-inch thick.

Heat the olive oil and butter in a large sauté pan over medium heat. Add the onions to the pan and stir well; sauté over medium heat for 5 minutes. Reduce the heat to medium-low, add the thyme sprigs, and cover. Stew the onions slowly, stirring every 10 minutes or so, for 45 to 50 minutes. The onions should be soft and tender, with some starting to turn golden. Season the onions with salt, pepper, and 1 tablespoon vinegar and cook, uncovered, for 5 more minutes. Taste for seasoning and adjust with salt, pepper, and vinegar.

The onions will keep in the refrigerator, tightly covered, for 3 or 4 days.

— *Recipe by Leslie Clapp*

Sweet Onions with Chile & Feta Stuffing

Preroasting onions not only allows them to develop a deliciously sweet, smoky flavor, it also makes them far easier to peel. Once the multiple layers hiding inside have been removed, there's room aplenty for this dish's savory stuffing.

Fresh from the garden: JALAPEÑOS, SWEET ONIONS, PARSLEY
4 servings| 270 calories, 20g fat, 300mg sodium

4 jalapeños or other fresh chile peppers, such as poblanos or Anaheims	1 teaspoon butter	Freshly ground pepper
2½ tablespoons olive oil	½ cup finely chopped fresh parsley	½ cup plus 4 teaspoons crumbled feta
4 medium sweet onions	¼ cup heavy cream	½ cup fresh breadcrumbs
	Salt	¾ cup chicken or vegetable stock

Preheat the oven to 500°F. Place the chiles on a cookie sheet, make a small slit in the side of each one, and roast for 10 minutes or until blackened on all sides. Remove the chiles and turn the oven down to 400°F. Wrap the chiles in foil for a few minutes, then peel and remove seeds, being sure to wear rubber gloves. Purée the chiles in a blender or food processor with 1½ tablespoons of the olive oil.

Wrap the onions, in pairs, tightly in tin foil and bake for 45 minutes. Remove from the oven and let cool slightly. When the onions are cool enough to handle, strip off the skins. Carefully slice off the root end at the base. Slice off the stem end about a quarter of the way down the onion. Scoop out the interior of the onion using a melon baller or a small, sharp knife. Reserve the insides of the onion. You want 4 hollow onion shells with sides about ¼ inch thick and the bottoms intact.

Finely chop the reserved onion and measure out ¾ cup. In a medium frying pan, heat the remaining 1 tablespoon olive oil and the butter over moderate heat. Add the onion and cook 5 minutes, stirring frequently. Add 1 to 1½ teaspoons chile purée, the parsley, and cream and cook another 2 minutes. Remove from the heat and cool slightly. Season with salt and pepper; add ½ cup feta and the breadcrumbs. Taste for spiciness. You want the stuffing to have a bite; stir in more chile purée if needed.

Divide the stuffing among the 4 onions, pressing down to pack the onion shells and doming the stuffing on top. Place the stuffed onions in a shallow casserole and pour the stock around the onions. Bake for 30 minutes, basting the onions once or twice. Sprinkle 1 teaspoon of the remaining feta on top of each onion, baste, and bake another 10 minutes, or until the cheese is melted and bubbling.

— *Recipe by Kathy Gunst*

Onion, Cabbage & Fennel Gratin

Baking mellows and melds the flavors of these three vegetables to a delicious sweetness. Scattering buttered breadcrumbs over the surface before baking makes a crisp topping that is a nice complement to the softened vegetables.

Fresh from the garden: SWEET ONIONS, CABBAGE, FENNEL

8 servings | 220 calories, 15g fat, 190mg sodium

9 tablespoons butter
3 large sweet onions, peeled and thinly sliced

1 medium cabbage, tough outer leaves removed
1 small bulb fennel, with lacy fronds
5 tablespoons flour

1½ cups milk
Salt and freshly ground pepper
Pinch freshly grated nutmeg, optional

Preheat the oven to 350°F. Butter a 2-quart gratin dish.

Melt 4 tablespoons of the butter in a heavy frying pan over medium-low heat. Add the onions and cook slowly until fragrant and translucent, about 25 minutes.

Remove the core from the cabbage and cut the leaves into 2-inch dice. Slice the fennel bulb very thin, and chop the fronds.

Make a thick béchamel by melting the remaining 5 tablespoons butter in a large, heavy pan over medium-low heat. When frothy, stir in the flour until no lumps remain. Let cook 1 to 2 minutes, but don't brown. Slowly whisk in the milk. Season the sauce with salt and pepper, and nutmeg if desired. Cook a few minutes, until thickened.

Add the onions, cabbage, and fennel bulb to the sauce and mix until the vegetables are evenly coated. Taste a piece of cabbage to check for seasoning and correct as needed. Turn the mixture into the buttered casserole, and sprinkle with fennel fronds. Bake 45 minutes to 1 hour. The cabbage should be tender but slightly crunchy. Cook longer for softer cabbage.

— *Recipe by Cynthia Hizer*

Deviled Tomato Slices

Pungent Dijon mustard and spicy cayenne are responsible for the kick in these savory tomatoes. They are a lusty and versatile accompaniment to everything from breakfast eggs to barbecue.

Fresh from the garden: THYME, TOMATOES, TARRAGON OR PARSLEY
4 servings | *190 calories, 9g fat, 540mg sodium*

½ cup flour
1 teaspoon fresh thyme
¼ teaspoon salt
⅛ teaspoon cayenne

1 tablespoon butter
1 tablespoon mild vegetable oil
4 large tomatoes (2 pounds), sliced
   ⅜ inch thick

¼ cup whole-grain Dijon mustard
1 lemon, cut lengthwise into quarters
Handful of fresh tarragon or flat-leaf
   parsley for garnish

In a large flat bowl, blend the flour, thyme, salt, and cayenne. Heat the butter and oil in a large cast-iron skillet or other heavy frying pan over high heat while you dredge each tomato slice in the flour mixture. When the butter has started to brown, add as many slices as you can fit in the frying pan. Sauté them just long enough to make the coating crispy and to warm the slices through, about 1½ minutes on the first side, then 1 minute on the second side.

Lift the slices onto a heated platter and quickly spread each with about ½ tablespoon mustard. Serve at once garnished with lemon wedges and herbs. A spritz of lemon over the mustard is delicious.

— *Recipe by Sylvia Thompson*

Rapid-Roasted Tomatoes

Cooked this way, the tomatoes are juicy and make a great quick, chunky tomato sauce. Toss them with fresh pasta, garden herbs, and feta for a quick lunch or dinner. If slow-roasted tomatoes are more your speed, see the Open-Face Cornbread Sandwiches with Goat Cheese & Slow-Roasted Tomatoes (p. 98).

Fresh from the garden: TOMATOES, ROSEMARY, GARLIC
Makes 3 to 4 cups | 160 calories, 14g fat, 20mg sodium; per ½ cup

12 medium tomatoes
2 sprigs fresh rosemary,
   about 4 inches long

½ cup olive oil
10 cloves garlic, sliced or chopped
¼ cup red-wine vinegar

Kosher salt and freshly ground pepper

Preheat the oven to 450°F. Wash and core the tomatoes, and cut them in half. If using plum tomatoes, cut from end to end; with regular tomatoes, cut through the middle. Remove and chop the leaves from the rosemary sprigs.

On a baking sheet or in a shallow casserole, pour half the olive oil and spread evenly. Sprinkle with the garlic and rosemary. Place the tomatoes cut side down and dab with the vinegar and the remaining olive oil. Salt to taste and add a few grinds from the peppermill.

Place in the preheated oven for a few minutes until the pulp has softened and the skin blistered. Remove from the oven, pick off the skins and discard them. You can serve the tomatoes right from the oven or store them in their own juices in the refrigerator.

— *Recipe by Carole Peck*

Roasted Asparagus

If you have never eaten roasted asparagus, you will be delighted by this cooking method. It takes the grassy green edge off the vegetable and deepens its flavor. Best of all, the seasoning is done up front, so once it's cooked, it's ready to eat.

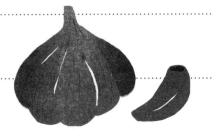

Fresh from the garden: ASPARAGUS, GARLIC

6 servings | *150 calories, 14g fat, 480mg sodium*

1 pound thin to medium asparagus

1 clove garlic, finely chopped

¼ cup vegetable or olive oil

1 teaspoon sea salt

Preheat the oven to 450°F. Wash the asparagus and remove the lower inch of stem if it's woody. In a medium bowl, mix the garlic, oil, and salt. Add the asparagus and toss until coated. Arrange the asparagus evenly on a baking sheet and roast for 8 to 10 minutes, or until tender. Serve warm or at room temperature.

— Recipe by Carole Peck

Roasted Cauliflower

Roasted cauliflower is a revelation to many of us, but has become the default way of preparing cauliflower in my kitchen. Cut into pieces, tossed with oil and seasonings, and roasted at high temperature until it's brown around the edges, the cauliflower develops a wonderfully nutty flavor. Lemon juice adds a bright counterpoint.

Fresh from the garden: CAULIFLOWER, OREGANO

8 servings | 140 calories, 14g fat, 260mg sodium

1 cauliflower head	½ cup olive or vegetable oil	1 teaspoon Kosher salt
Zest and juice of half a lemon	Leaves from 3 springs fresh oregano	Freshly ground pepper

Preheat the oven to 450°F. Remove the outer leaves from the cauliflower and cut the head into manageable pieces, then into ¼-inch slices.

In a medium bowl, mix the lemon zest and juice, oil, oregano, salt, and pepper. Add the cauliflower and toss until well coated. Spread evenly on a baking sheet.

Roast in the oven for about 12 minutes, until the cauliflower softens and browns around the edges.

— Recipe by Carole Peck

Potatoes with Cilantro & Garlic-Lime Butter

This festive potato dish can be served warm or cold, accompanied by small bowls of additional chili powder, sea salt, grated Parmigiano-Reggiano, and lime wedges. The recipe keeps for several days and is delicious reheated in ramekins and topped with additional crumbled bacon and Parmigiano-Reggiano.

Fresh from the garden: NEW POTATOES, GARLIC, SCALLIONS, CILANTRO
4 servings | *310 calories, 12g fat, 430mg sodium*

- 2 pounds medium-size new potatoes, quartered
- ½ teaspoon salt
- 4 tablespoons butter
- 3 to 4 cloves garlic, minced
- 3 tablespoons freshly squeezed lime juice
- 2 bunches scallions, chopped, including green tops
- 1 cup coarsely chopped fresh cilantro
- Sea salt
- Freshly ground pepper
- 1 tablespoon pure New Mexico chili powder, mild or medium heat
- 1 to 2 teaspoons paprika
- Grated Parmigiano-Reggiano
- Crumbled bacon or spicy, smoked meat, optional

Cover the potatoes with cold salted water and bring to a boil. Simmer about 12 minutes, but do not overcook.

Meanwhile, in a small saucepan, melt the butter with the garlic and the lime juice. Drain the cooked potatoes and toss gently with the garlic-lime butter. Continue tossing while adding the chopped scallions, cilantro, salt, pepper, chili powder, and paprika. Sprinkle generously with grated Parmigiano-Reggiano and crumbled bacon.

NOTE | Use pure chili powder, not one mixed with other spices.

— *Recipe by Lucinda Hutson*

Flavor booster

Bacon is a dual provider for the cook. When heated, it adds salt and flavor to a dish while releasing fat to cook with. Bacon fat provides just the right flavor and richness to coat and brown cold-weather vegetables, root crops in particular.

Bacon is brined and lightly smoked pork belly, and it comes in many versions, all of which are wonderful for cooking. Standard bacon comes in both regular and thick-cut slices. I use the thicker slices when sautéing vegetables like Brussels sprouts, carrots, and cabbage. A low-sodium variety is useful for dishes where you use a lot of bacon but want to avoid too much salt. There are also heavily smoked forms of bacon, which are pleasantly robust.

Pancetta is an Italian bacon that is salt cured, but not smoked. It is seasoned with pepper and rolled into a coil. When sliced very thin, pancetta can burn easily. Pair it with delicate vegetables like peas, beans, or baby onions.

Salt pork comes as a square slab. I find it much fattier than standard bacon, and often quite salty. Cut off what you need and blanch or soak it for a few minutes to get rid of excess salt. Salt pork is great in stews, hearty soups, and with lentils and beans.

When sautéing vegetables, start by placing a portion of bacon in a pan over medium-low heat, and then render, or melt, the fat from the bacon. Let the bacon simmer until it browns, then remove and reserve it. Use a small amount of the fat to sauté the vegetables over medium-high heat. When they're almost done, add the reserved bacon to the pan to heat through before serving.

For roasting, use thick-cut bacon, and add it to the roasting pan at the same time as the vegetables so that the fat will be rendered in the oven before the vegetables begin to cook. A favorite dish of mine is smoked bacon and small potatoes in a covered roasting pan, baked at 450°F, until the potatoes are tender. The bacon fat crisps the potato skin and at the same time infuses the tubers with smoky bacon flavor.

— *Amanda Hesser*

New Potatoes with Chervil Vinaigrette

It's important not to overcook the potatoes for this recipe; otherwise, they'll start to flake apart as you toss them with the dressing. If you choose potatoes that are nearly the same size, they'll be done at the same time. Depending on the moistness of the potatoes you use, they may not soak up all the dressing.

Fresh from the garden: NEW POTATOES, SHALLOTS, CHIVES, PARSLEY, CHERVIL

4 servings | *180 calories, 10g fat, 80mg sodium*

1 pound small new potatoes

3 tablespoons olive oil

1 tablespoon red-wine or sherry vinegar

⅛ teaspoon salt

1 pinch freshly ground pepper

1 tablespoon chopped shallots

1 tablespoon chopped fresh chives

1 tablespoon chopped fresh parsley

2 tablespoons chopped fresh chervil

Boil the potatoes until just tender. This may take 10 to 20 minutes, depending on size and freshness. Drain and set aside.

While the potatoes are cooling, whisk the oil, vinegar, salt, pepper, and shallots together in a small bowl. Taste for salt and correct if necessary. Set aside.

When the potatoes have cooled enough to handle, cut them in half and place them in a medium bowl.

Whisk the vinaigrette once more, and pour over the potatoes. Toss them gently until they are well coated. Just before serving, sprinkle the potatoes with the chives, parsley, and chervil, and toss again until the herbs are evenly distributed. Serve warm or at room temperature.

— *Recipe by Ruth Lively*

Potato Salad with Shallot & Mustard Dressing

For potato salads, you want a potato that has a creamy texture when cooked and that will also absorb dressing well. Good salad types include small round potatoes (either red- or white-skinned) and fingerlings.

Fresh from the garden: RED-SKINNED POTATOES, SHALLOTS, CHIVES, PARSLEY

4 servings | *490 calories, 21g fat, 700mg sodium*

3 pounds small, red-skinned potatoes, cut into irregular, bite-size pieces	1 teaspoon salt	6 tablespoons extra-virgin olive oil
½ cup finely chopped shallots	2 tablespoons tarragon-flavored white-wine vinegar	¼ cup chopped fresh chives
6 tablespoons dry white wine	1 tablespoon Dijon mustard	2 tablespoons minced fresh parsley
		Coarsely cracked black pepper

Put the potatoes in a vegetable steamer, cover and steam steadily until tender, 25 to 30 minutes. Remove from the steamer and pour the potatoes into a deep work bowl. Gently mix in the shallots so that the hot potatoes cook them slightly. Then sprinkle the mixture with 3 tablespoons of the white wine and set aside to cool.

Put the remaining wine, salt, vinegar, and mustard in a mixing bowl and whisk until the salt is dissolved. Add the oil and whisk again to emulsify.

Once the potatoes are cool or at room temperature, add the vinaigrette, chives, and parsley. Season with pepper to taste and serve.

— *Recipe by William Woys Weaver*

Roasted Potatoes with Sage

I make these so often I had to plant extra sage. Both the ingredients and the cooking times are flexible in this dish. I like to roast the potatoes until they've developed a deep brown crust on the bottom and the interiors are meltingly tender.

Fresh from the garden: POTATOES, SAGE

4 servings | *240 calories, 7g fat, 590mg sodium*

2 pounds small, waxy-fleshed
  potatoes (round reds, fingerlings,
  or yellow)

2 tablespoons extra-virgin olive oil
30 to 40 fresh sage leaves
1 teaspoon coarse sea salt

Preheat the oven to 425°F. Scrub and dry the potatoes. Pour the oil into a heavy ovenproof frying pan, preferably of cast iron, and spread evenly. Lay the sage leaves flat on the oiled surface, completely covering the bottom of the pan. Sprinkle the salt over the sage. It may look like too much salt, but it's not. Cut small potatoes in half or large ones in quarters and arrange, cut side down, on the sage. Bake, uncovered, until the potatoes are tender and the cut sides are crusty brown, about 35 minutes.

— *Recipe by Ruth Lively*

Garlic Mashed Potatoes

To my mind, garlic mashed potatoes are the ultimate comfort food. I try not to make them too often, but it's hard, because they are perfect with grilled steak or chops, pot roast, roast chicken, fork-tender pork braised with sauerkraut, and any kind of lamb. This recipe comes from Ravenous, a restaurant in Healdsburg, California.

Fresh from the garden: RUSSET POTATOES, GARLIC

6 generous servings | *300 calories, 13g fat, 110mg sodium*

10 medium Russet potatoes, peeled	2 heads garlic, or more	¼ cup butter
Salt	1 cup half-and-half	

Put the potatoes in a pan of cold, salted water and bring to a boil. While the water is heating, peel the garlic cloves. Add the garlic to the pan when the water has come to a boil, and cook until the potatoes and garlic are tender.

In another pan, heat the half-and-half and butter together.

Drain the potatoes and garlic, and put them through a ricer or food mill. Whisk in the hot cream and butter mixture.

NOTE | Garlic mashed potatoes can also be made using roasted garlic puréed with warm cream (see Oil-Simmered Garlic, p. 18, and Salt-Roasted Garlic, p. 20). Chopped chives are a nice addition, too.

— From Yael Bernier, based on a recipe by Joyanne Pezzolo

Butternut Squash with Cheddar & Sage

The basic goodness of butternut squash is enhanced with a stuffing of tomato, Cheddar, white wine, and sage. A drizzle of maple syrup over the top gives the dish a lovely glaze.

Fresh from the garden: BUTTERNUT SQUASH, SAGE, TOMATO
4 servings | *330 calories, 15g fat, 250mg sodium*

2 butternut squash, about
   1½ pounds each
Salt and freshly ground pepper
1 tablespoon finely chopped
   fresh sage

1 tomato, coarsely chopped
4 ounces Cheddar, cut into ½-inch cubes
1 cup dry white wine
4 tablespoons maple syrup

2 tablespoons butter,
   cut into small cubes

Preheat the oven to 400°F. Remove the stems from the squash, cut them in half lengthwise, and scoop out the seeds and stringy flesh from the cavities. Place the squash halves in a shallow roasting pan.

Sprinkle each of the cavities with salt, pepper, and a touch of the sage. Place 1 tablespoon chopped tomato in the bottom of each cavity. Divide the cheese among the 4 squash halves, add 2 tablespoons wine to each cavity, and top with the remaining tomato and sage. Sprinkle the squash with salt and pepper. Pour the remaining wine around the squash and bake for 1 hour, basting the squash several times. Check the bottom of the pan to make sure the liquid hasn't cooked away. Add more wine or water if necessary.

The squash should feel tender when pierced with a fork or sharp knife; if not, bake it for another 10 to 15 minutes. Drizzle 1 tablespoon maple syrup on top of each squash half and top with the cubed butter. Bake until the butter is melted and the syrup has formed a glaze on top, about 5 minutes. Serve hot.

— *Recipe by Kathy Gunst*

Butternut Squash with Dried Cherry Compote

A mélange of pan-toasted cloves, cardamom pods, cumin, and coriander seeds flavors this piquant cherry compote, which is used to anoint sautéed chunks of winter squash before baking into a gratin.

Fresh from the garden: CORIANDER SEEDS, APPLES, ONION, WINTER SQUASH
8 servings | 310 calories, 7g fat, 85mg sodium

½ teaspoon cumin seeds
½ teaspoon whole cloves
½ teaspoon cardamom pods
½ teaspoon coriander seeds
2 medium tart apples, peeled, cored, and chopped
1 cup dried sweet cherries

¾ cup brown sugar
1 teaspoon chile paste
¾ cup white-wine vinegar
3 cups chicken stock
1 cinnamon stick, about 1 inch long
4 tablespoons butter

1 small onion, chopped fine
1 cup fresh breadcrumbs
9 cups winter squash, seeded and cut into 1-inch chunks
Salt and freshly ground white pepper
Pinch of freshly grated nutmeg

Preheat the oven to 350°F. Butter a gratin dish. Toast the cumin seeds, cloves, cardamom pods, and coriander seeds in a small frying pan over medium-low heat until fragrant, stirring occasionally, about 4 minutes. Crush in a mortar and pestle and set aside.

Place the ground spices, apples, cherries, brown sugar, chile paste, vinegar, and stock in a small, heavy saucepan. Toss in the cinnamon stick and bring to a boil over medium heat. Simmer until the apples and cherries absorb the liquid and the mixture thickens slightly, about 15 minutes.

Melt 2 tablespoons of the butter in a large frying pan over medium heat. When the butter sizzles, sauté the onion and breadcrumbs for the topping until light golden brown, about 10 minutes. Remove from the pan and set aside. Add the remaining 2 tablespoons of butter to the frying pan and sauté the squash until it just begins to brown, about 10 minutes. Add salt, pepper, and nutmeg to taste.

Remove the cinnamon stick and stir the compote into the squash in the pan.

Pour the mixture into the gratin dish. Top with the onions and breadcrumbs. Bake until the squash is tender but still holds its shape, 10 to 15 minutes.

— *Recipe by Dorette Snover*

Brussels Sprouts Braised in Red Wine & 40 Cloves of Garlic

Forty cloves of garlic, red wine, and a basketful of shallots load the senses deliciously in this dish. But the secret decadence behind it is the rich flavor imparted by the duck or goose fat, making it a perfect complement to a holiday duck, goose, or turkey.

Fresh from the garden: SHALLOTS, GARLIC, BRUSSELS SPROUTS, TARRAGON
6 servings | *250 calories, 11g fat, 65mg sodium*

4 tablespoons rendered duck
   or goose fat, or fruity olive oil
1 tablespoon butter
12 large shallots, peeled and left
   whole, about ¾ pound

40 cloves garlic, peeled
   and left whole
2½ pounds Brussels sprouts,
   trimmed
1 cup red wine

1 cup chicken stock
2 tablespoons chopped
   fresh tarragon

In a heavy casserole with a tight lid, heat the fat or olive oil and butter over medium-high heat. Add the shallots and garlic, and sauté until lightly browned, about 5 minutes. Add the Brussels sprouts, toss to coat with the fat or oil, and cook about 5 minutes.

Deglaze the pan with red wine. Cook 5 more minutes, stirring occasionally. Add the chicken stock, stir well, and bring to a boil over high heat. Reduce heat, cover, and braise for 20 minutes. Garnish with tarragon.

— *Recipe by Dorette Snover*

Bread Stuffing with Quinces

A quince's flavor is similar to apples and pears (they're related), but with overtones of tropical fruit, too. The quince pieces lend their flavor and perfume to this dish, making it a stuffing like no other; perfect for baking in a 10- to 12-pound holiday turkey or goose.

Fresh from the garden: SHALLOTS, CELERY, QUINCES

12 servings | *200 calories, 11g fat, 430mg sodium*

1-pound loaf rustic whole-wheat or white bread, one or two days old	6 shallots, thinly sliced	⅓ cup chopped walnuts
8 tablespoons butter	3 celery ribs, thinly sliced	¾ teaspoon salt
	2 medium quinces	Several grinds of pepper

Cut the bread into ½-inch cubes and set aside. Melt 2 tablespoons of the butter in a frying pan over moderate heat. Add the shallots and celery and cook until softened, about 5 minutes. Wash the quinces. Cut the fruit from the core, leaving the skin intact. Cut the chunks into ½-inch pieces.

Combine the bread, vegetables, quinces, and walnuts in a large bowl. Melt the remaining butter and add it to the stuffing. Add the salt and the pepper to taste (don't taste the raw quince!).

Stuff the bird and roast as directed.

— *Recipe by Fran Gage*

Chunky Ratatouille

This rustic vegetable stew is a classic of southern French cooking. Serve it warm or at room temperature; make it ahead or eat it immediately. Leftovers can be used as a sandwich filling, on pizza or crostini, on a salad, in an omelet, or tossed with pasta.

Fresh from the garden: RED ONION, GARLIC, EGGPLANT, BELL PEPPERS, SUMMER SQUASH, TOMATOES, OREGANO, BASIL, THYME | **6 servings** | *220 calories, 14g fat, 190mg sodium*

6 tablespoons olive oil

1 small red onion, diced into ¼-inch pieces

6 cloves garlic, minced

3 small or 1 large eggplant, cut into 1-inch pieces

1 red bell pepper, cut into 1-inch pieces

1 yellow bell pepper, cut into 1-inch pieces

6 baby patty pan squash, cut in half from top to bottom, or 3 small yellow squash, cut into 1-inch pieces

3 medium tomatoes, cut into ½-inch pieces

½ teaspoon salt

¼ teaspoon freshly ground pepper

2 tablespoons chopped fresh oregano

2 tablespoons chopped fresh basil

2 tablespoons chopped fresh thyme

Heat 4 tablespoons of the olive oil in a large frying pan over medium-low heat. Add the onions and garlic, lower the heat, and sauté, stirring frequently, until the onions are translucent, about 5 minutes.

Raise the heat to medium-low and add the eggplant. Cover the pan and cook for 15 minutes. Stir in the remaining 2 tablespoons of olive oil and the peppers.

Cook for 5 minutes and then toss in the squash. Cover and cook for 8 minutes more.

Stir in the tomatoes, salt, and pepper. Turn the heat down and simmer for 15 minutes. Add the herbs and, if necessary, more salt and pepper, and serve.

— *Recipe by Sam Gittings*

Moroccan-Style Summer Vegetable Sauté

This colorful medley makes a quick, light meal served over couscous. You can start with powdered spices, of course, but grinding them by hand results in fresher flavor. Cut the squash and carrots in quarters lengthwise, then in thin slices. Slender pear slices make an unexpected, but tasty additional garnish.

Fresh from the garden: CORIANDER SEEDS, FENNEL SEEDS, CARROT, RED ONION, GARLIC, BELL PEPPER, ZUCCHINI, TOMATO, PARSLEY | **4 side servings, or 2 main-dish servings with rice or couscous** | *110 calories, 6g fat, 310mg sodium; per side serving*

¼ teaspoon coriander seeds

¼ teaspoon fennel seeds

¼ teaspoon caraway seeds

½ teaspoon cumin seeds

½ teaspoon ground turmeric

Pinch of cayenne or to taste

1 tablespoon olive oil

1 medium carrot, thinly sliced

1 medium red onion, quartered and thinly sliced crosswise

4 large cloves garlic, minced

1 medium red, orange, or yellow bell pepper, thinly sliced vertically, then cut into 1½-inch sticks

2 cups sliced green or gold zucchini or other summer squash

1 medium tomato, peeled and thinly sliced vertically

2 tablespoons dried currants

½ teaspoon salt, plus more to taste

2 tablespoons minced fresh flat-leaf parsley

Freshly ground black pepper

2 tablespoons coarsely chopped toasted almonds

With a mortar and pestle or spice grinder, grind together the coriander, fennel, caraway, and cumin seeds. Add the turmeric and cayenne and grind again.

Add the oil to a frying pan or sauté pan over medium-high heat. Add the carrot and sauté for 2 to 3 minutes. Stir in the onion and garlic and continue to sauté, gradually adding the bell pepper and squash. When the vegetables are almost tender, add the spice mixture and sauté briefly. Add the tomato, currants, and ½ teaspoon salt. Continue to cook, stirring, until the tomato juices and the flavors have melded, 2 to 3 minutes. Stir in the parsley and add pepper and more salt to taste. Serve immediately, topped with the almonds.

NOTE | See p. 179 for tips on how to easily remove tomato skin.

— *Recipe by Susan Jane Cheney*

Briami

Briami is a Greek dish of mixed garden-fresh vegetables, layered, seasoned, and baked like a gratin. And like a gratin, the name of the recipe—briami—derives from the name of the dish in which it's baked.

Fresh from the garden: OREGANO, ONION, TOMATOES, GARLIC, PARSLEY, POTATOES, EGGPLANT, ZUCCHINI, SWEET PEPPERS | **6 servings** | *340 calories, 20g fat, 220mg sodium*

8 tablespoons fresh oregano, stripped off stem and crushed between fingers

6 tablespoons extra-virgin olive oil, warmed

1 onion, chopped

6 tomatoes, coarsely chopped

2 cloves garlic, finely minced

2 tablespoons fresh flat-leaf parsley

Salt and freshly ground pepper

2 potatoes, cut into ½-inch slices

2 eggplants, cut into ½-inch slices

2 zucchini, cut into ½-inch slices

2 sweet red peppers, thickly sliced

1 cup fresh breadcrumbs

1 cup Kasseri or Pecorino Romano, coarsely grated

2 tablespoons fresh oregano, chopped

Add the 8 tablespoons oregano to the warmed olive oil and let steep for at least 1 hour. Sauté the onion in 2 tablespoons of the oregano-flavored olive oil until golden but not brown. Add the tomatoes and garlic, and simmer for about 15 minutes. Add the parsley and salt and pepper to taste. Set the sauce aside.

Place the sliced potatoes in a single layer in a baking dish. Sauté the sliced eggplant in the remaining oregano-flavored olive oil, then place the slices on top of the potatoes. Add half the tomato sauce. Follow with layers of zucchini and sweet peppers. Add the rest of the tomato sauce.

Bake at 375°F until bubbling and the potatoes are tender, about 1 hour. Combine the breadcrumbs, cheese, and the 2 tablespoons oregano. Top the dish with the mixture and bake an additional 15 to 20 minutes at 425°F.

— *Recipe by Jeanne Quan*

Roasted Vegetables with Balsamic Vinegar

In my kitchen, this is a standard technique for treating all kinds of root vegetables: potatoes, beets, carrots, turnips, parsnips, sweet potatoes, rutabagas, and onions.

Fresh from the garden: ASSORTED ROOT VEGETABLES, GARLIC, ROSEMARY, MARJORAM, OREGANO, OR SAGE | **6 servings** | *220 calories, 7g fat, 250mg sodium*

4 pounds assorted root vegetables

3 tablespoons olive oil

5 cloves garlic, minced

3 tablespoons chopped fresh rosemary, marjoram, oregano, or sage, or a combination

2 tablespoons balsamic vinegar

½ teaspoon salt

¼ teaspoon freshly ground pepper

Preheat the oven to 450°F. Scrub the vegetables and trim the tops and root ends. Cut into 1½- to 2-inch pieces. Toss with the oil. Spread on a baking sheet and roast for 15 minutes. Stir the vegetables, lower heat to 375°F, and continue roasting another 10 minutes. Add the garlic and herbs, and continue cooking until the vegetables are soft when pierced with a sharp knife, 15 to 30 minutes more. Pour on the vinegar, sprinkle with salt and pepper, and toss gently.

— *Recipe by Jesse Cool*

PASTA, GRAINS & BEANS

Pasta, grains, and beans, with their subtle flavors and neutral colors, make ideal canvases for vegetables and herbs. Because the starch provides the bulk of the dish, you can make good use of even small amounts of produce—perfect for when your garden is just gearing up or winding down. Think about using what you have in different ways. Many of us eat arugula primarily as a salad green, but it makes a zesty pasta sauce, too. The fact that it loves cool weather and grows quickly means that, in most regions, arugula season is longer than tomato season.

B ecause rice, noodles, cornmeal, couscous, beans, lentils, bulgur, and the like are bland, dishes with these as the main ingredients really benefit from good-quality supporting players. Use fruity extra-virgin olive oil, fresh butter, and flavorful cheeses. Be generous with herbs. Season with a free hand (this is especially important if the dish will be eaten chilled or at room temperature). If you're winging it, and your dish seems too bland, add a bit of something pungent or savory to punch up the flavor: diced, sautéed bacon; a mashed anchovy, chopped black olives or capers; slivers of sun-dried tomato; or perhaps even dried cranberries. Just be sure to stay in sync with your flavor profile. Often just a bit of acidity can pull a dish together. A squeeze of lemon juice and maybe a little grated zest can work wonders.

Most of the recipes collected here were written for dried pasta. If you want to use fresh pasta, keep in mind that, pound for pound, dried pasta cooks up to a greater quantity than fresh, so you'll need to use a little more fresh pasta. If a recipe calls for 12 ounces of dried pasta, 1 pound of fresh pasta will be about right. In recipes calling for 1 pound of dried pasta, you'll want to use 1⅓ (21 to 22 ounces) or even 1½ pounds of fresh, depending on your appetite. Don't try to use fresh pasta in the Broccoli Raab with Spaghettini, though; the risottolike cooking method works best with dried pasta. ⬦

Pasta with Fennel & Shellfish

The mild anise flavor of fennel is a natural complement to fish and shellfish. Add a little cream and you've got a delicate, elegant pasta sauce.

Fresh from the garden: FENNEL, GARLIC

4 servings | 620 calories, 15g fat, 340mg sodium

- ½ pound medium shrimp, peeled and deveined
- ½ pound bay scallops (or crab or other shellfish)
- 2 tablespoons butter
- 1 large or 2 medium bulbs fennel, trimmed, cut into ¾-inch cubes
- 4 cloves garlic, chopped
- 1 pound pasta (penne, shells, or noodles)
- ¼ cup cream
- Salt

Boil a large pot of well-salted water for the pasta.

In a large sauté pan, bring 1 inch of water to a boil and cook the shrimp just until opaque, 1 to 2 minutes. Reserving the cooking liquid, remove the shrimp from the pan and rinse them in cool water. Peel the shrimp and, if they are large, cut them in half.

In the same pan, sauté the scallops in the 2 tablespoons butter over high heat until barely cooked, about 3 minutes. Remove the scallops from the pan. Brown the fennel in the scallop butter. Then add the garlic and ½ cup of water, cover, and braise over low heat until very soft, 15 to 20 minutes. Remove the fennel from the pan.

Cook the pasta according to the package directions. While the pasta is cooking, add the reserved shrimp water to the sauté pan and cook until slightly syrupy. When the pasta is almost done, put the fennel, shrimp, and scallops back into the sauté pan and heat through. Taste and add salt if necessary.

Add just enough cream to thicken the sauce. Toss the pasta with the sauce and serve.

— Recipe by Ed Miller

Whole-Wheat Spaghetti with Arugula

Arugula's assertiveness goes well with the earthiness of whole-wheat pasta. This is an excellent way to use arugula that has started to bolt, when its flavor gets too pungent to enjoy raw.

Fresh from the garden: GARLIC, ARUGULA
4 servings | *580 calories, 21g fat, 260mg sodium*

4 tablespoons extra-virgin olive oil
12 cloves garlic, sliced thin
¼ teaspoon crushed red pepper flakes

¾ pound (about 7 heaping cups)
  arugula
Salt

1 pound whole-wheat spaghetti
¾ cup freshly grated Pecorino
  Romano

Preheat the oven to the lowest setting.

Heat 2 tablespoons of the olive oil in a 12-inch frying pan over moderately low heat. Add the garlic and red pepper flakes, and cook until garlic is soft, about 10 minutes. Add the arugula; salt to taste. The arugula will be bulky at first, but keep tossing it with tongs until it has just barely wilted, about 2 minutes. Remove from heat. Put the remaining 2 tablespoons of oil in a large bowl and set the bowl in the oven.

Cook the pasta in a large pot of boiling salted water according to the package directions. Just before the pasta is done, reheat the arugula gently. Remove the bowl from the oven and transfer the pasta to the bowl. Toss well. Add the arugula and ½ cup of the cheese and toss again. Serve on warm dishes. Top with the remaining cheese.

— *Recipe by Janet Fletcher*

Match the pasta shape to the sauce

The right shape of pasta can enhance a dish. To make the most successful matches, it helps to divide dried pasta into three categories: long (like linguine), short and stubby (like penne), and short with hollows (shells, fusilli). Long pasta is superb with tomato sauce and with cooked greens. Short, stubby shapes are well suited to chunky, tomato-based vegetable sauces and to baked pasta dishes. For short pasta with hollows, consider chunky vegetable sauces with peas, beans, and other small ingredients that can slip into the open spaces.

Sauce adheres better if noodles are a little wet, so remove long pastas with tongs rather than draining in a colander. Hollow shapes and those with crevices trap ample water and should be drained and tossed in a colander.

— *Janet Fletcher*

Linguine with Mixed Sweet Peppers, Feta & Oregano

Pasta and vegetables have an affinity that Italians have explored for generations. With pasta in my pantry and a vegetable garden in my backyard, I know I always have the makings of a feast. Here, a mix of red, green, and yellow peppers lends different flavors along with outstanding color.

Fresh from the garden: BELL PEPPERS, GARLIC, PLUM TOMATOES, OREGANO

4 servings | 730 calories, 25g fat, 490mg sodium

1 large red bell pepper

1 large green bell pepper

1 large yellow bell pepper

¼ cup olive oil

4 cloves garlic, minced

1 pound plum tomatoes, peeled, seeded, and chopped

2 teaspoons minced fresh oregano

Salt

1 pound linguine

6 ounces feta, crumbled

Halve the peppers through the stem end. Cut away the stem, core, and white ribs. Slice the peppers thin.

Heat the olive oil in a 12-inch frying pan over moderate heat. Add the garlic and sauté 1 minute. Add the tomatoes, raise the heat to moderately high, and cook, stirring constantly, until the tomatoes collapse and form a thick sauce, about 10 minutes. Add water as necessary to keep tomatoes from sticking.

When the sauce is thick and nearly smooth, stir in the peppers, oregano, and salt to taste. Cover, reduce to moderately low heat, and cook until the peppers are tender but not completely soft, 15 to 20 minutes. Uncover and check occasionally to make sure the peppers are not burning.

Cook the pasta in a large pot of boiling salted water according to the package directions. Transfer to a large warm bowl. Add the sauce and toss. Add the feta and toss again, adding a few tablespoons of hot pasta water as necessary to make the sauce a little creamy. Serve immediately on warm dishes.

— *Recipe by Janet Fletcher*

How to peel a tomato

Plunging a tomato into a pot of boiling water is often recommended to loosen its skin, but this isn't the best technique. Left in a bath of boiling water for more than 15 seconds, a tomato will become mushy. Better is a 5- to 10-second dip. Best is a quick scorching of the skin over a gas flame, the tomato stuck on the tines of a fork. Turn the fork quickly so the flesh doesn't begin to cook; it takes 5 to 15 seconds per tomato, depending on size. A water bath dilutes the tomato's flavor; the flame intensifies it.

With either method, set the tomatoes aside until they are cool enough to handle, after which the skins will pull away easily.

A well-grown, properly ripened tomato may not need extra peeling help; its skin should pull off easily with a sharp knife, though the process is a little slower than the water-dip or direct-flame method. To encourage the skin to loosen, rub the tomato with the dull edge of a knife, and then peel it.

— *Michele Anna Jordan*

Pasta with Uncooked Summer Tomato Sauce

This is one of the best ways to feature just-picked tomatoes. If you are pressed for time, don't peel the tomatoes, and chop them a little coarser than if you had peeled them. The sauce will be more rustic, but still wonderful. Although the sauce is not heated, this is a hot dish—the tomato sauce is warmed by the pasta. There are endless variations to this style of uncooked sauce: vary the herbs; add cheese, such as feta, cut into small cubes; toss in fresh corn just cut from the cob; or top the finished dish with tiny brisling sardines.

Fresh from the garden: TOMATOES, GARLIC, BASIL
4 servings | *640 calories, 30g fat, 25mg sodium*

2 pounds medium to large tomatoes (3 to 6 tomatoes, depending on size)	Kosher salt and freshly ground black pepper	2 or 3 ounces Parmigiano-Reggiano, Dry Jack, or aged Asiago, grated, optional
2 cloves garlic, peeled	12 ounces thin pasta (vermicelli, spaghettini, spaghetti)	
1 cup lightly packed fresh basil leaves		
½ cup best-quality extra-virgin olive oil		

Peel the tomatoes by placing one at a time on the tines of a large fork and holding it over a gas flame to quickly sear the skin (see p.179). Repeat until all tomatoes have been seared, let them cool, then remove the skins and stem core. (For a sauce of unpeeled tomatoes, simply remove and discard the stem end of the tomatoes.)

Cut each tomato in half horizontally and gently squeeze out the seeds and gel.

With a sharp knife, chop the tomatoes very fine and place them in a glass or stainless steel bowl.

Crush each garlic clove by putting it on your work surface, placing the side of your knife blade on it, and using your fist to press down firmly on the blade.

After smashing the garlic, chop it fine and add it to the tomatoes.

Cut the basil into julienne and toss with the tomatoes and garlic. Add the olive oil and toss again. Let the mixture rest in a cool spot, but not the refrigerator, for 1 to 2 hours. Cook the pasta and drain it. Season the tomato sauce with salt and black pepper, add the pasta to the sauce, and toss together. If you're using the cheese, scatter it over the pasta and serve immediately.

VARIATIONS | Mint: Use ½ cup julienned mint leaves instead of the basil. **Spicy:** Add 1 or 2 serrano chiles, seeded and minced, with the garlic, and use ½ cup cilantro leaves in place of the basil. **Anchovy:** Mince 3 small anchovy fillets and add them, with 1 tablespoon red-wine vinegar, to the sauce. Use 2 tablespoons fresh oregano leaves in place of the basil. **Olives:** Reduce the amount of tomatoes to 1½ pounds. Add ½ cup each of sliced pitted green olives and sliced pitted Kalamata olives; use 2 tablespoons chopped fresh oregano, 2 tablespoons chopped fresh basil, and 1 teaspoon fresh thyme leaves in place of the basil.

—Michele Anna Jordan

Broccoli Raab with Spaghettini

Broccoli raab, garlic, and hot red pepper flakes are one of the holy trinities of Italian cookery. The cooking method in this recipe is unorthodox for pasta, more like making risotto. For that reason, it works best with spaghettini, a thin pasta between the thickness of angel hair and that of plain spaghetti. If you can't find true spaghettini, try linguini, but don't try this technique with fresh pasta. It won't give the same results.

Fresh from the garden: GARLIC, BROCCOLI RAAB
4 servings | *490 calories, 15g fat, 280mg sodium*

12 ounces dried spaghettini	4 tablespoons extra-virgin olive oil	Salt
2 or more cloves garlic, chopped	8 cups chopped broccoli raab,	
Crushed red pepper flakes	cut into 1-inch pieces	

Break the spaghettini into 2-inch lengths. In a large frying pan, sauté the garlic and red pepper flakes in the oil. As soon as the garlic begins to brown, add 1 cup of water. When the water comes to a boil, add the spaghettini and salt to taste. Stir until all of the pasta is coated with oil and water. Don't worry if the spaghettini takes time to settle into the water—eventually it will.

When the water returns to a boil, add the broccoli raab. Cook over medium heat, stirring often and adding water—as much as ½ cup at a time—to keep the pasta from sticking. When the pasta is almost done, in about 10 to 15 minutes, stop adding water so that the remaining water is absorbed by the pasta, and the mixture becomes thick enough to eat with a fork. Serve immediately.

— Recipe by Edward Giobbi

Pasta with Savoy Cabbage, Black Kale & Sage

Black or Tuscan kale (also called *cavalo nero*) makes a striking combination with the cabbage, but any kind of kale will work. For pasta, choose substantial shapes, such as fusilli or gemelli.

Fresh from the garden: SAVOY CABBAGE, BLACK OR TUSCAN KALE, POTATOES, LEEKS, SAGE, ONION, GARLIC

6 servings | *610 calories, 20g fat, 1,010mg sodium*

1½ pounds Savoy cabbage
1 or 2 bunches black kale
½ pound Yukon Gold potatoes
2 large leeks, white parts only
3 tablespoons butter

⅓ cup chopped fresh sage
1 onion, diced
3 cloves garlic, finely chopped
1 teaspoon salt
Freshly ground pepper

1 pound pasta
5 ounces Fontina, grated
1 cup freshly grated
    Parmigiano-Reggiano

Bring a large pot of water to a boil for the pasta and greens. While it's heating, prepare all the vegetables. Quarter the cabbage, remove the core, and chop into 1-inch pieces. Slice the kale leaves from their stems and chop the leaves. Peel, then dice the potatoes into small cubes. Quarter the leeks lengthwise, then chop and wash them well. Drain and set aside.

When the water boils, add salt to taste and the cabbage and kale. Boil until tender, 6 minutes, then scoop out and transfer to a colander. Add the potatoes to the pot and boil until tender. Remove and set aside. Keep the water for the pasta.

Heat the butter in a large sauté pan over medium-high heat until it is golden brown and has a good nutty smell. Add the leeks, potatoes, sage, onion, and garlic. Cook until the vegetables are pale gold. Season the vegetables with 1 teaspoon salt and plenty of pepper. Add the cabbage and kale plus 1 cup of the cooking water. Cover and simmer over low heat until all the vegetables are completely tender.

Boil the pasta according to the package directions, then drain. Immediately toss the hot pasta with the vegetables and the Fontina. Garnish with the Parmigiano-Reggiano and serve.

— *Recipe by Deborah Madison*

Garlic-Lover's Pasta with Pancetta & Walnuts

This is the kind of recipe that can be a busy cook's salvation. When the cupboard is virtually bare, you're still likely to have these ingredients tucked in the pantry and the fridge, especially if you keep an extra bit of bacon or pancetta in the freezer. Be warned, this dish packs a real garlic punch. If you don't own a good mortar and pestle, grating garlic on a Microplane® grater will reduce it to a paste.

Fresh from the garden: GARLIC, PARSLEY
4 servings | *1,060 calories, 58g fat, 1,420mg sodium*

1 head garlic, cloves peeled
1 teaspoon Kosher salt
1 cup walnut pieces
½ cup minced fresh Italian parsley

4 ounces Parmigiano-Reggiano, grated
½ cup extra-virgin olive oil
Freshly grated black pepper
1 pound linguine

4 ounces pancetta or bacon, diced
½ teaspoon crushed red pepper flakes

Place 6 cloves of garlic and the salt in a mortar and grind it to a paste. Add half the walnuts, grind until well incorporated, add half the parsley, grind until well blended, and then use a rubber spatula to fold in about one-third of the cheese. Thin with 2 tablespoons of the olive oil, season with black pepper, and set aside. Mince the remaining garlic.

Cook the pasta in boiling salted water according to package directions. While it cooks, sauté the pancetta in 1 tablespoon of the olive oil in a medium saucepan. (If using bacon, do not add the olive oil. When the bacon is nearly crisp, drain off the fat before continuing.) When the pancetta is nearly but not quite crisp, add the minced garlic, sauté 1 minute (do not let it burn), add the remaining olive oil, heat through, and remove from the heat. Stir in the remaining parsley and the red pepper flakes.

Drain the pasta and place it in a large bowl. Pour the olive oil mixture over the pasta and toss well. Divide among individual plates, add a generous spoonful of the garlic-walnut sauce on top of each portion, and scatter some of the remaining walnuts and cheese on top. Serve immediately, with the extra garlic-walnut sauce alongside.

— *Recipe by Michele Anna Jordan*

Winter Lasagna

The colors of this vegetarian lasagna are simply stunning: golden butternut squash and deep green spinach sandwiched between ivory layers of pasta and oozing with cheesy béchamel sauce.

....

Fresh from the garden: BUTTERNUT SQUASH, ONION, GARLIC, SAGE, SPINACH

8 servings | 440 calories, 21g fat, 630mg sodium

....

One 3-pound butternut squash	4 cups milk	2 pounds spinach, or a mix of greens,
6 tablespoons butter	25 to 30 large fresh sage leaves,	stemmed and chopped
½ cup diced onion	chopped (about ¼ cup)	1 cup grated Parmigiano-Reggiano
1 to 2 cloves garlic, pressed or minced	Salt and freshly ground pepper	1 cup grated Pecorino Romano
4 tablespoons flour	8 ounces no-cook lasagna noodles	

....

Bake the squash, whole, at 350°F for 30 to 40 minutes. Let cool, then wrap in a plastic grocery bag and refrigerate until ready to use. (You can do this while you're baking something else; the temperature can vary up or down a little and not matter.)

To make the béchamel, melt the butter in a heavy saucepan over low heat. Add the onions and sauté for a few minutes, until they begin to turn translucent. Add the garlic and sauté 1 to 2 minutes. Whisk in the flour and cook until it thickens. Slowly whisk in the milk and the chopped sage. Let the sauce simmer and thicken for 5 minutes. Add salt and pepper to taste. Turn off the heat and let the sauce sit for 10 to 30 minutes. (You can make the béchamel ahead and refrigerate, but lay plastic right on top of the sauce so it won't form a skin.)

Soak the lasagna noodles in a bowl of hot water for about 10 minutes, while you prepare the squash.

Peel the squash, and discard the seeds and strings. Cut into ½-inch dice.

Preheat the oven to 350°F. Lightly butter or oil a 9x13-inch baking dish. Lift the noodles out of the water as you use them, and blot on a towel. Make a layer of noodles in the bottom, arranging so they do not overlap. Trim if necessary. Scatter one-third of the squash over the noodles, then top with one-third of the greens. Pour a ladleful of béchamel evenly over the contents, and sprinkle with ¼ cup each of Parmigiano-Reggiano and Pecorino Romano. Add another layer of noodles and filling. Repeat a third time, and then top with a last layer of noodles. Pour the rest of the béchamel over the top layer of noodles, and sprinkle with the last of the cheese.

Cover tightly with aluminum foil (stick toothpicks in the noodles to keep the foil off the lasagna if necessary) and bake for 45 minutes. Remove the foil and bake another 10 to 15 minutes to brown the top lightly.

— *Recipe by Cynthia Hizer*

Mema's Meatballs & Sausages in Tomato Sauce

The classic combination of beef, pork, and veal along with a good amount of seasoning in the meatballs imparts richness to the simple tomato sauce in this dish. Ladle over cooked spaghetti for a hearty Italian supper.

Fresh from the garden: PASTE TOMATOES, OREGANO, BAY LEAVES, ONIONS, PARSLEY, GARLIC

16 servings | 390 calories, 24g fat, 2,550mg sodium

FOR THE SAUCE

18 pounds paste tomatoes, peeled, seeded, and cored

4 tablespoons salt

2 tablespoons sugar

1 tablespoon freshly ground black pepper

1 tablespoon fresh oregano

1 tablespoon Worcestershire sauce

1 teaspoon crushed red pepper flakes

¼ teaspoon allspice

Pinch ground cloves

2 bay leaves, fresh if possible

FOR THE MEATBALLS AND SAUSAGES

1 pound ground beef

¼ pound ground pork

¼ pound ground veal

½ cup dried breadcrumbs

2 eggs, beaten

¼ cup finely chopped onion plus 2 large onions, diced

2 tablespoons chopped fresh parsley

2 tablespoons grated hard cheese, such as Parmigiano-Reggiano, Asiago, Dry Jack, or Grana Padano

1 tablespoon plus 1 teaspoon minced garlic

1 tablespoon Kosher salt

½ teaspoon freshly ground black pepper

¼ pound salt pork

2 tablespoons olive oil

1 pound sweet Italian sausage links

MAKE THE SAUCE | In a food processor, quarter the tomatoes and purée them. (If you don't have a food processor, finely chop the tomatoes and push them through a strainer to remove the seeds and skins.) Put the purée in a large saucepan and add the rest of the sauce ingredients. Bring to a boil. Turn the heat down and cook gently, uncovered, for 2 to 2½ hours.

MAKE THE MEATBALLS AND PREPARE THE SAUSAGES | In a large bowl, combine the beef, pork, and veal. In a small bowl, moisten the breadcrumbs with the egg and add to the meat mixture. Add the ¼ cup finely chopped onion, parsley, cheese, the tablespoon of minced garlic, salt, and pepper and combine, being careful not to overwork the meat. Form the meatballs by scooping up about 3 tablespoons of the mixture and rolling it in the palms of your hands. The meatballs should be a little smaller than golf-ball size. Set them aside.

continued

In a large frying pan, fry the salt pork in the olive oil. Add the two diced onions and the teaspoon of garlic and continue to cook for 1 minute. Add the sausages and cook until they are browned. Remove the onions, sausages, and salt pork and set aside. Carefully place the meatballs in the pan and brown. Remove them from the heat and set them aside until you are ready to add them to the sauce.

When the sauce has cooked for a couple of hours, slice the sausages into 1-inch lengths. Add the sausages, meatballs, and onions to the sauce and continue cooking gently for 1 hour longer.

— *Recipe by David Page and Barbara Shinn*

Parsley Gnocchi

Gnocchi—Italian dumplings—are usually the size of a large grape. These larger gnocchi work well as a side dish, and they're very pretty on the plate. Of course, if you prefer, you can shape smaller gnocchi.

Fresh from the garden: PARSLEY, SCALLION
Makes 20 gnocchi | *45 calories, 2g fat, 55mg sodium; per gnocco*

1 cup finely chopped fresh parsley	1 scallion, minced	⅛ teaspoon freshly grated nutmeg
1 cup low-fat ricotta cheese	1 tablespoon freshly squeezed lemon juice	Salt and freshly ground pepper
½ cup flour	¼ cup plus 2 tablespoons freshly grated	1 teaspoon olive oil
1 egg	Parmigiano-Reggiano	

Bring a pot of salted water to a simmer. In a large bowl, mix the chopped parsley, ricotta, ¼ cup of the flour, egg, scallion, lemon juice, ¼ cup of the Parmigiano-Reggiano, nutmeg, and salt and pepper to taste.

In another bowl, put the remaining ¼ cup of flour. Scoop up a rounded teaspoonful of the dough and drop it into the bowl of flour. Roll the dough gently in the flour, forming a 1x2-inch log shape. Continue to form the gnocchi, placing them on waxed paper as you go.

Gently place all the gnocchi in the simmering water. They will sink to the bottom, stay there a minute or two, and then slowly rise to the top. After they rise, simmer for 10 minutes. Remove them with a slotted spoon and drain on paper towels.

Coat a shallow baking dish with the olive oil. Arrange the gnocchi in the dish in one layer. Sprinkle the gnocchi with the 2 tablespoons grated Parmigiano-Reggiano cheese. Bake them at 400°F until the cheese is lightly browned, about 15 minutes.

— *Recipe by Ashley Miller*

Spring Couscous Salad

This salad tastes best at room temperature or chilled, which makes it perfect for those warm spring and early summer days. Make it ahead to let the flavors meld. As with all legumes, the flavor of snap peas deteriorates rapidly after picking, so seek out the freshest pods available.

Fresh from the garden: CARROT, SNAP PEAS, RED ONION, MINT, PARSLEY, GARLIC

6 servings | *280 calories, 10g fat, 20mg sodium*

½ cup diced carrots

2 cups snap peas, stringed
　and cut in half

1½ cups couscous

⅓ cup diced red onion

¼ cup olive oil

3 tablespoons chopped fresh mint

½ cup chopped fresh parsley

¼ cup freshly squeezed lemon juice

1 clove garlic, minced

Salt and freshly ground pepper

Bring 3 cups of water to a boil in a small saucepan. Briefly cook the carrots in the water until they're tender yet firm, about 2 minutes. Remove the carrots with a mesh strainer and set aside. Cook the peas in the same water about 1 minute. Reserve the water for the couscous.

Put the couscous in a heatproof bowl and pour on 1¼ cups of the boiling water. Cover the bowl with foil and set aside for 5 minutes. Fluff the couscous with a spoon to separate the grains. Mix together the remaining ingredients and toss with the vegetables and couscous. Serve at room temperature or chilled.

— *Recipe by David Hirsch*

Creamy Red Pepper Grits

Grits aren't what they used to be; new Southern cuisine has lifted the reputation of this humble starch. A red pepper purée with cream and Parmigiano-Reggiano gives grits an appealing elegance. The garlic and red pepper purées can be made ahead, which makes the final prep much simpler. If you have Oil-Simmered Garlic (p. 18) on hand, you can use it in place of the roasted garlic.

....

Fresh from the garden: GARLIC, BELL PEPPERS, SHALLOTS

4 servings | 270 calories, 18g fat, 140mg sodium

....

FOR THE ROASTED GARLIC PURÉE

1 to 2 heads garlic

½ teaspoon olive oil

FOR THE RED PEPPER PURÉE

2 tablespoons olive oil

1 cup sliced red bell peppers

2 sliced shallots

½ cup dry white wine

FOR THE GRITS

2 cups chicken or vegetable stock

½ cup stone-ground grits

2 tablespoons Roasted Garlic Purée

¼ cup Red Pepper Purée

2 tablespoons butter

¼ cup grated Parmigiano-Reggiano

⅛ cup light cream

Salt and freshly ground pepper

....

MAKE THE ROASTED GARLIC PURÉE | Preheat the oven to 350°F. Coat the garlic bulbs with olive oil. Place in a small, ovenproof pan, cover with foil, and roast until garlic is soft, about 45 minutes. Pass through a sieve to extract garlic paste.

MAKE RED PEPPER PURÉE | In a large, nonreactive sauté pan, heat olive oil over medium heat until shimmering. Add peppers and shallots, stir to combine, reduce to low heat, cover, and cook until softened, stirring occasionally. Add the wine, bring to a boil, and cook over medium heat until liquid is absorbed. Cool, purée in a blender or food processor, and reserve at room temperature if using immediately, or refrigerate for up to 3 days.

MAKE THE GRITS | In a 1-quart saucepan, bring the stock to a boil. Whisk in the grits and return to a boil, stirring. Lower the heat and simmer, stirring frequently, until grits have thickened. (If you aren't using quick grits, this may take 30 to 50 minutes.) When grits are the consistency of thick oatmeal, stir in the garlic and red pepper purées, and cook for 1 minute. Stir in the butter, Parmigiano-Reggiano, and cream. Season with salt and pepper to taste. Serve immediately or hold in a double boiler.

— Recipe by Ben Barker

Chardonnay-Lover's Creamy Corn Polenta

This dish combines four of my favorite foods: fresh corn, polenta, rich and tangy Parmigiano-Reggiano, and thyme. Pair it with a full-bodied, oak-aged Chardonnay, and you've got a match made in heaven. When using subtler, less oaky wines, substitute fresh goat cheese for some of the Parmigiano-Reggiano. A note about the corn: cut and scrape it from the cobs at the last minute—while the stock is heating—for the best, sweetest flavor.

Fresh from the garden: CORN, THYME

4 side or 2 main-course servings | *220 calories, 8g fat, 260mg sodium; per side serving*

½ cup reduced-fat ricotta cheese

3 tablespoons freshly grated Parmigiano-Reggiano or smoked mozzarella

2 cups chicken or vegetable stock

½ cup coarse cornmeal

2 cups fresh corn kernels (from about 4 medium ears)

1 tablespoon butter

1½ teaspoons fresh or ½ teaspoon dried thyme, optional

⅛ teaspoon salt

Blend the ricotta and Parmigiano-Reggiano in a small bowl and set aside.

In a heavy saucepan, bring the stock to a boil. Using a wire whisk, slowly add the cornmeal in a thin stream, stirring constantly to prevent lumps. Reduce heat to low and cook for a couple of minutes, whisking often, until the polenta reaches the consistency of thick mush.

Stir in the corn kernels, and continue cooking and stirring until the corn is tender-crisp, 3 to 5 minutes.

Remove from heat and stir in the ricotta mixture, butter, and thyme, if desired. Taste for seasoning and add salt as needed. Serve immediately.

— *Recipe by Andrea Immer*

Polenta with Broccoli Raab

Starches make an excellent foil for the assertive, slightly bitter, nutty flavor of broccoli raab. Here, polenta provides the canvas for broccoli raab's splash. Use fine-ground cornmeal for this recipe, which gives a quichelike texture.

Fresh from the garden: BROCCOLI RAAB, GARLIC

6 servings | 200 calories, 11g fat, 410mg sodium

12 cups chopped broccoli raab,
    cut into 1-inch pieces
2 cloves garlic, finely chopped
Crushed red pepper flakes

2 tablespoons olive oil, plus extra for
    drizzling
1 teaspoon salt
1 cup cornmeal

1 teaspoon olive oil
Freshly ground pepper

Cook the chopped broccoli raab in salted, boiling water for about 4 minutes. It will cook down dramatically. Drain and mix with the garlic, red pepper flakes to taste, and the 2 tablespoons olive oil; sauté over medium heat for 5 minutes. Set aside.

Bring 4 cups water and the salt to a gentle boil in a 2-quart or larger heavy saucepan. Stirring constantly with a wooden spoon, add the cornmeal gradually by letting it trickle from your hand in a slow, steady stream.

Stir vigorously, making sure to scrape the bottom of the pan. If lumps begin to form, break them apart by pressing them against the side of the pan. The polenta is done when it's the consistency of thick porridge and it begins to pull away from the pan. This should take 5 to 10 minutes from the time you began adding the cornmeal.

As soon as the polenta is cooked, thoroughly mix in the broccoli raab. Immediately pour the mixture into a 10-inch pie plate. Allow the mixture to sit for about 10 minutes, so that it firms up.

Meanwhile, preheat the broiler. Drizzle the polenta with about 1 teaspoon olive oil, season with pepper, and broil until the top is lightly crusted, about 3 minutes.

— *Recipe by Edward Giobbi*

Risotto with Spring Herbs

Creamy risotto makes an inviting showcase for a mélange of chopped herbs, which turn this dish a lovely springtime green. If you prefer, you can substitute fennel leaves for the mint.

Fresh from the garden: ARUGULA, PARSLEY, CHIVES, MINT, GARLIC, ONION
4 servings | 490 calories, 20g fat, 820mg sodium

4 tablespoons butter, softened
1 cup young arugula
½ cup fresh parsley
¼ cup chopped fresh chives
1 tablespoon chopped fresh mint

2 cloves garlic
2 cups chicken broth
1 small yellow onion, chopped
1½ cups Italian short-grain rice, such as Arborio

¼ cup heavy cream
3 tablespoons freshly grated Parmigiano-Reggiano
Salt and freshly ground pepper

In a food processor, combine 2 tablespoons of the butter with the arugula, parsley, chives, mint, and garlic. Process to a near-paste. Set aside.

In a saucepan, bring the broth and 3 cups water to a simmer over moderate heat. Keep the broth hot, but don't let it boil.

In a 4-quart saucepan, melt the remaining 2 tablespoons butter over moderately low heat. Add the onion and sauté until softened, 5 to 10 minutes. Add the rice; cook, stirring, until rice is hot, 2 to 3 minutes. Begin adding the hot broth ½ cup at a time, stirring frequently and adding more liquid only when the previous addition has been absorbed. Adjust the heat so the mixture simmers briskly. It should take about 20 minutes for the rice to absorb most of the broth and become al dente, creamy but firm. You may not need all the broth.

Just before the rice is done, heat the cream in a small saucepan. Stir the cream into the rice and cook briefly until it's mostly absorbed, then remove from heat and stir in the herb paste and cheese. Season the risotto with salt and pepper. Serve in warm bowls.

— Recipe by Janet Fletcher

Risotto with Leeks & Peas

Risotto is an ideal springtime food: the warm, creamy rice is sustaining, satisfying, and at the same time provides a perfect backdrop for spring delicacies like leeks and fresh peas.

....

Fresh from the garden: LEEKS, ENGLISH PEAS

4 servings | *530 calories, 16g fat, 1,350mg sodium*

....

4 tablespoons butter

3 cups thinly sliced leeks, white and pale green parts only

Salt and freshly ground pepper

¾ cup shelled English peas

2 cups chicken broth

1½ cups Italian short-grain rice, such as Arborio

3 tablespoons freshly grated Parmigiano-Reggiano

2 ounces prosciutto, cut into julienne

....

Melt 2 tablespoons of the butter in a 4-quart saucepan over moderate heat. Add the leeks and stir to coat with butter; season with salt and pepper. Cook the leeks, stirring occasionally, until tender, about 10 minutes.

While the leeks are cooking, bring a small amount of water to a boil in a small saucepan. Add the peas, cover, and steam just until tender, about 5 minutes. Drain and set aside.

In a saucepan, bring 3 cups of water and the broth to a simmer over moderate heat. Keep the broth hot, but don't let it boil.

Add the rice to the softened leeks; cook, stirring, until rice is hot, 2 to 3 minutes. Begin adding the hot broth ½ cup at a time, stirring frequently, and adding more liquid only when the previous addition has been absorbed. Adjust the heat so the mixture simmers briskly. It should take about 20 minutes for the rice to absorb most of the broth and become al dente, creamy but firm. You may not need all the broth.

Stir in the peas, the remaining 2 tablespoons butter, the Parmigiano-Reggiano, and the prosciutto. Season with salt and pepper. Serve in warm bowls.

— *Recipe by Janet Fletcher*

Risotto with Celery & Sorrel Pesto

This is two recipes in one: a fabulous and pretty risotto flecked with the pale green of celery, and a creamy pesto rich with sorrel's lemony tang. The sorrel pesto can be used in other ways. Try it as a topping for all kinds of fish and shellfish, or as a dressing for vegetables, or simply stir it into cooked rice.

Fresh from the garden: SORREL, PARSLEY, GARLIC, ONION, CELERY

6 servings | *270 calories, 6g fat, 150mg sodium*

FOR THE SORREL PESTO

2 cups packed sorrel

½ cup fresh parsley

2 cloves garlic

½ cup chicken stock, as needed

Salt

FOR THE RISOTTO

5 cups chicken stock

2 tablespoons butter

1½ cups Arborio rice

½ cup chopped onion

2 cups finely diced celery stalk

2 to 3 tablespoons chopped celery leaves

½ cup Sorrel Pesto

2 tablespoons freshly grated Parmigiano-Reggiano

Salt

MAKE THE PESTO | Combine all ingredients in a food processor, reserving ¼ cup of stock. If the pesto appears too dry, add additional stock. Set the pesto aside.

MAKE THE RISOTTO | Bring the stock to a boil in a saucepan, and then reduce the heat to a simmer. In another heavy-gauge pot, melt the butter over medium-high heat. Stir in the rice and toast it for a minute. Add the onion and stir for another minute. Add the celery and the celery leaves; cook, stirring often, for 3 minutes.

Add ½ cup of simmering stock to the pot, or just enough to cover the rice. When the stock has been absorbed, add another ½ cup. Maintain a vigorous sim-mer and stir occasionally to keep the risotto from sticking to the pot. Add additional stock each time the liquid is almost gone, ½ cup at a time, stirring to incorporate it into the risotto. Cook until the kernels become al dente—tender but firm to the bite. This will take about 20 minutes. If your risotto is done but there is too much liquid in the pot, let it sit off the heat for a minute. If there's still excess liquid, just pour it off.

Remove the risotto from the heat. Stir in 4 or 5 table-spoons of the pesto and the Parmigiano-Reggiano. Add salt to taste. Serve the risotto with the remaining pesto.

— Recipe by Louise Langsner

Garlic Chive & Rice Salad

Make this salad early, as the flavor develops on standing. If you don't have garlic chives, you can substitute regular chives.

Fresh from the garden: PEAS, MINT, CARROT, BELL PEPPER, TOMATO, GARLIC, GARLIC CHIVES, BASIL, TARRAGON | **8 servings** | *230 calories, 9g fat, 60mg sodium*

1 cup fresh or frozen peas

1 sprig fresh mint

5 cups cooked rice

1 large carrot, peeled

1 red or yellow bell pepper, roasted, seeded, and peeled

1 firm tomato

⅓ cup olive oil

1 tablespoon freshly squeezed lemon or lime juice, more to taste

3 or 4 dashes Angostura bitters

1 clove garlic, minced

Salt and freshly ground pepper

⅓ cup chopped fresh garlic chives

2 tablespoons minced fresh basil

2 tablespoons minced fresh tarragon

Chive blossoms for garnish

Place the peas in a small saucepan with the mint sprig, barely cover with water, bring to a simmer, and cook for 1 minute. Drain, remove the mint, and cool.

Put the rice in a large bowl. Cut the carrot into quarters lengthwise, and slice thin. Cut the pepper into ⅜-inch-wide strips and cut the strips into 1-inch lengths. Cut the tomato into ½-inch dice. Add the vegetables to the rice.

In a small bowl, stir the olive oil, lemon juice, and bitters together with a fork to emulsify. Add the garlic and season the dressing with salt and pepper.

Add the dressing, garlic chives, basil, and tarragon to the rice and vegetables and toss well. Taste for seasoning.

Refrigerate the salad for at least 2 hours or as long as overnight. Allow the salad to come to room temperature before serving, adjust the seasonings, and garnish with the chive blossoms.

NOTE | The original recipe appears in *Herbs in the Kitchen* by Susan Belsinger and Carolyn Dille (Interweave Press, 1991).

— Recipe by Susan Belsinger and Carolyn Dille

Cucumber & Noodle Salad with Satay Dressing

Don't hesitate to use pickling cucumbers in nonpickling recipes. Harvested young, when the seed cavities are small, any variety of pickler is fine for fresh eating—in a salad or out of hand. Picklers tend to be crunchier than slicing (also called salad) cucumbers—an added bonus, in my book.

Fresh from the garden: JALAPEÑO, GARLIC, BELL PEPPER, SCALLIONS, CILANTRO, CUCUMBER

4 servings | 470 calories, 27g fat, 310mg sodium

FOR THE DRESSING

¼ cup peanut butter

3 tablespoons rice vinegar

2 tablespoons canola oil

½ cup coconut milk

½ cup half-and-half or milk

1½ teaspoons grated fresh ginger

1 jalapeño pepper, seeded and minced

2 cloves garlic, pressed

FOR THE SALAD

Scant ½ pound Asian noodles

⅔ cup diced red bell pepper

2 scallions, thinly sliced

2 tablespoons chopped fresh cilantro

2 cups cucumber, peeled, quartered lengthwise, and sliced

2 tablespoons coarsely chopped peanuts

Fresh cilantro sprigs for garnish

MAKE THE DRESSING | Combine the peanut butter and rice vinegar and whisk together. Stir in the other dressing ingredients and set aside.

MAKE THE SALAD | Cook the noodles, drain, and add the dressing. Allow to cool while preparing the other ingredients. When the noodles are cool, add the other ingredients, except the cucumbers and peanuts, and stir to coat the vegetables. To serve, heap the noodles on a platter, put the cucumbers on top, and garnish with the peanuts and cilantro sprigs.

— *Recipe by Frederique Lavoiepierre*

Tuscan Beans

Tuscan beans are wonderfully versatile. In cool weather, they're delicious served hot, topped with a grilled sausage or a chop. A little extra cooking liquid turns them into a hearty soup. Cooked down and mashed, they're the basis for a vegetable dip. Or toss them with a flavorful vinaigrette for a hearty bean salad. To avoid tough beans, add salt only near the end of the cooking time.

Fresh from the garden: BAY LEAVES, SAGE, ONION, CARROT, CELERY
Makes 8 to 9 cups | *130 calories, 0g fat, 270mg sodium; per ½ cup*

1½ pounds (about 3 cups) dried cannellini beans	10 fresh sage leaves	1 stalk celery
2 bay leaves	1 whole onion, peeled	1 teaspoon peppercorns
	1 carrot	2 teaspoons salt

Rinse the beans under cold water and pick through, discarding any that are shriveled or discolored. Turn into a large pot, cover with at least 2 inches of water, and allow to stand overnight.

Drain and rinse the beans again, turn them back into the large pot, cover with about 2 inches of water, and add the bay leaves, sage, onion, carrot, celery, and peppercorns, but not the salt. Bring to a boil, reduce the heat, and simmer for 45 to 50 minutes, partially covered. Stir in the salt and continue cooking until the beans are firm on the outside and creamy within, about 10 more minutes. Remove the pot from the heat. Discard the bay leaves, sage, onion, carrot, and celery.

Serve immediately or cool the beans, then store them in their broth, covered, in the refrigerator.

NOTE | This recipe may be cooked a day or two ahead and kept in the refrigerator. If you don't have time to soak the beans overnight, put them into a pot, cover with about an inch of water, and bring to a boil for about 3 minutes. Cover, remove from the heat, and allow them to stand for 1 hour. Then proceed with the recipe.

— *Recipe by Beth Dooley and Lucia Watson*

White Bean Salad
with Rosemary-Balsamic Vinaigrette

For this flavorful salad, toss the beans with the vinaigrette while they are still hot from cooking. Let the beans cool, and then add the rest of the ingredients. The salad tastes even better the second day. The dressing keeps for several days in the refrigerator, so can be made ahead.

Fresh from the garden: GARLIC, ROSEMARY, CARROTS, GREEN BEANS, BROCCOLI, SCALLIONS, CHERRY TOMATOES, BELL PEPPERS, PARSLEY, MINT, BASIL, SALAD GREENS | 6 servings | *370 calories, 19g fat, 380mg sodium*

FOR THE VINAIGRETTE

¼ cup balsamic vinegar

2 tablespoons red-wine vinegar

2 cloves garlic

1 tablespoon freshly cracked pepper

Dash of hot sauce

Dash of Worcestershire sauce

1 tablespoon chopped fresh rosemary

½ cup extra-virgin olive oil

FOR THE SALAD

4 cups cooked – or white beans

2 cups mixed, diced, blanched vegetables, such as carrots, green beans, and broccoli

2 cups diced raw vegetables, such as scallions, cherry tomatoes, and bell peppers

1 tablespoon chopped fresh rosemary

1 tablespoon chopped fresh parsley

2 tablespoons chopped fresh mint

2 tablespoons chopped fresh basil, plus extra for garnish

Salt and freshly ground pepper

Salad greens

Grated Pecorino Romano, optional

MAKE THE VINAIGRETTE | Whisk together the ingredients in a medium bowl and set aside.

MAKE THE SALAD | In a large bowl, toss together the beans and the blanched and raw vegetables with the dressing, the fresh herbs, a couple of pinches of salt, and a few grinds of black pepper.

To serve, turn onto a large platter or individual plates lined with salad greens. Garnish with extra chopped fresh basil and grated cheese.

NOTE | Homemade croutons are a wonderful addition to this salad. See p. 83 for how to make them.

— *Recipe by Beth Dooley and Lucia Watson*

Lentils with Mint, Cider & Ginger

Two out-of-the-ordinary ingredients—mint and ginger—add bright flavor to lentils stewed with smoky bacon. This can be eaten as a main dish or a side; it goes particularly well with lamb or pork.

Fresh from the garden: GARLIC, ONION, CARROT, MINT
6 servings | *160 calories, 2g fat, 240mg sodium*

1 cup dried lentils
3 slices smoked bacon, finely diced
1 teaspoon minced garlic
1 tablespoon minced fresh ginger
¼ cup finely diced onion
½ cup finely diced carrots

1 cup apple cider
½ teaspoon salt
½ teaspoon freshly ground black pepper
Pinch of sugar
¼ teaspoon ground cumin

2 tablespoons sherry vinegar or red-wine vinegar
½ cup chopped fresh spearmint
Shredded fresh spearmint leaves for garnish

Bring a large saucepan of salted water to a boil. Add the lentils. Boil until just tender, about 20 minutes. Drain, rinse under cold running water, and drain well.

Heat the saucepan over medium heat. Add the bacon and cook, stirring often, until crisp. Drain half the fat. Add the garlic, ginger, onion, and carrots, and cook for 3 minutes, stirring frequently. Add the lentils, cider, and salt, and cook over low heat until the liquid is absorbed, stirring occasionally, about 10 minutes. Stir in the pepper, sugar, cumin, vinegar, and spearmint. Transfer to a serving bowl and garnish with shredded spearmint leaves.

— *Recipe by Jerry Traunfeld*

Which mint for the kitchen?

No kitchen garden should be without a few mint plants, but there are so many kinds! Which to choose? Spearmint and peppermint are the two mainstays. Spearmint is an all-purpose mint. Its flavor accentuates the subtle, natural sweetness of meats and vegetables, so it's a good match with savory fare. It also blends well in sorbets and dessert sauces. Peppermint, with its pungent aroma and sweet, cooling flavor, is great for tea, dessert, and for taming spicy dishes. Chocolate peppermint is a good choice for desserts and confections. True mint and curly mint can substitute for spearmint. Exotic mints, such as pineapple, lemon, apple, and ginger mints, are often more aromatic than spearmint and peppermint, but they are usually less flavorful.

— *Ron Zimmerman*

Tabbouleh with Garbanzos

This is a traditional-style tabbouleh with the added flavors of garbanzos, pine nuts, and currants. It can stand on its own as a vegetarian main course served on fresh greens with good, crusty bread or warm pita, and perhaps olives and cheese. If you have them on hand, scallions are a nice substitute for the onion.

From the garden: TOMATO, CUCUMBER, ONION, GARLIC, MINT, PARSLEY

6 to 8 servings | *280 calories, 11g fat, 360mg sodium*

1½ cups bulgur wheat

1 medium-large tomato, diced

1 medium cucumber or 2 pickling cucumbers, peeled and diced

Generous ½ cup diced onion

¼ cup olive oil

¼ cup freshly squeezed lemon juice

1 teaspoon salt

Freshly ground black pepper

1 large clove garlic, minced

One 15-ounce can garbanzo beans, drained or 1 cup cooked

⅓ cup lightly toasted pine nuts

⅓ cup currants, soaked in water for 10 minutes and drained

½ cup chopped fresh spearmint

½ cup minced fresh parsley

A few pinches each: cinnamon, allspice, and cayenne

Put the bulgur in a large bowl and add 1½ cups boiling water. Stir and let stand for 30 minutes to 1 hour. If necessary, drain excess water from the bulgur. Add the tomato, cucumber, and onion, and season lightly with salt and pepper.

In a small bowl, combine the oil, lemon juice, salt, pepper, and garlic and stir well with a fork.

Add the garbanzos, pine nuts, and currants to the bulgur. Sprinkle with the mint and parsley and add the spices. Drizzle the dressing over the tabbouleh and toss well. Let the salad stand for about 30 minutes before serving and taste again for seasoning; you may need a little more oil, lemon juice, salt, or pepper.

The salad can be prepared in advance and kept at cool room temperature, or if refrigerated, allowed to come to room temperature before serving.

— *Recipe by Susan Belsinger*

Golden Squash & Split Pea Dal

Serve this spicy Indian dish over fragrant basmati or jasmine rice. Legumes and grains together combine to form a whole protein, providing all the essential amino acids in adequate proportions.

From the garden: ONION, BUTTERNUT SQUASH, GARLIC, CORIANDER SEEDS

4 servings | *240 calories, 3g fat, 20mg sodium*

1 cup dry yellow split peas
2 teaspoons sesame oil
1 medium to large onion, chopped
2 cups peeled, butternut squash,
   cut into 1-inch cubes

4 cloves garlic, minced
1 teaspoon finely grated fresh ginger
½ teaspoon ground cumin
½ teaspoon ground coriander
½ teaspoon ground turmeric

Pinch of cayenne
Freshly ground pepper
½ cup vegetable stock
Salt

Combine the split peas and 3 cups of water in a medium saucepan. Bring to a boil, and then lower the heat and simmer, loosely covered, for 30 to 40 minutes, or until tender.

Heat the oil in a large frying pan set over medium heat. Add the onion and sauté until it's translucent, 3 to 4 minutes. Add the squash, garlic, ginger, cumin, coriander, turmeric, cayenne, and pepper. Continue to sauté for about 1 minute, taking care not to burn the spices.

Add the stock and bring to a simmer. Cover the pan and cook the mixture gently for 5 to 10 minutes, until the squash is tender. Stir in the cooked peas, and season with salt and more pepper, if necessary.

— *Recipe by Susan Cheney*

Dishes that are satisfying, easy, and have a little something special thrown in—those are the kind of meals we all want to bring to the table for ourselves and for our families. Here, you'll find familiar favorites like Herb-Encrusted Pork Tenderloin and Chicken Pot Pie with Rosemary Biscuit as well as exotic and ethnic-inspired recipes like Lamb & Fava Pod Sauce and Asian-flavored Grilled Eggplant Stacks. There are dishes with the French elegance like Salmon Scallops with Sorrel Sauce and ones with down-home Southern goodness like Collards & Andouille Sausage Casserole under a cornbread crust.

These dishes make the most of luscious produce, and all of them build on fresh flavors that will invigorate your meals, season in and season out. I think you'll be delighted with Deborah Madison's three vegetable ragouts, geared toward spring, summer, and fall. The Romesco Sauce that accompanies her Potato and Chickpea Stew is outrageously good. You'll find yourself looking for other ways to use it. And, of course, you'll find things that work well as sides or even appetizers, like the Moroccan–Spiced Vegetable Kebabs or Spanakopita.

Moroccan-Spiced Vegetable Kebabs

Baby root vegetable kebabs make an appealing presentation, and the sweetness of the roots plays off nicely against the warmth of the spices. I like to serve these over couscous or rice, with a yogurt sauce for dipping or drizzling.

Fresh from the garden: TURNIPS, POTATOES, BEETS, ONIONS OR SHALLOTS, GARLIC

4 servings | 210 calories, 11g fat, 340mg sodium

8 young turnips

8 new potatoes

8 young beets

8 pearl or small onions,
   or whole shallots

3 tablespoons olive oil

2 cloves garlic, minced

½ teaspoon cumin

½ teaspoon sweet paprika

½ teaspoon cinnamon

½ teaspoon salt, or to taste

Pinch of cayenne

4 long or 8 short bamboo
   or metal skewers

Preheat the oven to 450°F. Wash and trim the turnips, potatoes, and beets. Peel the onions or shallots. Lightly coat the vegetables with about 1 tablespoon of the oil and roast on a baking sheet until the vegetables are soft enough to pierce with the skewers, 10 to 15 minutes. Lower the heat to 375°F.

Toss the partially cooked vegetables with the rest of the oil, the garlic, and all of the spices. Let the vegetables marinate until cool enough to handle, and then thread them onto the skewers. Put the skewers on the baking sheet and then back into the oven, cooking them until all the vegetables are soft, about 15 to 20 minutes. Save the remaining spiced oil to drizzle over the cooked vegetables.

— Recipe by Jesse Cool

Sweat your vegetables!

When I'm cooking with aromatic vegetables like onions, garlic, carrots, and celery, often the first thing I do is make them "sweat." Perhaps you are using this technique, too. To sweat vegetables, simply cook them over low heat, covered, in a little fat or fat combined with a liquid, until the vegetables are soft. The fat can be butter or oil; the liquid is usually water or stock. This simple procedure allows the vegetables to give off, or sweat, their natural juices.

Why cook vegetables this way? The natural juices exuded from sweated vegetables give great flavor to soups, stews, and sauces. The sweated vegetables themselves are tasty, too. I like to blanket fish fillets with a colorful trio of sweated leeks, carrots, and peppers. After sprinkling them with garden herbs, I wrap the fillets in parchment or foil packets. I bake them briefly, and dinner is ready in minutes.

Sweating is also a good way to reduce the fat but not the flavor in a dish. Just take any of your favorite recipes that start with sautéed vegetables, but instead of sautéing, sweat them. Do this by cutting way down on the suggested amount of oil or butter and adding a splash of water or stock. Cook over low heat, covered, until the vegetables exude their savory juices, and then proceed with the recipe.

— *Amy Cotler*

Braised Artichokes with Leeks & Peas

During springtime, take advantage of fava beans, baby carrots, asparagus, spring turnips, or the first zucchini for this dish. For a fall stew, add diced celery root along with the artichokes.

....

Fresh from the garden: ARTICHOKES, SHALLOTS, LEEKS, FENNEL, POTATOES, PEAS OR FAVA BEANS, PARSLEY | 4 generous servings | *410 calories, 17g fat, 880mg sodium*

....

4 large artichokes

Juice of 1 large lemon or
    4 tablespoons vinegar

2 tablespoons butter

¼ cup diced shallots

2 leeks, using the white part plus
    1 inch of the green, sliced into
    ¼-inch rounds

½ cup Riesling

2 bulbs fennel, cut into 1-inch
    wedges, joined at the root end,
    leafy greens reserved

1 teaspoon salt

Freshly ground pepper

¾ pound new red potatoes,
    cut into quarters

½ to ¾ cup crème fraîche

1 teaspoon Dijon mustard

1 cup peas or shelled and peeled
    fava beans

3 tablespoons chopped fennel greens
    or fresh parsley

....

Cut off the upper two–thirds of each artichoke. Snap off and discard the tough outer leaves. With a paring knife, trim the base and stem to reveal the pale, tender interior. Finally, cut each artichoke into sixths and cut out the choke. As you finish each piece, drop it into a bowl of water that's been acidulated with the lemon juice or vinegar. Set aside.

Melt the butter in a wide soup pot over medium-high heat. Add the shallots and leeks and cook for 3 to 4 minutes, stirring frequently, without browning. Add the wine, raise the heat, and simmer 2 minutes. Drain the artichokes, discarding the soaking water, and add them to the pan, along with the fennel and 2½ to 3 cups water, or vegetable or chicken stock. Season the vegetables with salt and pepper, and then press a piece of crumpled parchment or wax paper directly over them

so they stay bathed in steam. Bring the liquid to a boil, then cover the pan, lower the heat, and simmer until the artichokes are tender, about 25 minutes. Meanwhile in another pan, steam or boil the potatoes until tender, 10 to 12 minutes.

When the vegetables are tender, remove and discard the parchment. Transfer the vegetables to a dish using a slotted spoon. Whisk the crème fraîche and mustard into the broth and boil briskly to make a thin sauce, about 10 minutes. Add the peas and cook until tender, then return the vegetables and potatoes to the broth. Chop the reserved fennel greens and stir in just before serving.

— *Recipe by Deborah Madison*

Summer Vegetables Stewed in Their Own Juices

There's no rule that a vegetable stew must be eaten piping hot. This one, in particular, is delicious warm or at room temperature. Leftovers make a good sandwich filling or addition to a salad plate.

Fresh from the garden: BAY LEAVES, ONIONS, GARLIC, THYME, SAGE, CARROTS, POTATOES, STRING BEANS, TOMATOES, BELL PEPPER, SUMMER SQUASH, PARSLEY | 4 *generous servings* | *290 calories, 12g fat, 570mg sodium*

3 tablespoons extra-virgin olive oil

2 bay leaves

2 onions, coarsely chopped or sliced

6 plump cloves garlic, peeled and halved, plus 1 clove for garnish

6 fresh thyme sprigs

6 fresh sage leaves

12 small carrots

¾ pound small new potatoes

1 teaspoon salt

Freshly ground pepper

½ pound yellow wax beans, or a mixture of varieties, ends trimmed

5 tomatoes, peeled, seeded, and coarsely chopped

1 yellow bell pepper, cut into 1-inch strips

1 pound summer squash, cut into large pieces

3 tablespoons chopped fresh parsley

1 teaspoon lemon zest

In a wide soup pot or casserole, warm the oil with the bay leaves over low heat until fragrant. Add the onions, 6 cloves garlic, thyme, and sage; cover and cook while you prepare the vegetables. Cut fat carrots in half lengthwise; leave small ones whole. If the potatoes are small, like large marbles, leave them whole; quarter larger ones or cut fingerlings in half lengthwise. Lay the carrots and potatoes on top of the onions and season with a little salt and pepper. Cut the beans into 3-inch pieces. Add them with the rest of the vegetables to the pot. Season each layer with a little salt and pepper, then cover and cook until tender, about 40 minutes. If tightly covered, the vegetables themselves will produce plenty of flavorful juices. If the pot seems dry, though, add a few tablespoons water.

For the garnish, chop the parsley with the last clove garlic and the lemon zest until all are in fine pieces. Serve the stew in bowls topped with the parsley mixture.

— *Recipe by Deborah Madison*

Potato & Chickpea Stew with Romesco Sauce

Who would have thought two such humble ingredients—potatoes and chickpeas—could be combined so satisfyingly? Saffron, paprika, and sherry add rich color and complexity, and a little hot red pepper flake contributes a minor kick. This dish is especially attractive when made with fingerlings or small yellow potatoes like Yukon Gold.

Fresh from the garden: POTATOES, ONION, GARLIC, BELL PEPPERS, PARSLEY, TOMATOES

4 generous servings | *530 calories, 13g fat, 1,740mg sodium*

1 pound waxy-fleshed potatoes

3 tablespoons extra-virgin olive oil

1 large onion, diced

2 large cloves garlic, minced

2 generous pinches saffron

2 large red bell peppers, diced

1 large yellow or red bell pepper, cut into 1-inch-wide strips

1 heaping teaspoon sweet paprika

¼ cup chopped fresh parsley

¼ teaspoon crushed red pepper flakes

½ cup medium-dry sherry

2 cups crushed tomatoes with juice

2½ cups cooked chickpeas or two 15-ounce cans, rinsed

3 cups chickpea broth or water

1½ teaspoons salt

Freshly ground pepper

Romesco Sauce (on the facing page)

Chopped fresh parsley for garnish

If using fingerling potatoes, halve them lengthwise. Large round potatoes can be cut into thick rounds or quartered.

Warm the oil in a wide pot with the onion, garlic, saffron, peppers, and potatoes. Cook over medium-low heat, stirring gently every now and then, until the potatoes are tender-firm, about 25 minutes. Add the paprika, parsley, and red pepper flakes, and cook 3 to 4 minutes. Add the sherry and cook until the juices are thick and syrupy, about 12 minutes.

Add the tomatoes, chickpeas, and broth or water to cover. Season with salt and plenty of freshly ground pepper, then cover and cook over low heat until the potatoes are completely tender, about 20 minutes.

Serve in soup plates with the chopped parsley sprinkled over the top. Add a spoonful of the Romesco Sauce to each bowl and pass the rest.

Romesco Sauce

This Catalan sauce is utterly delicious with the chickpea and potato stew. For other ways to use it, I suggest placing a dollop on grilled or oven-roasted vegetables (especially leeks), meats, or seafood.

Fresh from the garden: BELL PEPPERS, GARLIC, PLUM TOMATOES, PARSLEY
Makes 2 cups | *60 calories, 6g fat, 45mg sodium; per tablespoon*

2 red bell peppers, roasted, peeled, and seeded
¼ cup almonds, roasted
¼ cup hazelnuts, roasted and peeled
1 slice country-style white bread
Olive oil for the pan

3 cloves garlic
1½ teaspoons ground red chile or crushed red pepper flakes
4 small plum tomatoes, coarsely chopped
1 tablespoon chopped fresh parsley

½ teaspoon salt
Freshly ground pepper
1 teaspoon sweet paprika
¼ cup sherry vinegar
½ cup plus 2 tablespoons extra-virgin olive oil

To roast the peppers, place them under a broiler or over a gas flame until the skins are charred. Put them in a bowl, cover with a plate, and set aside to cool for 15 minutes. Peel and seed the peppers.

Roast the nuts in a 350°F oven until they smell toasty, 7 to 10 minutes. Let them cool slightly, and then rub the hazelnuts between the folds of a towel to remove loose skins. (The almonds don't need peeling.)

Fry the bread in a little olive oil until golden and crisp. When the bread is cool, grind it with the nuts and garlic in a food processor or a mortar until fairly fine. Add everything else but the vinegar and oil and process or work with the pestle until smooth. With the machine running, or your arm working if you're using a mortar and pestle, gradually pour in the vinegar, then the oil. Taste to make sure the sauce has enough salt and plenty of piquancy.

— *Recipe by Deborah Madison*

Grilled Eggplant Stacks

This combination of eggplant, mushrooms, bell peppers, smoked cheese, and soy sauce is rich with umami, the so-called fifth taste, which translates from Japanese as "savory" or "deliciousness." And savory and delicious these stacks are, indeed. Serve them in a nest of Japanese noodles tossed with Cilantro Pesto (p. 135) spiked with freshly squeezed lime juice and a dash of Thai hot chile sauce like Sriracha.

Fresh from the garden: EGGPLANT, SCALLIONS, BELL PEPPERS

4 servings | 310 calories, 22g fat, 880mg sodium

1 tablespoon vegetable oil, plus more for grilling	1 medium eggplant	4 slices good-quality smoked mozzarella cheese, each ¼ inch thick
3 tablespoons sesame oil	8 scallions	
3 teaspoons Thai hot chile sauce	3 bell peppers, 1 each red, yellow, and green	
3 tablespoons tamari or soy sauce	4 large, whole white mushrooms	

Preheat a gas grill, with all burners on high, for 10 to 15 minutes. If using charcoal, prepare a medium-hot fire with all the coals banked on one side. In a small bowl, stir together the vegetable and sesame oils, hot chile sauce, and tamari. Set aside.

Cut the unpeeled eggplant crosswise into ⅜-inch-thick slices, and paint both sides of each slice with the chile sauce mixture. Trim the onions and slice them in half lengthwise. Cut the peppers vertically into quarters, discarding the stem, core, and seeds. Clean and trim the mushrooms.

Assemble the vegetables into stacks on a large plate, painting each layer generously as you go. Start with a slice of eggplant, then a slice of mozzarella, then four scallion halves, trimmed to fit. Add three pieces of pepper, laid so they overlap in the center. Top with a whole mushroom, and run a bamboo skewer through the stack to hold it together. Break off the top of the skewer so you can close the grill lid.

Turn one grill burner off and all others to medium. Just before standing the stacks on the grill, with the skewers vertical, dunk the bottom layer in a shallow plate of vegetable oil to prevent sticking. Grill for 20 minutes over indirect heat, lid down, without turning.

— *Recipe by Cort Sinnes*

Turkish Stuffed Peppers

This dish is fresh, exotic, and delicious. Serve it hot or let the peppers cool to room temperature.

....

Fresh from the garden: BELL PEPPERS, ONIONS, GARLIC, CORIANDER SEEDS, OREGANO, MINT

8 servings | *380 calories, 13g fat, 570mg sodium*

....

3 cups cooked white rice, cooled

8 green, red, or yellow bell peppers, or a combination

2½ tablespoons olive oil, more for garnish

2 medium onions, chopped

4 cloves garlic, chopped

Salt

Freshly ground pepper

2 teaspoons ground coriander

2 teaspoons ground cumin

2 tablespoons dried oregano

1 teaspoon cinnamon

1 cup cashews or walnuts, chopped

1 cup dried currants or raisins

1 cup chopped dried apricots

¼ cup plus 2 tablespoons chopped fresh mint

¼ cup freshly squeezed lemon juice, more for garnish

Dash cayenne

2½ cups tomato sauce, homemade or canned

Fresh mint for garnish

....

Preheat the oven to 400°F.

Place the cooled rice in a large bowl, stirring to separate the grains. Cut the tops off the peppers and use a small knife to remove the ribs and seeds from inside the peppers, being careful not to pierce the skins. Very carefully, cut a thin slice off the bottom of each pepper so they sit flat.

In a large frying pan, heat 1½ tablespoons olive oil over moderate heat. Add the onions and half the garlic, season with salt and pepper, and sauté, stirring occasionally, for 8 minutes. Add the coriander, cumin, oregano, cinnamon, and the remaining tablespoon of oil, and cook for 30 seconds. Stir in the nuts, the remaining garlic, currants, apricots, and ¼ cup of the mint, and cook until the scent of the spices is released into the air, about 5 minutes.

Add the onion-spice mixture to the rice and stir well. Add the remaining mint, the lemon juice, and cayenne; taste for seasoning.

Divide the mixture among the 8 peppers, pressing down on the stuffing to pack well. Place the stuffed peppers in a shallow roasting pan and top with half the tomato sauce. Add the remaining sauce and ½ cup water to the bottom of the pan and bake about 45 minutes. Baste the peppers with the sauce once or twice.

If the sauce appears to be drying out, add ½ cup water. Serve hot, or at room temperature, drizzled with olive oil and lemon juice, and garnished with the mint.

— *Recipe by Kathy Gunst*

Spanakopita

For this oven-baked spinach pie, there's no need to brush every layer of phyllo with butter. Instead, stack 4 sheets, brush the top with butter, and fold in half. They'll fit perfectly in a 9x13-inch pan.

Fresh from the garden: SPINACH, SCALLIONS, PARSLEY

12 servings | *230 calories, 15g fat, 450mg sodium*

2¼ pounds spinach, coarsely chopped
¼ cup extra-virgin olive oil
¾ cup chopped scallions
½ pound feta, crumbled
1¼ cups whole milk ricotta, drained

3 tablespoons grated Kefalotyri, Parmigiano-Reggiano, or Pecorino Romano
½ cup chopped fresh parsley
4 large eggs, beaten
¼ teaspoon freshly ground nutmeg

¼ teaspoon finely ground white pepper
¼ teaspoon salt
1 teaspoon ouzo or anise liqueur
5 tablespoons butter, melted
8 phyllo sheets

Preheat the oven to 375°F.

Place the spinach in a medium saucepan and add ½ cup water. Cover and steam over medium heat until limp but still bright green, 5 to 7 minutes. Remove the pan from the heat and spoon the spinach into a colander to drain.

Heat the olive oil in a medium frying pan. Add the scallions and cook over medium-low heat for 3 to 4 minutes.

Place the spinach, scallions (with olive oil), feta, ricotta, Kefalotyri, parsley, eggs, nutmeg, pepper, and salt in a large bowl. Blend well with a slotted spoon, until everything is coated with the cheese and the egg. Add the ouzo and mix well.

Brush the bottom of a glass 9x13-inch baking dish with a little of the butter.

Stack four of the phyllo sheets and brush the top of the stack with melted butter. Fold the phyllo in half and place it in the baking dish. Spoon the spinach mixture onto the phyllo.

Stack another four sheets of phyllo and brush with butter. Fold the phyllo in half and place it on top of the spinach mixture.

Brush the top of the spanakopita with the remaining butter. Bake until puffy and golden brown, about 45 minutes.

Remove from the oven and set aside for 10 minutes before serving.

— *Recipe by Barbara Ciletti*

Monkfish Malabar

Regular spinach can replace the heat-tolerant Malabar spinach (not a true spinach). If you can't get monkfish, fillets of other mild fish like halibut, cod, or sea bass work well.

....

Fresh from the garden: MALABAR OR REGULAR SPINACH, ONIONS, GARLIC, TOMATOES, PARSLEY
6 servings | *300 calories, 13g fat, 340mg sodium*

....

6 cups Malabar spinach leaves
3 yellow onions, thinly sliced
2 cloves garlic, minced
¼ cup olive oil

6 slicing tomatoes, peeled, seeded, and diced
One 2-ounce can anchovy fillets, mashed

1 cup white wine
1 cup finely chopped fresh parsley
Freshly ground pepper
6 monkfish fillets, about 6 ounces each
Juice of 1 lemon

....

Set a steamer pot to boil for the spinach. In a large frying pan, heat the olive oil over medium heat and add the onion and garlic; sauté until the onion is translucent. Add the tomatoes, anchovies, white wine, parsley, and 3 or 4 grinds of pepper. Stir. Add the fish fillets in a single layer, spooning the vegetables on top. Lower the heat, cover, and simmer until the fillets are done, 10 to 12 minutes. Remove the fish and vegetables to a low heat oven to keep warm. Increase the heat under the frying pan and reduce the sauce by half.

Just before serving, take the boiling steamer pot off the heat. Add the spinach and cover for 2 to 3 minutes, until just wilted. Sprinkle with lemon juice. For each serving, spoon a portion of spinach onto a plate, top with a fillet, and spoon the vegetables and sauce over the fish.

— *Recipe by Jack Staub*

Grilled Fish Wrapped in Mammoth Basil Leaves

This treatment works for a whole range of fish. Wrapping the fish in large basil leaves gives you the opportunity to cook fragile, white-fleshed varieties like cod, tilapia, and halibut on the grill. The variety Mammoth has the largest leaves of all basils, so it's particularly well suited for this recipe.

Fresh from the garden: MAMMOTH BASIL

4 servings | *220 calories, 8g fat, 150mg sodium*

12 Mammoth basil leaves	1½ pounds boneless fish	¼ cup Classic Basil Pesto (p. 47)

Light a charcoal grill or fire up a gas grill. Soak the basil leaves in water.

Slice the fish into 2-inch-wide strips, making 12 strips. Dry the basil leaves on paper towels and lay them flat on a board or dish. Place a slice of fish on each leaf and spread a dollop of pesto on the fish. Wrap the basil leaf around the fish so that the edges overlap, and secure by piercing the leaves with a toothpick or a wooden skewer.

Place the wrapped pieces of fish on the hot grill, 6 inches from the heat. Cover the grill and cook the fish for 5 minutes. Carefully turn the fish and cook for another 5 minutes.

— Recipe by Ellen Ogden

Grilled Fish with Cilantro Rub

When cilantro goes to flower in hot weather, fresh coriander seed isn't far behind. Here, the ground seeds are highlighted in a tangy citrus rub for fish. You can grind coriander seeds along with the dried chile in a small electric coffee grinder or spice mill, or do it the traditional way with a mortar and pestle. The fish is great hot off the grill or served cold in salads with fresh cilantro sprigs for garnish.

Fresh from the garden: CORIANDER SEEDS, GARLIC, CILANTRO, SERRANO CHILES

4 servings | 380 calories, 22g fat, 95mg sodium

FOR THE CILANTRO CITRUS RUB

Freshly grated zest of 1 navel orange, about 1½ teaspoons

2 teaspoons freshly grated lemon zest

1 tablespoon ground coriander

1 dried hot red chile

3 cloves garlic, minced

⅓ cup finely chopped fresh cilantro

Sea salt

Freshly ground pepper

1 tablespoon sesame oil

1½ pounds fresh fish, such as halibut, mahi mahi, or tuna

FOR THE MARINADE

2 tablespoons each freshly squeezed orange, lime, and lemon juice

1 teaspoon brown sugar

2 serrano chiles, seeds and ribs removed, minced

2 tablespoons canola oil

2 tablespoons sesame oil

3 tablespoons chopped fresh cilantro plus sprigs for garnish

MAKE THE RUB | In a small bowl, mix together the ingredients for the rub; distribute and work it evenly into both sides of the fish.

MAKE THE MARINADE | In another small bowl, whisk together the ingredients for the marinade. Place the fish in a glass dish or in a zip-top bag and cover with the marinade. Refrigerate for 30 minutes, turning occasionally.

Grill or broil the fish until it can be flaked with a fork, about 6 minutes per side. Turn once and baste with the marinade. Garnish with cilantro sprigs.

NOTE | The citrus marinade "cooks" the fish, so be careful not to overcook it on the grill.

— *Recipe by Lucinda Hutson*

Winter Salade Niçoise

Gently poaching tuna in olive oil gives the fish a melt-in-your-mouth texture and a delicious, moist flavor. But you could also get good results by using a high-quality canned tuna packed in olive oil.

....

Fresh from the garden: BAY LEAVES, SHALLOT, LETTUCE, CARROTS, TURNIP OR RUTABAGA, CELERY ROOT, POTATOES | 4 servings | *470 calories, 35g fat, 560mg sodium*

....

FOR THE TUNA

2/3 pound fresh tuna

Extra-virgin olive oil

4 bay leaves

Several peppercorns

FOR THE VINAIGRETTE

1 finely minced shallot

2 tablespoons champagne or
   white-wine vinegar

½ tablespoon freshly squeezed lemon juice

6 tablespoons extra-virgin olive oil

¼ teaspoon salt

Freshly ground pepper

FOR THE SALAD

One head of lettuce

2 carrots, peeled and sliced thin

1 turnip or rutabaga, peeled and julienned

1 celery root, peeled and julienned

Juice of half a lemon

2 medium red potatoes, unpeeled
   and sliced

2 hard-boiled eggs, halved

4 anchovy fillets (preferably
   salt-packed)

Small handful of Niçoise olives,
   or combination Niçoise and small
   brine-cured cracked green olives

....

COOK THE TUNA | To cook the tuna, put it in a small pot just large enough in diameter to contain it and add enough olive oil to completely cover the fish. Add bay leaves and peppercorns. Slowly heat the oil and simmer the tuna until just cooked, 7 to 10 minutes. Remove from the heat.

MAKE THE VINAIGRETTE | Place all of the vinaigrette ingredients in a small bowl and whisk to combine.

MAKE THE SALAD | Line a large, low pottery bowl with washed and dried lettuce leaves and set aside.

Blanch carrots in boiling salted water for 2 minutes. Drain and refresh under cold running water. Pat dry and in a small bowl toss the carrots with 1 tablespoon of

the vinaigrette. Do the same with the turnip or rutabaga. Put the celery root in a small bowl, lightly salt it, squeeze the lemon juice over it, and toss.

Cover the potato slices with cold water and slowly bring to a boil. Add salt. Cook until just done. Drain and refresh under cold water. Toss with 3 tablespoons of the vinaigrette.

Distribute the vegetables artfully over the lettuces. Flake the tuna in large chunks and add to the salad. Garnish with the eggs, anchovies, and olives. Drizzle the vinaigrette over all to taste. Serve with a baguette or slices of sourdough country bread.

— *Recipe by Maggie Blyth Klein*

Salmon Scallops with Sorrel Sauce

The lemony tang of sorrel is perfect with fish, but cooking turns it a drab color. To pretty it up, reserve a few leaves of raw sorrel, finely chop them, and stir them into the sauce once it is off the heat.

Fresh from the garden: SORREL, SHALLOT

4 servings | *410 calories, 27g fat, 95mg sodium*

3 ounces sorrel (about 5 handfuls)	1 medium shallot, minced	Salt and freshly ground white pepper
One 1½-pound salmon fillet, skin removed	½ cup dry white wine	Freshly squeezed lemon juice
	¾ cup heavy cream	Cooking oil for the pan, if necessary

Heat the serving plates in a warm oven or in the microwave. Wash the sorrel and pat dry. Remove the stems and cut the leaves into chiffonade. Set aside.

Wash the salmon fillet under cold water and dry it on paper towels. Remove any small bones from the center of the fillet; to find them, run your finger along the thickest part of the fillet and then pull them out with tweezers. Cut the fillet into four pieces. Place each piece between two sheets of wax or parchment paper and carefully flatten with a mallet until each piece is an even thickness of about ⅜ inch. Be careful not to shred the fish. Set aside.

To make the sauce, put the shallots and wine in a heavy, 1-quart saucepan. Bring to a boil, and cook until the liquid has almost evaporated, leaving only about a tablespoon. Add the cream, generous pinches of salt and white pepper, and bring to a rolling boil. Add the sorrel, give it a stir, bring back to a boil, and turn off the heat. Give the sauce a few squirts of lemon juice, and taste for salt and pepper. Cover to keep warm while cooking the salmon.

Use a nonstick frying pan if you have one. Otherwise, any lightly oiled frying pan will work. The pan should be large enough to hold two pieces of fish. Heat the pan over medium-high heat until hot. Add the fish and cook for about 1 minute.

Turn the fish and cook for another minute. Remove the fillets from the frying pan, loosely cover them with foil, and set aside. Cook the remaining two pieces without delay. Spoon the sauce onto the serving plates. Set a piece of salmon on the sauce, the former skin side down. Season with salt and pepper, and serve at once.

— *Recipe by Fran Gage*

Stir-Fried Shrimp & Asparagus

Total cooking time for this dish is super quick—less than 10 minutes—so be sure to coordinate the cooking of your starch accompaniment.

Fresh from the garden: ASPARAGUS, HOT CHILE, SCALLIONS, GARLIC
4 servings | *220 calories, 8g fat, 690mg sodium*

1 pound asparagus
1 small hot chile, optional
6 scallions
2 tablespoons oil

1 pound medium shrimp, peeled
  and deveined
1 clove garlic, chopped fine
1 tablespoon Chinese oyster sauce

1 tablespoon soy sauce
1 tablespoon dry sherry

Slice asparagus diagonally into 1½-inch pieces, keeping the tips whole. If using hot chile, cut into thin slivers and remove seeds. Trim scallions and cut into 1-inch pieces, including green tops.

Set a wok or large frying pan over high heat, add oil, and heat until sizzling hot. Stir-fry shrimp until they turn pink, 2 to 3 minutes. Remove with a slotted spoon and set aside on a plate. Add the garlic and asparagus, and stir-fry until tender-crisp, about 3 to 4 minutes. Return shrimp to pan along with the scallions, oyster and soy sauces, and sherry. Cook until the shrimp are heated through. Serve at once with rice or noodles.

— Recipe by Karen Pendleton

Chicken Pot Pie with Rosemary Biscuit

For vegetarian pot pie, omit the chicken and increase the vegetables by about 4 cups. Substitute rich vegetable stock for the chicken stock. For beef pot pie, use pot roast and beef broth. And for any version, small mushrooms, quartered and sautéed in butter or oil, would be a wonderful addition.

Fresh from the garden: ROSEMARY, LEEKS, CARROTS, POTATO, ONION, TURNIPS

8 servings | 610 calories, 31g fat, 930mg sodium

FOR THE BISCUIT TOPPING

3 cups flour

3 teaspoons baking powder

1¼ teaspoons salt

1 tablespoon finely minced
    fresh rosemary

4 ounces cold butter,
    cut into pieces

¼ cup cold shortening

1 cup milk

FOR THE POT PIE

4 cups diced, cooked chicken
    (6 large thighs)

2 large leeks, root and coarse top
    removed, remainder thinly sliced,
    rinsed and drained

4 large carrots, thinly sliced

1 large Yukon Gold potato, diced

1 medium onion, diced

1 medium or 2 small turnips, diced

1 teaspoon salt

¼ teaspoon freshly ground black pepper

2 tablespoons butter

2 tablespoons flour

2 teaspoons Dijon mustard

1 cup milk

1 cup chicken broth

1 tablespoon finely minced
    fresh rosemary

Preheat the oven to 350°F.

MAKE THE BISCUIT TOPPING | Combine the flour, baking powder, and salt in a large mixing bowl. Stir in the rosemary. With a pastry blender or your fingers, cut the butter, then the shortening, into the flour until it resembles small peas. Pour the milk over and let it sit for a few minutes, while the flour absorbs the moisture. With a fork, gently combine the mass to form a ball. If the dough is still dry, add 1 or 2 tablespoons more milk. Pat the dough around a bit to help it hold together. Set aside.

MAKE THE POT PIE | Arrange the chicken pieces, leeks, carrots, potato, onion, and turnip in a shallow, 2-quart casserole; season with salt and pepper. Melt the butter in a saucepan over medium heat. Add the flour and whisk to a smooth paste. Cook 1 to 2 minutes but don't brown. Increase heat to medium-high and whisk in the mustard, milk, and broth, a little at

a time. Add the minced rosemary and let the mixture bubble for a couple of minutes. Pour the sauce over the contents of the casserole.

Pat the biscuit dough out on a lightly floured board until it is slightly larger than the opening of the casserole. Transfer the biscuit to the casserole, pressing the edges to form a seal.

Bake for 45 minutes to 1 hour. Cover loosely with aluminum foil if the biscuit threatens to get too brown.

NOTE | This dish really benefits from rich, homemade stock. If you don't have any on hand, you can cook the chicken and get great stock in one step. Lay the chicken atop a bed of chopped onion, carrot, and celery; several cloves of garlic; and a few sprigs of herbs. Season everything with salt and pepper. Bake at 350°F for about 1 hour. If the thighs are skinless, cover with foil so they don't dry out. This yields about 1 cup of stock.

— *Recipe by Cynthia Hizer*

Quick Chicken Breasts with Chervil

This dish takes all of about 10 minutes to make, but the result is moist, delicious, and elegant. For a slightly crisp exterior to the chicken, remove the meat from the pan before adding the lemon juice. Pour the sauce over the chicken, and then sprinkle with the chervil. Whichever method you follow, be sure your pan is up to temperature before putting in the butter. I've had best results using enameled cast iron.

Fresh from the garden: CHERVIL
4 servings | 310 calories, 15g fat, 180mg sodium

4 skinless, boneless chicken breast halves	Salt and freshly ground pepper	Juice of half a lemon
4 tablespoons butter	½ cup flour	½ cup chopped fresh chervil

Set a heavy, nonreactive pan, wide enough to hold all 4 chicken breasts without crowding, over medium-high heat. Trim any bits of fat from the chicken. Put the butter in the hot pan to melt. Season the chicken with salt and pepper, and dredge in flour to lightly coat the breasts. When the butter is melted, lay the breasts in the pan; don't overlap them. Sauté until golden, about 3 minutes. Turn the chicken over and cook for another 3 minutes.

Turn the heat off, quickly pour in the lemon juice, and swirl the pan to mix the butter and lemon juice. Sprinkle most of the chervil over the chicken, and turn each piece once to coat with the sauce. Serve immediately, topped with the remaining fresh chervil.

— *Recipe by Ruth Lively*

Chicken Sautéed with Cider Vinegar & Shallots

Onions and garlic are usually used to create foundation flavors in a dish, whereas shallots are often incorporated to add "finish," that extra polish that pushes a good recipe over the top.

Fresh from the garden: SHALLOTS, BAY LEAVES, TOMATOES, PARSLEY, ROSEMARY

6 servings | *380 calories, 24g fat, 90mg sodium*

One 4– to 4½–pound stewing chicken, cut into 8 pieces
Juice of 1 lemon or lime
4 tablespoons butter
2 tablespoons olive oil

1 cup chopped shallots
6 fresh bay leaves
2 cups tomatoes, seeded and chopped, (preferably a mix of mostly yellow and some red varieties)

¼ cup apple-cider vinegar, or more to taste
½ cup chopped fresh parsley
1 tablespoon minced fresh rosemary
Salt and freshly ground pepper

Put the chicken in a deep, nonreactive work bowl and squeeze the citrus juice over it. Let the chicken marinate in the juice for 15 to 20 minutes.

Heat the butter and olive oil in a large sauté pan. Drain the chicken, pat it dry, and brown in the butter and oil mixture for about 20 minutes.

Add the shallots, cover, and sweat over medium-high heat for 10 minutes. Add the bay leaves, tomatoes, and vinegar. Cover and cook over medium-low heat until the chicken is tender, about 30 minutes.

Add the parsley and rosemary, and season to taste with salt and pepper. Serve immediately, or cool and store overnight in the refrigerator to reheat the next day.

— *Recipe by William Woys Weaver*

Tarragon-Stuffed Roasted Chicken

Just a few well-chosen ingredients can make a truly outstanding meal. The anise flavor of tarragon is particularly good with mild-flavored foods like chicken, turkey, eggs, fish, and fresh cheeses.

Fresh from the garden: BAY LEAVES, TARRAGON

4 servings | *500 calories, 31g fat, 135mg sodium*

1 whole chicken, about 3 pounds
Salt
2 bay leaves

At least 2 cups fresh tarragon sprigs
2 tablespoons olive oil
1 lemon, cut in half

Freshly ground pepper
1 cup dry white wine

Preheat the oven to 400°F.

Rinse the chicken in cold water and pat it dry inside and out with a paper towel. Sprinkle the interior with salt and place the chicken in a roasting pan on top of bay leaves and a handful of tarragon sprigs in order to flavor the pan drippings. Rub the chicken with the olive oil and squeeze the juice from the lemon over the chicken. Place the squeezed lemon halves in the chicken cavity along with a generous handful of tarragon. With your fingers, slide some sprigs of tarragon under the breast skin. Sprinkle with pepper. Pour the wine into the pan.

Put the chicken in the oven and cook for 1½ hours, basting occasionally. Add extra water, wine, or stock if the liquid in the roasting pan dries up.

Serve the chicken on a platter, garnished with sprigs of fresh tarragon. Skim the fat from the pan juices and serve the juices with the chicken.

— *Recipe by Noel Richardson*

Herb-Encrusted Pork Tenderloin

This is an easy way to cook pork tenderloin—no stovetop searing, no pan to clean. It's great for company, too. Just double or triple the recipe, roasting each tenderloin in its own foil packet.

Fresh from the garden: OREGANO, THYME, ROSEMARY, GARLIC

4 servings | *220 calories, 11g fat, 690mg sodium*

1 small pork tenderloin, about 1 pound	1 tablespoon fresh oregano	1 tablespoon honey
1 teaspoon salt	1 tablespoon fresh thyme	1 tablespoon Dijon mustard
1 tablespoon coarsely ground pepper	1 teaspoon fresh rosemary	6 sprigs fresh rosemary,
2 tablespoons pine nuts	2 cloves garlic, peeled	each 6 inches long

Preheat the oven to 450°F.

Sprinkle the pork tenderloin lightly with some of the salt and pepper, and let it come to room temperature.

Place the rest of the salt and pepper, the pine nuts, herbs, garlic, honey, and mustard in the bowl of a food processor or blender, and process until the nuts are well chopped and all the ingredients have blended. You may need to stop the machine and scrape down the sides with a spatula several times.

Use a double layer of aluminum foil cut 4 inches longer than the tenderloin. Place the rosemary sprigs in the center of the foil and position the tenderloin on top of the rosemary. Coat the top and sides of the tenderloin with the herb paste. Join the foil together at the top and at the ends, making a tent so the tenderloin is completely enclosed but the herb crust does not touch the foil.

Place the package on the top rack of the oven and bake for 20 minutes. Carefully open the foil and fold back the sides so the tenderloin can brown. Bake for an additional 10 minutes. Let the pork cool for 5 minutes, and then slice and serve.

— *Recipe by Mimi Luebbermann*

Collards & Andouille Sausage Casserole

Collards are a quintessentially Southern vegetable. This casserole combines them with another Southern favorite, cornbread.

Fresh from the garden: SWEET ONION, BELL PEPPERS, CELERY, GARLIC, COLLARDS

10 servings | 260 calories, 14g fat, 510mg sodium

FOR THE FILLING

¼ cup peanut oil

½ pound andouille sausage (or Italian sausage or Portuguese linguiça), quartered lengthwise then cut crosswise into ¼-inch pieces

1 cup sweet onion, diced small

½ cup red bell pepper, seeded and diced small

½ cup green bell pepper, seeded and diced small

½ cup celery, diced small

¼ cup chopped garlic (about 7 cloves)

1 teaspoon crushed red pepper flakes (optional)

3½ pounds young collards, cleaned, stemmed, and cut crosswise into 1-inch pieces

3½ cups chicken stock or water

Apple-cider vinegar

Salt and freshly ground black pepper

Hot sauce

FOR THE CORNBREAD

1 cup stone-ground yellow cornmeal

¾ teaspoon salt

1 teaspoon sugar

⅛ teaspoon baking soda

1½ teaspoons baking powder

2 eggs

1 cup buttermilk

1 tablespoon melted butter

1 tablespoon melted bacon fat or an additional 1 tablespoon melted butter

Preheat the oven to 350°F.

MAKE THE FILLING | In a heavy-bottomed, 4-quart pot heat the oil over medium heat. Add the sausage and cook over medium-low heat until browned. Remove the sausage to drain, leaving the fat in the pot.

Add the onions, peppers, and celery to the pot. Cook over medium heat until softened and lightly colored. Add the garlic and pepper flakes and cook for 1 more minute. Add the collards in 2- to 3-cup increments and stir to wilt. Continue adding collards until all are wilted. Add the chicken stock and bring to a simmer. Cook over low heat, adding additional stock or water if necessary, until the collards are tender, about 20 minutes.

Season to taste with vinegar, salt, pepper, and hot sauce if desired. Be cautious with the pepper and pepper sauce if the andouille sausage is spicy. Stir in the reserved sausage and transfer the mixture to a 9x13-inch casserole dish.

MAKE THE CORNBREAD | In a large bowl, combine the cornmeal, salt, sugar, baking soda, and baking powder.

In a second bowl, whisk the eggs, then whisk in the buttermilk, melted butter, and melted bacon fat. Fold the egg mixture into the cornmeal mixture until well combined. Spread the cornmeal mix on the surface of the greens until the casserole is covered to the edges.

Bake until the cornbread is set and a toothpick inserted into it withdraws clean, approximately 30 minutes. Cool slightly before serving.

— *Recipe by Ben Barker*

Lamb Roasted in Parchment

This lamb dish is cooked until spoon tender and all its gaminess is gone, making it appealing to those who tend to avoid lamb. The packages may be prepared ahead of time and refrigerated for later roasting.

Fresh from the garden: SWEET ONIONS, GARLIC, ROSEMARY, MARJORAM OR OREGANO

6 servings | *450 calories, 26g fat, 180mg sodium*

2½ to 3 pounds boneless leg of lamb

2 very large sweet onions

¼ cup olive oil

6 cloves garlic, in slivers

2 tablespoons freshly squeezed lemon juice

Pinch of salt

Freshly ground black pepper

4 ounces mild melting cheese, such as Gruyère, Jack, or Kasseri, cut into 6 wedges

6 generous teaspoons fresh rosemary or two teaspoons dried

6 generous teaspoons fresh marjoram or oregano, or 2 teaspoons dried

6 large squares cooking parchment

Preheat the oven to 325°F.

Cut the meat into 6 uniform pieces. The shape of the lamb will determine the manner in which you cut—try to keep the pieces as equal as possible so they will finish cooking at the same time. Cut three ¼-in.-thick slices from the center of each onion.

Brush one side of the parchments with some of the oil and place a slice of onion in the center of each oiled side, then a portion of lamb on the onion. Make small slashes in the lamb and bury slivers of garlic in each piece, the equivalent of 1 clove per portion. Brush the lamb with oil and sprinkle with lemon juice, salt, and pepper. Lay a wedge of cheese on the lamb and top with the rosemary and marjoram.

Gather the edges of the paper together, being careful not to dislodge the cheese, twist firmly, and tie securely with string, finishing with a bow. You want not one drop of juice to escape. Brush the packages with oil, including the bottoms, and arrange them in a small shallow baking pan so they all touch—you don't want them to dry out.

Bake the packets uncovered, without disturbing, for 3 or even 4 hours if the pieces of lamb are especially large. This is not lamb in the pink French manner but in the melting Greek way, so if you're in any doubt, longer roasting won't hurt. Serve the packages as they are, passing a tray to collect wrappings.

— *Recipe by Sylvia Thompson*

Lamb & Fava Pod Sauce

This Mideastern dish, in which young fava pods are cooked like green beans, makes a quick and simple meal when served over rice or couscous.

Fresh from the garden: ONION, GARLIC, SMALL FAVA PODS, CILANTRO
4 servings | *380 calories, 22g fat, 650mg sodium*

3 tablespoons olive oil

1 pound lean lamb, such as boneless shoulder, cut into ½-inch cubes

1 onion, coarsely chopped

8 cloves garlic, peeled and chopped

1 teaspoon salt

1 pound small fava pods, up to 6 inches long

¼ cup chopped fresh cilantro

Heat the olive oil in a Dutch oven or flameproof casserole set over medium-high heat. Add the lamb and brown on all sides. Add the onion, garlic, and salt, reduce heat to medium-low, and cook until onions are lightly browned, about 10 minutes.

Add the favas and ½ cup water. Cover, reduce heat to low, and simmer until the pods are very soft, about 30 minutes. If necessary, adjust the consistency of the stew either by cooking down or by adding water—you want a gravy with the lamb and beans to moisten the accompanying starch. Remove from the heat, stir in the cilantro, and serve.

NOTE | If you don't have enough small, tender fava pods, flat Italian beans make a good substitute.

— *Recipe by Ed Miller*

Saltimbocca

Saltimbocca means "jump in the mouth," and this Italian classic is so good it wants to do just that. You can make this dish with boneless, skinless chicken breasts instead of veal. Flatten them as much as possible without destroying the meat. You'll need to cook them a little longer, about 15 to 18 minutes.

Fresh from the garden: SAGE
4 servings | 310 calories, 16g fat, 930mg sodium

1 pound veal cutlets
6 thin slices prosciutto

12 large fresh sage leaves
2 tablespoons butter

¼ cup dry Marsala wine

Cut the veal so you have 12 portions of roughly equal size. Lay each piece between sheets of waxed paper and pound them with the flat side of a meat mallet until they're a uniform thickness. Cut the prosciutto in half and cover each piece of veal with prosciutto, trimmed to fit. Lay a sage leaf crosswise at one end of the veal, and roll into a bundle, with the sage in the middle. Secure with a toothpick.

Melt the butter in a large sauté pan over medium-high heat. Brown the veal bundles in the butter, turning to color them on all sides. This should take about 5 minutes. Add the Marsala and shake the pan to coat the bundles. Cook until the Marsala has reduced to a syrupy glaze, 2 to 3 minutes. Remove the toothpicks and serve immediately with the sauce.

— *Recipe by Ruth Lively*

DESSERTS

&

SWEETS

The end of a meal can be just the beginning of something positively decadent. In this chapter you'll find all manner of treats to satisfy the palate. Naturally, fruits figure big in the recipes. There are lots of desserts to make with berries, plus recipes calling for cherries, plums, peaches, apples, and pears. But don't overlook the recipes that showcase the sweeter side of herbs. Besides the ones you'd expect, like mint or lemon-flavored herbs, there's the lovely Peach Crisp with Lavender. You'll also find sage-infused syrup in the Pear Burgundy Granita; aromatic rosemary that flavors butter-cookie dough; fennel seeds that perfume biscotti; and lemon basil that creates a delicately delicious ice cream.

Let your sweet tooth be inspired by the season. Summer is for berries and stone fruits. At the height of berry season, when the fruit is most flavorful, just puree berries with a bit of sugar. These sauces can be used to top ice cream, breakfast breads, yogurt parfaits, and more, so you'll want to have lots on hand; stash cupfuls in the freezer to pull out in winter for a taste of summer. Fall fruits keep well, so apple and pear desserts are in season for months. And in the depths of winter, bake those Orange Peel and Rosemary-Scented Butter Cookies, or a rich cake flavored with Fig Preserves from the fall harvest.

Chocolate Mint Truffles

Peppermint, with its head-clearing aroma and expansive, menthol-cool flavor, is the perfect match for rich, dark chocolate. When infusing mint in a liquid, as you do here, no need to strip the leaves from the stem. Just use whole sprigs.

Fresh from the garden: MINT

Makes 16 truffles | *100 calories, 7g fat, 0mg sodium*

½ cup heavy cream
Four 4-inch-long sprigs of fresh
   peppermint or chocolate mint

½ pound good-quality semisweet
   chocolate, chopped
Cocoa for rolling

Bring the cream to a boil in a small saucepan. Add the mint. Turn the heat off and let it steep for 15 minutes. Strain the cream and return it to the saucepan.

Place the chocolate in the bowl of a food processor. Bring the mint-flavored cream to a boil again. Pour it over the chocolate and process until smooth. Transfer the mixture to a small mixing bowl and chill until solid.

Scoop out tablespoon-size dollops of the chocolate and place them on a plate. Chill for 10 minutes. Dip your hands in ice water and dry them. Roll the chocolate into uniform balls and toss them in a bowl of the cocoa. Chill and dry your hands again if the chocolate begins to melt. Shake off any excess cocoa and store the truffles in the refrigerator.

— *Recipe by Jerry Traunfeld*

Blondies with Orange Mint & Apricots

Orange mint gives these chewy bar cookies—non–chocolate cousins of brownies—a citrus flavor and scent. In place of the apricots, try plump, ruby-red dried plums (not prunes; these are dried red plums— very plump, jammy, and yummy), dried cranberries, or dried sour cherries. A cup of broken pecans would be a nice addition, too.

Fresh from the garden: ORANGE MINT, APRICOTS
Makes 32 bars | *150 calories, 6g fat, 100mg sodium*

1 cup butter
1⅓ cups packed light brown sugar
⅔ cup sugar
1 cup dried apricots

½ cup fresh orange mint leaves, loosely packed
2½ cups flour
2 teaspoons baking powder

1 teaspoon salt
3 eggs
1½ teaspoons pure vanilla extract

Preheat the oven to 350°F. Butter a 9x13-inch pan.

In a heavy-bottomed saucepan, melt the butter over medium-low heat. When melted, add the brown sugar and stir. Cook over medium-low heat, stirring, until the mixture is thick and syrupy, about 4 minutes. Add the granulated sugar and stir until it's dissolved. Remove the pan from the heat to cool.

Thinly slice the apricots crosswise. Wash, dry, and coarsely chop the orange mint; there should be about 3 tablespoons.

Combine the flour, baking powder, and salt in a bowl and stir to blend. Sprinkle 1 tablespoon of the flour mixture over the apricots and toss to coat them lightly.

Beat the eggs into the warm sugar and butter mixture (it should not be hot) and blend thoroughly. Add the vanilla and stir well.

Pour the liquid ingredients into the flour and stir until just blended. Add the apricots and mint and stir until just mixed in. Pour the batter into the prepared pan and bake in the oven until the top is a deep golden brown, about 35 minutes. Allow to cool completely on a baking rack before cutting into bars.

— *Recipe by Susan Belsinger*

Orange Peel & Rosemary–Scented Butter Cookies

Orange and rosemary is a lovely combination for these tender cookies. They're fragile, so when transferring the just-baked cookies to a cooling rack, handle them with a light touch.

Fresh from the garden: ROSEMARY

Makes about 2 dozen cookies | *120 calories, 8g fat, 55mg sodium; per cookie*

½ pound butter, at room temperature	2 eggs, beaten	1½ cups flour
1 teaspoon pure vanilla extract	Grated zest of 1 orange	½ teaspoon salt
⅔ cup sugar	1 teaspoon minced fresh rosemary	

Preheat the oven to 375°F. Lightly butter two cookie sheets.

Cream the butter and vanilla, then add the sugar, eggs, orange zest, and rosemary, and blend well. Sift the flour and salt together and add to the creamed ingredients; combine thoroughly.

Drop by teaspoonfuls onto the prepared sheets. Bake until the cookies brown slightly around the edges, 15 to 18 minutes. Remove the cookies from the oven, allow to cool for 2 minutes, and then transfer to a rack to cool completely. Store in a tin. Freeze if desired.

— Recipe by Janet Jemmott

Anise Seed Biscotti

Seeds from the herb fennel, or sweet anise, flavor these simple but sophisticated cookies. Because of their freshness, homegrown seeds are much more flavorful than store-bought.

Fresh from the garden: ANISE SEED

Makes about 6 dozen | *25 calories, 0.5g fat, 10mg sodium; per biscotti*

A little butter for the pan	2 teaspoons sweet Marsala, sherry,	1½ cups flour
3 eggs	or Madeira	¼ cup cornstarch
2 tablespoons plus ½ teaspoon	¾ cup sugar	½ teaspoon baking powder
dried anise seeds	Pinch of salt	

Line a heavy baking sheet with waxed paper and lightly butter it. Position a rack in the center of the oven, and preheat the oven to 350°F. Cover the eggs in their shells with hot water to warm them while preparing the remaining ingredients.

With a mortar and pestle or the back of a spoon in a bowl, crush half the anise seeds to a powder, leaving the rest in bits.

Run hot water in your mixer bowl until the bowl is warm. Wipe it dry, and then combine the eggs, anise, Marsala, sugar, and salt. Using the whisk attachment if you have one, or beaters, beat on low speed until the eggs are foamy, then gradually raise the speed to high. Beat until the mixture is light and very thick, 6 to 7 minutes.

Sift the flour, cornstarch, and baking powder together onto waxed paper.

Sift the dry ingredients into the egg mixture in 3 parts, folding them in with a rubber spatula after each addition until just blended. The batter will be thick but soft. Place the batter in a pastry bag (or a bag folded from parchment paper) with a plain ¾-inch opening. Pipe evenly onto the baking sheet in straight logs 1½ inches wide—3 strips about 12 inches long should do it. If necessary, take a table knife and smooth the edges and tops.

Bake the strips until golden, about 20 minutes. Leave the oven on. Slide the paper onto the counter, pull the paper off the logs, and turn the logs bottom-side-up to cool. In about 10 minutes, with a sharp serrated knife, cut slices on the diagonal, ½ inch thick. Lay the cut sides down on the baking sheet (no paper needed) and bake until lightly toasted, 10 to 15 minutes. Cool thoroughly on the pan, then store in an airtight tin.

— *Recipe by Sylvia Thompson*

Lemon Verbena Flan

The flowery citrus flavor of lemon verbena is nicely complemented by the rich warmth and sweetness of caramel—just right for this flan.

Fresh from the garden: LEMON VERBENA

6 servings | 420 calories, 20g fat, 65mg sodium

1 cup sugar

3 cups half-and-half

1 cup loosely packed fresh lemon
   verbena leaves, crushed;
    1 sprig for garnish

1 teaspoon freshly grated lemon zest

7 egg yolks

½ cup sugar

¼ teaspoon mace

Pinch of salt

Preheat the oven to 325°F.

Caramelize 1 cup of sugar by heating it in a small, heavy pan over medium heat, stirring as it melts to a deep golden brown. Quickly pour it into six ramekins, swirling it around the sides of each.

Heat the half-and-half until hot to the touch; add the lemon verbena and lemon zest and turn off the heat. Let steep 15 minutes, releasing the flavor of the herbs by bruising them with a wooden spoon. Remove the herbs. Over medium-high heat, scald the half-and-half; your clue that it has reached scalding will be tiny bubbles forming at the sides of the pan. Remove from heat. Mix the yolks with the ½ cup sugar; whisk in the half-and-half, mace, and salt. Strain into the ramekins and place them in a hot-water bath. Bake until set, 45 to 50 minutes; a knife inserted near the center should come out clean. Chill several hours or overnight.

To serve, run a knife around the inside of the ramekins and place them briefly in a pan of warm water; 30 seconds should do it. Unmold on dessert plates and garnish with a sprig of lemon verbena.

— Recipe by Lucinda Hutson

Sweet Cherry Clafouti

Clafouti is a traditional French dessert from the cherry-growing region of Limousin. This simple baked custard goes together in a flash. It's meant to be eaten warm, so put it in the oven just before sitting down to dinner.

Fresh from the garden: CHERRIES

8 servings | *150 calories, 4g fat, 95mg sodium; with low-fat milk*

Butter for the pan	¼ cup flour	2 tablespoons brandy
¼ cup sugar	⅛ teaspoon salt	1 tablespoon pure vanilla extract
2 cups pitted dark cherries	1⅔ cups milk, low-fat or whole	1 tablespoon confectioners' sugar
4 eggs at room temperature		

Preheat the oven to 350°F. Butter the bottom and sides of a 10-inch quiche dish and sprinkle with 1 tablespoon of the sugar. Arrange the cherries in a single layer in the dish.

In the bowl of an electric mixer, beat the eggs and the remaining sugar at high speed until light and slightly thickened, about 3 minutes. Reduce the speed to medium and gradually incorporate the flour and salt. With the mixer off, pour in the milk, brandy, and vanilla. Mix just until the ingredients are blended.

Carefully pour the mixture over the cherries. The batter should come nearly to the top of the dish.

Place in the center of the oven and bake until puffed and golden, about 50 minutes. Do not underbake; the batter puffs in the last 15 minutes of baking. Remove to a wire rack and cool for 10 minutes. The clafouti will sink slightly. Sift the confectioners' sugar over the top and serve warm.

— *Recipe by Edon Waycott*

Berry Trifle

This summer party dessert looks spectacular in a traditional 12-cup trifle bowl. Make it with any combo of berries, or even a single kind.

Fresh from the garden: RASPBERRIES, BLUEBERRIES, STRAWBERRIES

10 generous servings, or 16 smaller ones | *260 calories, 14g fat, 100mg sodium; per small serving*

FOR THE CUSTARD

2 cups milk

¾ cup sugar

½ cup flour

2 egg yolks

1 tablespoon butter

2 teaspoons pure vanilla extract

2 cups whipping cream

FOR THE FRUIT

1 pint raspberries

1 pint blueberries

1 pint strawberries

2 tablespoons confectioners' sugar

2 tablespoons medium-dry sherry or freshly squeezed orange juice

FOR THE CAKE

One 3-ounce package lady fingers

Half a 9-ounce angel food cake

¼ cup medium-dry sherry or freshly squeezed orange juice

MAKE THE CUSTARD | Scald the milk in a heavy pot. Mix the sugar and flour together and place in the top of a double boiler over barely simmering water. Whisk in the scalded milk, then quickly whisk in the egg yolks. Cook, stirring, until the mixture becomes thick enough to coat the back of a spoon. Remove from the heat and whisk in the butter and vanilla. Pour the custard into a bowl and lay plastic wrap or waxed paper right on the surface of the custard to prevent a skin from forming on top. Refrigerate until cool.

PREPARE THE FRUIT | Reserve a few whole berries to decorate the top. Place the rest of the raspberries and blueberries in a bowl. Slice the strawberries and add them to the bowl. Add the sugar and the 2 tablespoons sherry. Let the mixture steep until some of the fruit juices have been drawn out, about 30 to 45 minutes.

ASSEMBLE THE TRIFLE | Whip the cream and mix one-third of it into the custard; reserve the rest.

Place 1 cup of the fruit mixture in the bottom of a 12-cup trifle bowl. Arrange the ladyfingers around the outer sides of the bowl. Add 2 cups more berries to the bowl. Spoon half the custard mixture into the center of the bowl, distributing it evenly. Cut a couple of slices of angel food cake into pieces and scatter them on top of the custard. Drizzle half the sherry on it and top with the remaining fruit. Cover the fruit with slices of angel food cake and drizzle it with the remaining sherry. Add the remaining custard to the dish, and then spread the rest of the whipped cream evenly over the top.

Garnish the trifle with the reserved berries. Cover lightly with plastic wrap and refrigerate for several hours to allow the flavors to meld.

— *Recipe by Darlene White*

Strawberry Mascarpone Trifles

This easy twist on the English classic departs from tradition in a few ways. Yogurt and mascarpone cheese replace the usual custard; it's made as individual servings instead of one large trifle; and it can be served immediately after assembling. Traditionalists might gasp, but there's no arguing these are fun to make and delicious to eat.

Fresh from the garden: STRAWBERRIES

4 servings | *440 calories, 22g fat, 35mg sodium*

1½ pints fresh strawberries, rinsed, drained, and hulled

½ cup sugar

Juice of half a lemon

6 ounces mascarpone

¼ cup plain low-fat yogurt

1 or 2 drops pure vanilla extract

8 whole ladyfingers

Slice one pint of the strawberries thin and put them in a bowl. Sprinkle with 2 tablespoons of the sugar and the lemon juice, toss lightly, and set aside for 15 minutes.

Coarsely chop the remaining strawberries and put them in a small, nonreactive saucepan with 2 tablespoons of the sugar. Cover and heat gently, stirring occasionally, until the berries give off a fair amount of liquid, about 2 to 3 minutes. Transfer the contents of the saucepan to a food processor and process to a smooth purée. Scrape the purée into a small bowl.

Put the mascarpone, yogurt, vanilla, and remaining 4 tablespoons sugar in a small bowl and stir with a rubber spatula or wooden spoon just until smooth.

To assemble the trifle, split the ladyfingers in half and lay 4 halves in each of 4 individual dessert bowls. Divide the strawberry purée among the bowls, spreading it over the ladyfingers. Cover each one with some of the strawberries and their juice, then top with a generous spoonful of the mascarpone mixture. Serve immediately, or let sit briefly before enjoying.

— *Recipe by Ken Haedrich*

Blackberry Summer Pudding

Make this homey dessert the day before you want to serve it so the ingredients come together properly. You can also make this pudding with a mélange of summer berries and other soft fruits, such as red or black currants.

Fresh from the garden: BLACKBERRIES

6 servings | *400 calories, 2.5g fat, 280mg sodium*

About ½ loaf firm, white bread, such as Pepperidge Farm or challah	6 cups blackberries	Whipped cream
1 cup sugar	¼ cup Grand Marnier® or strained freshly squeezed orange juice	

Line the bottom and sides of a 5- to 6-cup deep bowl or mold with plastic wrap, allowing enough excess wrap so it will cover the top of the container completely. Remove the crusts from the bread, trimming as many slices as needed to line the bottom and sides of the bowl completely. Cut and place the bread so there are no gaps between the pieces.

Place the sugar and ½ cup water in a heavy saucepan and cook over medium heat until the sugar is completely dissolved, about 3 minutes. Add 5 cups of the berries, reduce the heat, partially cover, and simmer for 5 minutes. Spoon the cooked berries into the lined bowl, reserving the excess juice. Measure out ¾ cup juice and stir in the Grand Marnier.

Cover the berries with additional slices of crustless bread, cut to fit, and again make sure there are no gaps. Spoon the juice and Grand Marnier mixture over the bread. Cover with the overhanging plastic wrap. Weight the pudding with a 1-pound weight, such as an unopened can placed on a small plate, and refrigerate overnight.

At serving time, remove the weight, fold back the plastic wrap, and invert the pudding onto a serving plate. Remove the plastic wrap from the sides of the pudding. Cut into wedges and serve, garnished with the remaining berries and whipped cream.

— *Recipe by Jane Adams Finn*

Sweet Plum Soufflés

Soufflés are fun to eat, and you can't dispute the "wow" factor. Despite the mystique surrounding them, they're easy to make. Just be sure your bowl and beaters are clean before whipping the whites, and then be gentle when folding them into the flavor base. Use sweet, yellow mirabelle or greengage plums, if you can find them, for this delicate dessert.

Fresh from the garden: PLUMS

8 servings | *130 calories, 2.5g fat, 30mg sodium*

FOR THE PLUM PURÉE

7 to 8 small plums, peeled
   and quartered, pits removed
¼ cup brandy
¼ cup sugar

FOR THE SOUFFLÉ BATTER

Butter, for the ramekins
7 tablespoons sugar, plus extra
   for the ramekins
4 egg yolks

1 cup Plum Purée
4 egg whites

MAKE THE PLUM PURÉE | Cook the plums with the brandy and sugar in a small saucepan over medium heat, stirring occasionally, until the plums are tender, about 20 to 30 minutes. Remove the mixture from the heat, cover, and let the plums macerate for 30 minutes. Purée in a food processor or blender until smooth. Set aside.

MAKE THE SOUFFLÉS | Preheat the oven to 400°F. Butter and sugar eight 4-ounce soufflé ramekins.

Using a whip attachment on high speed, beat 4 tablespoons of the sugar with the egg yolks until the mixture forms ribbons when dripped from the end of the whip. Fold the plum purée into the yolk and sugar mixture.

In a clean bowl, whip the egg whites on high speed until frothy. Slowly add the remaining 3 tablespoons sugar while the egg whites are being whipped. Continue whipping to a medium peak. Fold the whites gently into the yolk base. Immediately spoon the batter into the prepared ramekins. Bake the soufflés for 15 minutes. Serve at once.

— *Recipe by Meredith Ford*

Peach Crisp with Lavender

Nothing compares with fresh, ripe peaches at the height of summer. Their fragrance, flavor, and mouthwatering sweetness are enhanced by a hint of perfume from lavender flowers. Serve with lightly whipped cream and a lavender bloom for garnish.

Fresh from the garden: PEACHES, LAVENDER FLOWERS

8 servings | *360 calories, 12g fat, 50mg sodium*

6 cups peeled and sliced peaches (about 2½ pounds) (see Note)

1 tablespoon freshly squeezed lemon juice

⅓ cup sugar

1 tablespoon plus 2 teaspoons cornstarch

1 scant tablespoon fresh lavender flowers or 1 teaspoon dried

1 cup flour

1 cup packed light brown sugar

⅛ teaspoon salt

Few fresh gratings of nutmeg

8 tablespoons butter, cut into pieces

Preheat the oven to 400°F and butter a 2½-quart baking dish.

Combine the peaches, lemon juice, sugar, cornstarch, and lavender flowers in a bowl and toss well. If the peaches are tart, add another tablespoon or two of sugar. Put the mixture in the baking dish.

Combine the flour, brown sugar, salt, and nutmeg in a bowl and stir to blend. Cut the butter into the dry ingredients with a pastry blender or two knives until just blended. Spread the mixture evenly over the fruit and bake until the crisp is golden brown and the peaches are bubbling, about 40 minutes. Serve warm or at room temperature.

NOTE | Dip the peaches briefly into boiling water for easier peeling.

— *Recipe by Susan Belsinger*

Raspberry Frangipane Cake

This cake is so moist and rich that it needs no icing. It's divine on its own or spectacular served in a pool of Raspberry Sauce (p. 242). You can also cut the cake into two layers and fill it with whipped cream and whole berries.

Fresh from the garden: RASPBERRIES

12 servings | *330 calories, 20g fat, 30mg sodium*

7 ounces almond paste
7 ounces butter, softened
1 cup plus 2 tablespoons sugar

1 teaspoon pure vanilla extract
5 eggs

1 cup sifted cake flour
1½ cups whole raspberries

Preheat the oven to 350°F. Butter and flour a 9-inch cake pan.

Use a food processor or a mixer with a paddle attachment to cream the almond paste, butter, and sugar until smooth and light. Add the vanilla and eggs, beating well and scraping down the sides of the bowl after each addition. By hand, gently fold in the flour until the batter is just barely combined. Fold in the raspberries. Avoid overmixing, or the cake will be tough. Pour the batter into the prepared pan and bake until the top is nicely browned and a toothpick comes out clean, about 50 to 55 minutes. Cool completely before removing from the pan.

— *Recipe by Sarah Wood*

Raspberry Sauce

This sauce has a flavor as profound as its color. Making this recipe is a lovely way to preserve the taste of fresh berries because the sauce freezes so well. Pour spoonfuls over ice cream, sorbet, or poached fruit. It is divine under a dense chocolate indulgence like truffle cake or mousse cake, too.

Fresh from the garden: RASPBERRIES
Makes 1¼ cups | *15 calories, 0g fat, 0mg sodium; per tablespoon*

2 cups raspberries | ¼ cup sugar

Press the berries through a fine mesh strainer to purée them and to remove all the seeds. Be patient, as it may take 10 or 15 minutes before you have nothing left in the strainer but seeds. Set aside. Make a simple syrup by stirring together 3 tablespoons of water and the sugar in a small saucepan; bring to a boil. Cool. Stir the purée and simple syrup together. Store in the refrigerator for up to a week. For longer storage, freeze in airtight containers (it will keep up to a year). After thawing, stir well before using.

— Recipe by Sarah Wood

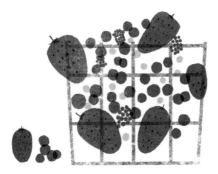

Fig Cake with Orange-Caramel Sauce

Make Fig Preserves for this cake (p. 244), or use store-bought preserves. If your homemade preserves are less than a month old, strain and withhold the sugar syrup from the preserves before adding them to the cake batter.

Fresh from the garden: FIGS

15 servings | *520 calories, 22g fat, 180mg sodium*

FOR THE FIG CAKE

¾ cup butter, softened, more for the pan

2½ cups sugar

4 eggs

3 cups flour

¼ teaspoon salt

1 teaspoon baking soda

1 teaspoon nutmeg

1 teaspoon allspice

1 teaspoon cinnamon

½ teaspoon cloves

1 teaspoon pure vanilla extract

1 cup chopped pecans

2 cups fig preserves, coarsely chopped

FOR THE SAUCE

1 cup sugar

½ cup heavy cream

4 tablespoons butter

¼ cup freshly squeezed orange juice

MAKE THE CAKE | Preheat the oven to 325°F. Butter and flour a bundt pan.

In a large bowl, cream the butter and sugar until light and fluffy, scraping the bowl occasionally. Add the eggs, one at a time, scraping after each addition.

Sift together the flour, salt, baking soda, and spices. Add the sifted dry mixture to the creamed mixture in three stages, mixing well after each addition.

In a medium bowl, combine the vanilla, pecans, and fig preserves. Add this mixture to the cake batter, stirring until just combined.

Pour the batter into the prepared bundt pan and bake until a toothpick inserted in the center comes out barely clean, about 1 hour. Do not overbake, or the cake will be too dry. Let the cake rest for 5 to 10 minutes, then turn it out of the pan and cool it on a cake rack.

MAKE THE SAUCE | Put the sugar in a small saucepan over high heat, stirring occasionally, until the sugar melts and begins to caramelize and turn a light amber color. Do not let the sugar burn. Add the cream and the butter, stirring carefully (the mixture will bubble and foam) until smooth. Add the orange juice and stir until smooth. Cover and let sit at room temperature until cool. Drizzle the sauce over the cooled fig cake and serve.

NOTE | If the sauce is too thin after it has cooled, place it in the refrigerator for a few hours and it will thicken.

— *Recipe by Meredith Ford*

Fig Preserves

As well as being a scrumptious addition to plain cake batter, these special preserves can be enjoyed as you would any jam—spread over warm toast, biscuits, or croissants, or in jam-filled cookies. You can eat them on crostini with a rich, aged cheese like manchego or a delicious blue for an unusual appetizer or sophisticated dessert.

Fresh from the garden: FIGS
Makes 4 to 5 pints | *20 calories, 0g fat, 0mg sodium; per tablespoon*

6 cups barely ripe figs
3 cups sugar

2 fresh lemon slices, seeded

Trim the stems from the figs and wash the fruit. Place the figs in a large bowl and cover them with the sugar. (As a rule of thumb, use ½ cup sugar for each cup of figs.) Cover the bowl, and let the figs sit in the sugar overnight.

Place the figs, sugar, and lemon slices in a large saucepan and bring the mixture to a boil, stirring frequently. Reduce the heat and let the mixture simmer over low heat, stirring frequently, until a thick syrup forms and the figs soften, about 1 hour. Take care that the syrup does not stick and burn; if it seems to, reduce heat further.

Ladle the figs and syrup into hot, sterilized jars, filling the jars to within ¼ inch of the top. Slide a wooden spoon or skewer down the inside of the jars to release any air bubbles. Seal the jars with sterile lids and bands, and then process in a boiling-water bath for 5 to 10 minutes.

Remove the jars from the water bath and allow them to cool completely. The jars are sealed if the lid does not pop back when pressed with a finger or thumb (wait 12 to 24 hours before testing). Any jar of preserves that doesn't seal should be stored in the refrigerator. Sealed jars will keep indefinitely; once opened, however, they should be refrigerated. (For more information about water-bath canning, see Water-bath canning basics, p. 270.)

— *Recipe by Meredith Ford*

Lemon Verbena Pound Cake

Decorative arcs of lemon verbena leaves accent and flavor this pound cake, which is served with a sauce made from an infusion of the herb. Remove the fibrous leaves before eating.

Fresh from the garden: LEMON VERBENA

12 servings | *490 calories, 19g fat, 210mg sodium*

FOR THE CAKE

20 fresh lemon verbena leaves, all about 3 inches long

1 cup butter, at room temperature

2 cups sugar

3 eggs

3 cups flour

½ teaspoon baking soda

½ teaspoon salt

1 cup buttermilk

2 tablespoons finely chopped fresh lemon zest

2 tablespoons freshly squeezed lemon juice

½ teaspoon pure vanilla extract

FOR THE SAUCE

1 cup sugar

1 tablespoon flour

¼ cup freshly squeezed lemon juice

20 fresh lemon verbena leaves

2 tablespoons butter

Preheat the oven to 325°F.

MAKE THE CAKE | Lightly butter and flour a 10-inch tube pan or standard bundt pan. Place the lemon verbena leaves, rib side up, around the bottom of the pan like the spokes of a wheel.

In a large bowl, use an electric mixer to cream the butter, then slowly add the sugar. Beat until the mixture is light and fluffy. Add the eggs one at a time, beating well after each addition.

In a small bowl, stir together the flour, baking soda, and salt. Add the flour mixture alternately with the buttermilk to the creamed mixture, beginning and ending with the flour and beating thoroughly to incorporate each addition. Mix in the zest, lemon juice, and vanilla.

Pour the batter into the prepared pan and bake in the center of the oven until a toothpick inserted in the middle comes out clean, 60 to 70 minutes. Cool the cake in the pan for 10 minutes, then invert onto a plate.

MAKE THE SAUCE | Combine the sugar and flour in a small saucepan, off the heat. Stir in ¾ cup boiling water and cook several minutes over moderate heat. Add the lemon juice and lemon verbena leaves and bring to a boil. When the sauce has thickened, remove the leaves with a fork. Add the butter and stir until it is melted. Remove the sauce from the heat and cool to room temperature or chill before serving. Serve slices of the cake napped with sauce.

— *Recipe by Edon Waycott*

Spiced Buttermilk Pound Cake

This cake is wonderful plain, but it also makes a perfect vehicle for strawberry sauce or lemon-verbena sauce, a purée of mixed berries and sugar, or a vanilla-scented custard sauce.

8 to 10 servings | *310 calories, 11g fat, 290mg sodium; per serving, based on 10 servings*

4 ounces butter, softened
1¼ cups sugar
3 eggs, at room temperature
1 teaspoon pure vanilla extract
Freshly grated zest of 1 orange

2 cups flour
2 tablespoons cornstarch
1 teaspoon baking soda
½ teaspoon salt
1½ teaspoons ground cardamom

½ teaspoon cinnamon
½ teaspoon powdered ginger
1 scant cup buttermilk

Preheat the oven to 350°F. Lightly butter a 5x9-inch loaf pan. Line the pan with waxed paper and butter the paper.

In a bowl, cream the butter, gradually adding the sugar. Add the eggs, one at a time, beating until smooth and fluffy after each addition. Blend in vanilla and zest.

Sift the dry ingredients into a separate bowl. Add the dry ingredients alternately with the buttermilk, beginning and ending with the dry ingredients. Mix until uniformly blended.

Scrape the batter into the pan and level the top. Bake until a toothpick inserted in the center of the cake comes out clean, about 60 to 70 minutes.

Cool the cake in the pan, on a rack, for 15 minutes. Turn out of the pan and peel down the waxed paper. Finish cooling, slice, and serve.

— *Recipe by Ken Haedrich*

Two quick strawberry sauces

Summer berries full of flavor and at peak ripeness are what you want for making berry sauces. Here are two strawberry sauces, one uncooked, the other cooked and thickened with cornstarch. Use them over cake or poached fruit, on top of ice cream or an old-fashioned soda, on cheesecake or yogurt, on pancakes or waffles, or inside crêpes.

UNCOOKED STRAWBERRY SAUCE

Rinse and hull a quart of ripe strawberries. Using the food processor, make a purée with slightly more than half of the berries, 3 tablespoons sugar, and the juice of half a lemon. Transfer to a bowl. Coarsely chop the remaining berries by hand and fold them into the purée.

QUICK COOKED STRAWBERRY SAUCE

To make the thickened version, do the same thing, using 2 tablespoons of sugar. Mix the third table-spoon of sugar with 2 teaspoons of cornstarch. Transfer the purée to a small, nonreactive saucepan, and stir in the cornstarch mixture. Slowly bring to a boil and then boil for 1 minute; the sauce will lose its chalky appearance and turn shiny. Serve hot, warm, or cold.

— *Ken Haedrich*

Country Blueberry Pie

Pies are a great way to use a lot of berries, so make this at the height of blueberry season, when you have them in abundance. The edges of this pastry aren't trimmed; instead, they're simply folded over and pinched to create a wonderfully rustic look.

Fresh from the garden: BLUEBERRIES

One 9-inch pie, 8 servings | *410 calories, 18g fat, 170mg sodium*

FOR THE DOUGH

2 cups flour

½ teaspoon salt

⅓ cup butter

⅓ cup shortening

FOR THE FILLING

6 cups blueberries

¾ cup sugar

Pinch of salt

Pinch of nutmeg

1 egg

½ teaspoon pure vanilla extract

1 teaspoon flour

½ tablespoon butter

MAKE THE DOUGH | Using a food processor or mixing by hand, combine the flour and salt. Cut in the butter and shortening until the mixture consists of pea-size pieces.

Add ¼ cup plus 2 tablespoons cold water and mix until just combined. Wrap in plastic and refrigerate for at least 1 hour. Preheat the oven to 400°F.

Remove the dough from the refrigerator. Using a well-floured rolling pin on a well-floured surface, roll out the pastry crust in a circle about 12 inches in diameter and about ⅛ inch thick. Place the pastry in a 9-inch pie plate, allowing the edges to hang over the sides. Set aside.

MAKE THE FILLING | Mix the blueberries, sugar, salt, nutmeg, egg, vanilla, and flour in a medium-size bowl.

Pour the blueberry mixture into the prepared pie shell and dot with the butter. Carefully fold over the pastry, allowing it to cover most of the blueberries.

Bake on the bottom rack for 15 minutes. Then turn the oven down to 350°F and bake until the pie crust is golden brown and the juices are bubbling, about 1 hour. Allow the pie to cool slightly before cutting.

NOTE | Dough can be made a couple of days ahead but should be taken out of the refrigerator to soften slightly before trying to roll it out.

— Recipe by Elizabeth Holland

Country Apple Pie

Tart apples, elegant spicing, and the intriguing flavor of sage make this one of the tastiest apple pies. And when embellished with fanciful pastry decorations, it is one of the most beautiful.

Fresh from the garden: APPLES, SAGE

One 9-inch pie, 8 servings | *400 calories, 17g fat, 350mg sodium*

Enough short pastry dough
   for a double-crust pie
2 tablespoons freshly squeezed
   lemon juice
2¼ pounds juicy apples; all tart
   or a mix of tart and sweet
1 cup sugar

¼ cup sage leaves,
   cut into thin ribbons
2½ tablespoons flour
¾ teaspoon ground mace
   or freshly grated nutmeg
¼ teaspoon salt
4 tablespoons cold butter

OPTIONAL TOPPINGS
¼ teaspoon cinnamon
   and 1 tablespoon sugar
¼ cup apple or quince jelly

Divide the dough in half. If the dough is chilled until brittle, soften at room temperature until workable. Roll out one piece and line a 9-inch pie pan with it. Roll out the other half and drape it over the back of a large plate. Cover both with plastic and refrigerate.

Put the lemon juice in a large bowl. Quarter and core the apples, then slice into the bowl. Toss them to coat with lemon juice so the flesh won't darken. Sprinkle the sugar and sage over the apples, and toss again to mix. Let stand to let the sugar dissolve and to slightly soften the apples, about 10 to 15 minutes. Sprinkle on the flour, mace, and salt, and blend well.

Set the oven rack in the lower third of the oven and slip a heavy rimmed baking sheet (or 2 light sheets, stacked) onto it. Preheat the oven to 450°F.

Heap about one quarter of the apples into the pie dish then closely arrange the slices over the bottom, being careful not to tear the dough. Cut 1 tablespoon of the butter in thin flakes over the apples. In three more parts, add the remaining apples and butter the same way, mounding the slices slightly in the center. Trim excess dough ¼ inch past the edge of the dish. Use a finger to moisten the border with sugary juices from the filling or cold water. Cover with the remaining dough and trim, leaving ¼-inch margin. Press the edges to seal, then flute a decorative border, or crimp the edges with a fork. Patch as needed, using a touch of cold water for glue.

If desired, stack dough scraps and roll out, then cut out an apple with a leafy twig, or a big A finished with apple leaves and twigs. Lightly brush the surface of the pie with water, and then arrange your decorations on top. Press down gently until the pieces stick.

continued

Cut 6 to 8 vents in the top of the pie to let steam escape. When the oven is ready, set the pie in the center of the baking sheet, rest a sheet of foil on top, and bake 20 minutes. Reduce heat to 375°F, remove the foil, and bake until juices bubble through the vents, and a thin metal skewer meets no resistance when slipped into the apples, about 40 minutes more. Do not overbake. Should the rim be in danger of darkening, tuck strips of foil loosely around its edges.

If the pie is undecorated, in the last 5 to 10 minutes of baking, dust the top of the pie with cinnamon and sugar. If there is a pastry decoration, do not do this.

Instead, after the pie comes out of the oven, melt a little light-colored jelly, such as apple or quince, and brush over the top for a handsome glaze.

Cool on a rack. Apple pie tastes best 1 to 4 hours after baking; juices are thickest after 3 to 4 hours. Serve drizzled with heavy cream, with a wedge of Cheddar, or with a scoop of vanilla ice cream. Apple pie can be kept in a cool place or refrigerated up to 3 days.

NOTE | At high altitude, add 20° to all temperatures.

— *Recipe by Sylvia Thompson*

Apples for pie

Many antique apples are incomparable when cooked. For pie, apples should be juicy and rich. If I'm going to use a single variety, I prefer the tartness of Rhode Island Greening, Bramley's Seedling, Northern Spy, Jonathan, or any Pippin. For a greater depth of flavor, however, I add tangy-sweet varieties like my grandmother's favorite, Yellow Bellflower, or something perfumed, like Grimes Golden.

For a sumptuous tall pie, I further slice each apple quarter into thirds. I'm crazy about apple pie made with unpeeled fruit, but cooked peel is slick, and broad surfaces of peel keep nearby slices from adhering. In serving, chunks glide off on their own and you've suddenly got *dessert* instead of *pie*. Nothing wrong with a luscious apple dessert, but for tidy pie, slice apple pieces ¼ inch thick, or peel the fruit.

Something else about apple pie: Brown sugar seems the natural choice, but white sugar is more subtle, giving a purer apple flavor.

— *Sylvia Thompson*

Cookie Crust Tart Dough

The key to success in working with this dough is its temperature. If the dough crumbles and breaks, it's too cold. Knead it a few turns to warm it, and then try rolling again. If the dough is too sticky, sprinkle it lightly with flour. If it's impossibly sticky, refrigerate it until it firms up a bit. Use the dough for Individual Apple Tarts (p. 252) or Poached Pear Tarts (p. 254).

Makes eight 4-inch tarts or one 9-inch tart | *300 calories, 17g fat, 85mg sodium; per 4-inch tart*

3 tablespoons ground blanched almonds	¾ cup unsifted confectioners' sugar	1 egg, at room temperature, lightly beaten
10 tablespoons butter, at room temperature	¼ teaspoon salt	1¾ cups flour
	¾ teaspoon pure vanilla extract	

Using a coffee mill, blender, or food processor, grind the almonds fairly fine but not to a powder.

To mix by hand: In a large mixing bowl, beat the butter with a whisk until soft. Beat in the powdered sugar until creamy. Mix in the almonds, salt, and vanilla. Add the egg in two portions, blending thoroughly after each addition. Add the flour, switch to a wooden spoon, and stir until the ingredients are just combined. The dough will be soft and sticky.

To make with a stand mixer: Use the paddle attachment to mix all the ingredients except the flour, stopping to scrape down the sides of the bowl once or twice. Turn off the mixer to add the flour, and then mix on low speed until just combined. Don't overmix, or the gluten in the flour will become activated, toughening the dough.

Remove the dough from the bowl, flatten it, wrap it in plastic, and chill until firm, at least 1 hour. It can be refrigerated for several days or frozen for 2 months.

When you're ready to line the tart pans, remove the dough from the refrigerator. Put it on a lightly floured work surface, and if it is very cold, beat it a few times with a rolling pin to soften it. Roll to ⅛ inch thick. Pick up the dough after each stroke and give it a quarter turn to make sure it isn't sticking to the work surface.

For individual tarts, cut disks from the dough slightly larger than the tart pans. To get eight disks, you'll have to gather the scraps into a ball and roll it a second time. Line each tart pan with a disk of dough, pressing it into the crannies and up the sides. Prick the bottoms a few times with the tines of a fork. Refrigerate or freeze

continued

until firm. The tart pans can be lined a few days ahead of baking. Wrap them with plastic wrap if you plan to store them.

For a large tart with lattice, roll the dough into a disk larger than the tart pan. Roll about half of the dough onto the rolling pin, lift the entire piece from the work surface, and unroll it over the tart pan. Press it firmly into the bottom edges and sides of the pan, and then trim away the excess. Refrigerate or freeze the pan until the dough is firm. Roll the remaining dough ⅛ inch thick, transfer to a parchment- or foil-lined cookie sheet and chill. This dough will be used for the lattice.

— Recipe by Fran Gage

Individual Apple Tarts

The apples are cooked in two ways: some in their own juices to make an applesauce for the base, the rest sliced and baked on top of the sauce. Many recipes pair apples with cinnamon, but sugar and a hint of brandy bring out the taste of the fruit rather than masking it. Use the Cookie Crust Tart Dough (p. 251), which is more forgiving of rough handling than flaky dough. The empty crust is partially baked before the fruit filling is added, which helps it to get fully cooked and makes for a nice crisp crust.

....

Fresh from the garden: APPLES
Eight 4-inch tarts | *500 calories, 18g fat, 90mg sodium; per 4-inch tart*

....

FOR THE APPLESAUCE
2½ pounds apples (7 medium), peeled, cored, and cut into 1-inch chunks
½ cup sugar
2 tablespoons brandy or Calvados

FOR THE TARTS
8 individual tart pans, lined with Cookie Crust Tart Dough (p. 251) and chilled
⅓ cup apricot preserves

1½ pounds apples (4 medium), peeled, cored, and cut in half top to bottom

Neat tricks for handling tender dough

- To line a pie pan without tearing the dough, roll the dough halfway over the rolling pin, then unroll it over the pan.

- Gently press the dough against the sides of the pan, holding the dough edge vertically to prevent it from tearing.

- Roll the pin firmly over the top of the pan; excess dough just falls away.

- Before prebaking an unfilled tart shell (also called blind baking), line the pan with parchment or foil and fill with dried beans or rice so the crust keeps its shape.

MAKE THE APPLESAUCE | Put the apple chunks in a large, heavy-bottomed saucepan. Add the sugar and brandy and stir a few times to mix everything together. Cover the pan and cook over very low heat, stirring occasionally until the apples are quite soft and falling apart. They will look like chunky applesauce. The apples will give off liquid as they cook; if they become dry before they are soft, add a very small amount of water. When finished, you should have moist, but not watery, applesauce. Set aside. This can be prepared several days in advance.

ASSEMBLE AND BAKE THE TARTS | Position a rack in the middle of the oven and preheat the oven to 400°F. Put the chilled tart pans filled with dough into the oven and bake until the dough is set but not browned, about 10 minutes.

Meanwhile, prepare the glaze. Combine the apricot preserves with 2 tablespoons water, and heat gently until warm. Stir until well mixed, and then push the warm mixture through a sieve.

Put an apple half, cut side down, on a work surface. Starting at the stem end, cut the apple into 1/16-inch slices, trying to keep the slices together. Repeat with the remaining apples.

Divide the applesauce among the tart pans. It should come close to the top. Flatten each sliced apple slightly, slide a knife or spatula under it, and carefully transfer to a tart pan. Using a pastry brush, coat the sliced apples with a thin layer of apricot glaze. Return the pans to the oven and bake until the apples are soft and the pastry is browned, 30 to 40 minutes.

Cool on a rack, and then remove the tarts from the pans. Brush them again with the apricot glaze.

— *Recipe by Fran Gage*

Poached Pear Tarts

The pears are poached in vanilla-infused red wine, which imparts a flavorful sweetness as well as color. Depending on the ripeness and density of the pears, the color may penetrate the whole pear or be more pronounced on the outside, yielding to pale pink in the middle.

Fresh from the garden: PEARS
Eight 4-inch tarts | *470 calories, 18g fat, 90mg sodium; per 4-inch tart*

FOR THE POACHED PEARS
3 cups fruity red wine
   (Beaujolais, Syrah, or Zinfandel)
⅓ cup sugar
1 vanilla bean

8 medium pears (3 pounds),
   peeled, cored, and cut in half
   top to bottom
1 lemon

FOR THE TARTS
8 individual tart pans, lined with
   Cookie Crust Tart Dough (p. 251)
   and chilled
½ cup of glaze from the reduced
   poaching liquid

MAKE THE PEARS | Mix the wine, sugar, and 1 cup water in a heavy, nonreactive pan that will hold 8 pear halves in one layer. Split the vanilla bean lengthwise. Using a sharp knife, scrape the seeds into the pan, and then add the pod. Bring to a simmer, stirring to dissolve the sugar. Put 8 pear halves, cut side down, into the pan. (Let the remaining pears sit in a bowl of water into which you have squeezed the juice of a lemon.) I put a piece of parchment paper directly on top of the pears in the pan because it helps cook them more evenly. Bring to a simmer and cook until the pears are easily pierced with the tip of a knife, but not falling apart. Turn them

over halfway through the cooking time (which can vary from 10 to 25 minutes, depending on the pears).

Transfer the cooked pears to a bowl, and repeat the process with the second batch. After they are cooked, add them to the bowl, pour on the cooking liquid, cover, and refrigerate until cool, or up to 4 days.

ASSEMBLE AND BAKE THE TARTS | Position a rack in the middle of the oven and preheat the oven to 400°F. Put the chilled tart pans filled with dough into the oven and bake until the dough is set but not browned, about 10 minutes.

Remove the pears from the poaching liquid. Chop half of the pears into ½-inch pieces. Thinly slice each of the remaining pears crosswise and set aside, keeping each half together and the slices in order. Boil the poaching liquid until it is reduced to ½ cup.

Divide the chopped pears among the prebaked tart pans. Arrange the slices from one pear half over each filled pan, so the slices overlap at the center and fan out toward the sides. Using a pastry brush, coat each fanned pear with the reduced poaching liquid. Bake the tarts for 30 minutes, and then transfer them to a rack to cool. Remove them from the pans and brush once more with the glaze.

— *Recipe by Fran Gage*

Quince Tarte Tatin

It is a good idea to make a trial arrangement of the fruit in the pan before caramelizing the sugar, so you can proceed quickly once the pan is ready. The quinces must be thoroughly cooked in advance, before starting the tart recipe; you may want to make them a day or two ahead. If making puff pastry seems too daunting, buy it from a favorite bakery.

Fresh from the garden: QUINCES
One 9-inch tart, 8 servings | *500 calories, 25g fat, 150mg sodium*

1 pound puff pastry made with butter	2 tablespoons butter
1 batch Quinces Cooked in Honey Syrup (see facing page)	9 tablespoons sugar

Position a rack in the middle of the oven and preheat the oven to 400°F.

Roll the dough to ⅛ inch thick on a lightly floured surface. Transfer to a baking sheet and refrigerate while you prepare the rest of the recipe.

To test-fit the quinces in the pan, arrange them tightly in one layer, core sides facing up, in the bottom of a heavy 9-inch cake pan or a 10-inch cast-iron skillet. (You may want to cut the quince halves in two pieces to make a tight fit.) Take them out and wipe out the pan. Put the butter and the sugar in the pan and cook over medium heat, stirring occasionally, until the sugar turns a light caramel color. Remove from the heat and again arrange the quince pieces in the pan.

Take the dough out of the refrigerator and, using a sharp knife or a pizza cutter, cut out a disk that is 1 inch larger in diameter than the pan you're using. Be decisive and cut through the dough in one motion, or the edges might fuse and prevent the dough from rising as it bakes. Drape the dough over the quinces.

Bake until the pastry is brown and the caramel under the fruit is bubbling, about 50 minutes.

Remove from the oven and let cool for about 10 minutes. Shake the pan slightly. If the quinces are sticking, heat the pan over a burner gently until they are free. Put a serving plate upside down over the pan. Using an oven mitt, grasp the bottom of the pan and turn it over onto the plate. Serve warm or at room temperature.

NOTE | This dish is best served the day it's made, but if there is any left over, eat it for breakfast the following morning.

— *Recipe by Fran Gage*

Quinces Cooked in Honey Syrup

Raw quinces, though fragrant, are rock hard and so astringent as to be inedible. But once cooked, they are delectable, with a flavor something like apples or pears but with tropical overtones. When quinces are in season, cook them in honey syrup and store them in the refrigerator in order to have them on hand. This master recipe can be used to make both sweet and savory dishes.

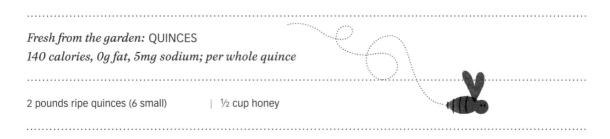

Fresh from the garden: QUINCES
140 calories, 0g fat, 5mg sodium; per whole quince

2 pounds ripe quinces (6 small)	½ cup honey

Preheat the oven to 350°F. Wash the quinces to remove any dirt and fuzz. Cut them in half vertically, and cut out the core. Leave the skin intact. Bring the honey and 1 cup water to a boil in a casserole with a lid. Add the quinces and bring the liquid back to a boil. Cover and put on the middle shelf of the oven. Bake until the quinces are soft, but not falling apart, and have deepened in color, about 1½ hours. Cool them, then transfer with the syrup to a bowl and refrigerate until needed.

— *Recipe by Fran Gage*

Three Refreshing Fruit Ices

No special equipment needed for these frozen treats. Just stir sugar syrup into puréed fruit, freeze in a shallow container, then scrape into shavings, and serve. If you prefer substitute water or fruit juice for the alcohol.

Mixed Berry Granita

Chambord®, a raspberry liqueur, deepens and enriches the berry flavor of this granita.

Fresh from the garden: BLUEBERRIES, RASPBERRIES, BLACKBERRIES, STRAWBERRIES
Makes 5 cups | 130 calories, 0g fat, 0mg sodium; per ½ cup

1 cup sugar
Juice and grated zest of 1 lemon

2 pints ripe berries, puréed

¼ cup Chambord or other fruit liqueur, or fruit juice

Bring the sugar, 1¾ cups water, and the lemon juice and zest to a boil in a medium saucepan over high heat. Reduce the heat and let the syrup boil for 1 minute. Let the mixture cool, and then add the berry purée and the Chambord or juice. Stir well.

Freeze in a large, shallow pan for 24 hours or overnight. Stir the mixture once or twice during the freezing process if it begins to separate.

To serve, let the mixture sit at room temperature for 10 to 20 minutes, then scrape with a chilled metal spoon or ice cream scoop into chilled glasses.

— *Recipe by Meredith Ford*

Pear Burgundy Granita

Sage-infused syrup enhances the autumnal flavor of the pears in this icy treat.

Fresh from the garden: SAGE, PEARS
Makes 6½ cups | 150 calories, 0.5g fat, 0mg sodium; per ½ cup

1 cup sugar
¾ cup red Burgundy wine, or fruit juice

10 fresh sage leaves
4 pounds Bosc or Bartlett pears, peeled, cored, and diced

2 teaspoons freshly squeezed lime juice

Combine all the ingredients with 1¾ cups water in a large pot over high heat and bring to a boil. Reduce the heat and boil for 5 to 10 minutes, or until the pears are tender. Let cool, then remove the sage leaves and purée the mixture. Freeze in a large, shallow pan for 24 hours or overnight. Stir the mixture during the freezing process if it begins to separate.

To serve, let the mixture sit at room temperature for 10 to 20 minutes, then scrape with a chilled metal spoon or ice cream scoop into chilled glasses.

— Recipe by Meredith Ford

Strawberry Champagne Granita

Strawberries and champagne make a decadent granita to toast early summer.

Fresh from the garden: STRAWBERRIES
Makes 5 cups | *100 calories, 0g fat, 0mg sodium; per ½ cup*

1 cup sugar Juice and grated zest of 1 lemon	2 pints ripe strawberries, puréed	½ cup dry champagne or other sparkling wine, or fruit juice

Bring the sugar, 1¾ cups water, and the lemon juice and zest to a boil in a medium saucepan over high heat. Reduce the heat and boil for 1 minute. Let the mixture cool, and then add the strawberry purée and the champagne or fruit juice. Stir until well combined.

Freeze in a large, shallow pan for 24 hours or overnight. Stir the mixture once or twice during the freezing process if it begins to separate.

To serve, let the granita sit at room temperature for 10 to 20 minutes, then scrape with a chilled metal spoon or ice cream scoop into chilled glasses.

— Recipe by Meredith Ford

Melon Mint Sorbet

This sorbet is light and refreshing—the essence of summer. Use any kind of melon, so long as it is ripe and flavorful. Cantaloupes and crenshaws yield a peach-colored sorbet; made with honeydew, the sorbet is cool, icy green. Add a little sparkling wine to give the sorbet a bit of a tingle.

Fresh from the garden: SPEARMINT, MELON

10 servings | *80 calories, 0g fat, 10mg sodium*

½ cup sugar

Six 4-inch fresh spearmint sprigs

2 small or 1 large very ripe melon, such as cantaloupe, honeydew, or crenshaw

2 tablespoons freshly squeezed lemon juice

½ cup champagne or other sparkling wine, optional

Bring ½ cup water and the sugar to a boil in a small saucepan. Once the sugar has dissolved, add the spearmint sprigs and turn off the heat. Let the spearmint steep for 30 minutes. Strain.

Meanwhile, cut the melon in half, remove the seeds, and scoop out the flesh with a large spoon. Place the flesh in a food processor or blender and purée. Measure out 3 cups of purée. Stir in the spearmint syrup, the lemon juice, and, if desired, the champagne. Freeze the mixture in an ice cream maker according to the manufacturer's instructions.

— *Recipe by Jerry Traunfeld*

Strawberry Soft-Serve Yogurt

You don't need special equipment to make this summer treat, just a food processor or blender and juicy, sun-ripened berries. For an even creamier and thicker treat, use Greek yogurt.

Fresh from the garden: STRAWBERRIES
6 servings | *130 calories, 1g fat, 0mg sodium*

1 quart fresh strawberries, rinsed, drained, and hulled	½ cup sugar Juice of 1 lemon	1 cup plain low-fat yogurt Several tablespoons skim milk

Halve about half of the berries and combine them with the sugar in a medium, nonreactive saucepan. Bring to a simmer over low heat, stirring occasionally for about 5 minutes. When the sugar has dissolved, transfer the mixture to a food processor and add the remaining berries.

Process the berries to a smooth purée, then transfer to a shallow bowl and whisk in the lemon juice and the yogurt. Place the bowl in the freezer and let the mixture freeze solid, taking the bowl out and stirring the mixture about every 30 minutes. When the mixture is solid—3 to 4 hours—transfer the strawberry ice to the food processor. Process the mixture in 5- to 8-second bursts, adding a teaspoon or so of milk at a time to make the mixture smooth.

NOTE | This dish can also be made in a blender.

— *Recipe by Ken Haedrich*

Ice Cream Base

In this simplified technique, you don't cook the custard. Instead, you whisk scalding milk into egg yolks, add cold cream, and chill the mixture. It's much quicker, and you don't have to worry about overcooking the custard.

Makes about 1 quart | *400 calories, 33g fat, 60mg sodium; per ½-cup serving*

1½ cups milk
¾ cup sugar

6 egg yolks
2½ cups cream

In a heavy-bottomed, nonreactive pan, heat the milk and sugar to boiling. Put the egg yolks in a mixing bowl and whisk lightly to break them up. When the milk-sugar mixture is boiling, quickly add about ¼ cup of it to the egg yolks and whisk in to temper. Then, whisking constantly, add the remaining milk in a steady stream to the yolks. Strain this mixture into a clean bowl. Stir in the cream and chill thoroughly.

— *Recipe by Kathleen Stewart*

Apricot Ice Cream

Make this icy treat when you have fully ripe, truly flavorful apricots. For really good ice cream, the fruit doesn't have to look great, but it should taste wonderful. Steeping the pits in the cooked fruit imparts a deliciously subtle bitter-almond flavor.

Fresh from the garden: APRICOTS

Makes about 2 liquid quarts | *280 calories, 17g fat, 30mg sodium; per ½-cup serving*

2 pounds apricots

1 cup sugar

1 recipe Ice Cream Base
(see facing page)

Wash, halve, and pit the apricots. Put the fruit in a heavy-bottomed, nonreactive pan with a tiny bit of water. (If you want, tie the pits in cheesecloth and add to the pot.) Over medium-low heat, warm the apricots slowly until they are hot but not boiling. Cool in the pot with the pits, if used. Remove the bag of pits and discard. Purée the fruit either in a food mill or food processor. Add 1 cup sugar to 1 quart purée and warm slightly to dissolve the sugar. Add the purée to an equal amount of base (approximately 1 quart). Chill the mixture, and then freeze in an ice cream maker according to the manufacturer's directions.

— *Recipe by Kathleen Stewart*

Lemon Verbena Ice Cream

Lemon verbena leaves make an ice cream that is lemony in both taste and fragrance. You can use the preparation technique for infusing other flavors, such as cinnamon, hazelnut, or mint.

Fresh from the garden: LEMON VERBENA
Makes 1 liquid quart | *400 calories, 33g fat, 60mg sodium; per ½-cup serving*

1½ cups milk

¾ cup sugar

¾ cup torn fresh lemon
   verbena leaves

6 egg yolks

2½ cups cream

In a heavy-bottomed, nonreactive pot, put the milk, sugar, and lemon verbena leaves. Bring to a boil, turn off the heat, and let sit at least 1 hour. Taste the mixture. If you want it stronger, add more lemon verbena leaves, reheat, and let it stand again for 15 minutes or so before tasting again. You don't want the flavor to be too strong at this point because it continues to develop as the custard chills. When the flavor is right, heat the mixture once again just to boiling. Put the egg yolks in a bowl and whisk slightly to break up. Remove the hot milk from the heat, and whisk a small amount of it into the yolks to temper them, then immediately whisk the remaining milk into the yolks in a slow, steady stream. Strain into a bowl. Stir in the cream. Chill thoroughly before freezing in an ice cream maker according to the manufacturer's directions.

— Recipe by Kathleen Stewart

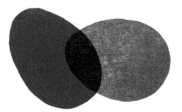

Lemon Basil Ice Cream

This velvet-textured ice cream leaves a delightful perfume on the palate. The method used here is the traditional one of cooking the custard.

Fresh from the garden: LEMON BASIL

Makes about 1 quart | *330 calories, 25g fat, 40mg sodium; per ½ cup*

2 cups whipping cream	Twelve 3- to 4-inch sprigs fresh	3 egg yolks
1 cup milk	lemon basil	
¾ cup sugar		

Combine the whipping cream, milk, sugar, and basil in a heavy-bottomed, nonreactive saucepan. Bring the contents of the pan to a simmer and then remove from heat. Let the herbs steep in the liquid for 30 minutes.

Reheat the mixture over low heat. Lightly whisk the eggs in a small bowl and add about ¼ cup of the warm cream to the eggs and whisk; add another ¼ cup and whisk again. Pour the egg and cream mixture into the saucepan and cook, stirring constantly, until the custard lightly coats a metal spoon, about 5 minutes.

Strain the cream mixture into a bowl, pressing on the leaves to release their flavor, and chill. Discard the leaves. Freeze the custard in an ice cream maker according to the manufacturer's instructions.

— *Recipe by Susan Belsinger*

PRESERVING

There are all manner of ways of keeping the harvest. The easiest techniques include pickling in a salty-sour brine, cooking with sugar, freezing, and drying. With just a little effort, your pantry will fill with tangy pickles, sweet jams, and frozen or dried vegetables, fruits, and herbs.

Does the idea of preserving bring to mind images of heaps of produce, phalanxes of mason jars, and you, sweating for hours over a steaming cauldron? If so, you should take a fresh look at the pickle recipes here. You can make several jars of dill Pickled Green Beans or Zesty Pickled Garlic or Bread and Butter Pickles in just an hour. Jams and fruit preserves take a little longer, but are no more difficult. And if water-bath canning puts you off, you can simply stash your pickles or preserves in the fridge until you're ready to eat them. You won't be able to store them on a pantry shelf, but that might be a good trade-off for not having to process them.

You'll also find wonderful condiments, including salsa-like Green Tomato Relish, Tarragon Mustard, and Preserved Lemon, a superb flavor booster for all kinds of foods, from stews, beans, and grains to braises and roasts. And there's a wide range of fruit spreads, from old-fashioned Apple Butter to sophisticated Pear Preserves with Crystallized Ginger. Plums pickled in cinnamon-spiked brine will spice up a holiday ham or turkey dinner. And speaking of holidays, these home-made goodies are ideal for gift giving.

Pickled Green Beans

These salty, sour vegetable snacks are addictive. You can use the same technique and brine recipe to make pickled okra, asparagus, hot peppers, pearl or cippolini onions, or an antipasto mix of carrots, celery, peppers, and cauliflower.

Fresh from the garden: GREEN BEANS, GARLIC, HOT CHILES, DILL
Makes 4 pints | *20 calories, 0g fat, 800mg sodium; per ¼ cup*

2½ cups cider or white-wine vinegar
¼ cup salt
3 to 4 pounds green beans
4 large cloves garlic, peeled

4 long, thin, red chiles, fresh or dried
1 tablespoon peppercorns,
    preferably mixed or pink

4 fresh dill sprigs or 4 teaspoons
    dried dill weed

Fill a canning kettle two-thirds full of water and bring to a boil. Wash, rinse, and sterilize the canning jars and lids.

Combine 2½ cups water with the vinegar and salt in a nonreactive saucepan, and bring to a simmer over medium heat.

Trim and string the beans, and rinse under cold water. I prefer very young, thin beans. If you use mature, large beans, blanch them for 1 to 2 minutes in boiling, salted water and then plunge them in ice water.

When the sterilized jars are just cool enough to handle, pack them with beans until they're comfortably tight. To each jar add a garlic clove and insert two chiles, preferably around the outside. Then add one-quarter of the peppercorns and the dill. Ladle the hot brine over the beans, leaving ½ inch of headspace. Wipe the jar rims clean and screw on the two-piece lids. Process in a boiling-water bath for 10 minutes. Allow the jars to cool, and then label and store in a dark place for one month for the flavors to develop.

— *Recipe by Jane Selover*

Zesty Pickled Garlic

These chile-spiked cloves are the perfect gift for garlic lovers. Eat them alongside sandwiches, or set them out with nuts and olives at cocktail time and watch them disappear.

Fresh from the garden: GARLIC, HOT CHILES
Makes 4 to 5 pints | *100 calories, 0g fat, 5mg sodium; per ¼ cup*

3 pounds cloves of garlic, about 20 heads	2½ cups white-wine vinegar 2½ cups sugar	10 long, thin, red chiles, fresh or dried

Fill a canning kettle two–thirds full of water and bring to a boil. Wash, rinse, and sterilize the canning jars and lids.

Separate and peel the garlic cloves. Although it takes longer, peeling by hand is better than using a mechanical peeler, which can leave bruises or cuts on the cloves. Discard badly discolored cloves; small blemishes can be cut out. Rinse the cloves under cold water.

Combine the vinegar and sugar in a nonreactive saucepan and stir. Bring to a simmer over medium heat. When the sterilized jars are just cool enough to handle, fill with the garlic cloves and insert two chiles in each jar. Try to keep the chiles visible for both decorative purposes and to warn eaters that the pickles will be spicy. Fill each jar with simmering brine, leaving ½ inch of headspace. Wipe the rim and screw on a sterilized lid and band. Transfer to the boiling-water bath and process for 10 minutes. Allow to cool. Label and store in a dark place for one month for flavors to develop.

— *Recipe by Jane Selover*

Water-bath canning basics
YOU NEED THE RIGHT EQUIPMENT

If you're going to can pickles or preserves, you'll need a few special items. All are available where housewares are sold, and none are expensive.

GLASS CANNING JARS– in quart or pint capacities. You can reuse canning jars if they have no nicks or stains on the rims, which might prevent a tight seal.

TWO-PIECE LIDS– called dome lids, which consist of a flat lid with a rubber gasket on the underside, and a screw-on ring or band to hold the lid down. You must use a new flat lid each time, but the ring can be reused if it's in perfect shape. If it's rusty or bent, don't use it. New jars come with lid sets.

A JAR LIFTER– which is like a pair of tongs for jars. Its vinyl-coated ends securely grip the jar's neck for safe trips in and out of the boiling-water bath. Don't even think of canning without this tool.

A CANNING FUNNEL– which has an extra wide mouth, for filling jars cleanly.

REGULAR TONGS OR A MAGNETIC WAND– for fishing lids and rings out of simmering water.

A CANNING KETTLE– or a water-bath canner, with a wire rack. Most canning-kettle racks will hold seven jars. In a pinch, you can substitute a large stockpot with a cake rack in the bottom. The important thing is that boiling water needs to envelop the jars completely, which is why the rack is necessary and why the jars must be covered with at least 1 inch of water. They also mustn't touch each other during boiling, or they might crack. If you don't have a deep canning kettle, you may be limited to pints and half pints to get the necessary water coverage.

A KITCHEN TIMER– for timing the water bath.

WATER-BATH CANNING IN DETAIL

Regardless of what you're canning—pickles, preserves, fruits, or vegetables—the hot-water-bath method of sealing jars is the same. Wash the jars, lids, and bands in hot, soapy water and rinse them. Then sterilize the jars in boiling water. Keep the lids and rings in a pan of simmering water on the stove until needed, but don't boil them; the water should stay at about 180ºF. The empty jars go into the boiling water bath for at least 10 minutes. Remove them only when you're ready to fill them.

It's important to be organized, because once you start filling the jars, you must work quickly.

IF YOU'RE MAKING PICKLES

While the water heats, make the brine, clean and trim the produce, and measure out the spices and herbs that you'll add to each jar.

When the jars are sterilized, lift them from the canning kettle and begin filling them one by one. Pack them tightly with the produce, fitting as many pieces as possible, and then add the spices and herbs. Ladle in hot brine, leaving ½ inch of headspace. To ensure a good seal, wipe the rim of the jar with a clean towel dipped in hot water. With the tongs, get a lid from the hot water and set it on the jar, then screw on a ring securely but not overly tight.

IF YOU'RE MAKING PRESERVES

Timing isn't as critical with preserves because you can reheat them if needed, although ideally you don't want to cook them any longer than necessary. Get your jars, lids, and water bath ready while the preserves are cooking. As soon as they've reached the desired stage, start filling your hot jars as above.

It's important to get the jars filled before they cool completely, or they're liable to crack. If a jar no longer feels warm, dunk it in hot water briefly before filling it. When you've filled seven jars, load them in the wire rack and lower them into the boiling water. When the water returns to a boil, begin timing— 10 minutes for pints and 15 minutes for quarts.

MY LIDS ARE SEALED

When the timer goes off, pick the jars out of the water with the jar lifter and set them on a clean, dry towel somewhere out of the way and protected from drafts. Allow space between the jars for air to circulate. Let the jars sit undisturbed until completely cool. As the contents of the jar cool, they shrink, creating a vacuum that holds the lid tight to the jar. The lid makes a popping sound as the seal is achieved, sometimes as soon as the jar is out of the water.

When the jars are cool, push down in the center of each lid. If there is no movement, you have a good seal and may store the jar in your pantry. Occasionally, a lid springs back, indicating that the jar isn't sealed. Just put that jar in the fridge. If it's pickles, you'll need to wait a month before eating to give the flavoring enough time to permeate to the center of the pickle. Preserves can be consumed right away. Failure to seal is usually due to an unclean rim or an overly full jar.

Before storing, label the jars with their contents and the date. Some cooks also remove the rings before storing their canned goods. A ring's purpose is simply to hold the lid in place until the seal is completed. I think it's handy to have the ring, though, in case there are leftovers.

— *Jane Selover*

Zucchini Pickles

Baby zucchini are ideal for these turmeric-flavored, sweet-sour pickles, but if you can't get them, use the youngest fruits you can find, and cut them diagonally into 3-inch pieces.

Fresh from the garden: ZUCCHINI, FENNEL SEED, GARLIC
Makes 6 pints | *40 calories, 0g fat, 15mg sodium; per ¼ cup*

3 pounds small zucchini
4 cups white-wine vinegar
2 cups sugar

2 teaspoons ground turmeric
¼ cup pickling spice
1 tablespoon fennel seed

12 cloves garlic, peeled

Fill a canning kettle two–thirds full of water and bring to a boil. Wash, rinse, and sterilize the canning jars and lids.

Trim the stem ends of the zucchini and rinse under cold water. Set aside.

Combine 4 cups water with the vinegar, sugar, and turmeric in a nonreactive saucepan. Bring the mixture to a boil over medium heat.

Pack the zucchini upright into the sterilized canning jars. Add 2 teaspoons pickling spice, ½ teaspoon fennel seed, and 2 garlic cloves to each jar. Fill to ½ inch from the top with the simmering brine. Wipe the rims with a clean, damp towel, and screw on the lids and bands. Transfer jars to the boiling-water bath and process for 10 minutes. Allow to cool, then label and store in a dark place for one month before eating.

— *Recipe by Jane Selover*

Bread & Butter Pickles

This sweet-sour mix of cucumber and onion flavored with whole mustard seeds and turmeric is undoubtedly an all-time favorite. Pair the pickles with a barbecued pork sandwich, hot dogs, hamburgers, or, as the name suggests, eat them on bread and butter. Chop them up and add them to chicken, tuna, pasta or potato salad. Jars of pickles also make great gifts.

Fresh from the garden: MUSTARD SEEDS, CELERY SEEDS, PICKLING CUCUMBERS, ONIONS
Makes 5 pints | *25 calories, 0g fat, 0mg sodium; per 2 tablespoons*

2 cups apple-cider vinegar	2 teaspoons celery seed	2 cups sliced onions
2 cups sugar	1 tablespoon ground turmeric	
2 tablespoons whole mustard seed	8 cups sliced pickling cucumbers	

Fill a canning kettle two–thirds full of water and bring to a boil. Wash, rinse, and sterilize the canning jars and lids.

In a large, nonreactive pot, stir together the vinegar, sugar, and spices. Boil for about 5 minutes. Add the cucumbers and onions, and return to a boil, stirring and turning the vegetables to mix them evenly and coat them with the brine. Let them boil until the color of the cucumbers changes from green and white to an even yellow-green, 5 to 8 minutes.

Pack into sterilized pint jars, leaving ½ inch of headspace. Process in a hot-water bath for 10 minutes. Let the jars cool, then label and store in a cool, dark place. You can eat them right away, but they're even better after a few weeks.

— Recipe by Patricia Bass

Tips for great bread & butter pickles

- Always use pickling cucumbers, immediately recognizable by their prickly warts and blocky shape. Picklers don't hold as much water as slicing cucumbers, so they make meatier, more substantial pickles.

- Try to get cucumbers the same size; 4 to 5 inches long is ideal.

- Slice cucumbers and onions thin, no more than ⅛ inch thick. For best results, use a hand-operated vegetable slicer or a food processor fitted with a slicing blade.

- For the best-tasting pickles, use apple-cider vinegar. Second choice would be distilled white vinegar. For pickling, vinegar must be at least 5 percent acidity.

— Patricia Bass

Sweet Pickled Jalapeños

Handle hot peppers with respect. It's best to wear gloves to keep from transferring the juice to your eyes or nose. Goggles are a good idea, too. Don't use a food processor to slice the chiles because it creates too many fumes. A mandolin makes fast work of slicing the chiles. Try these as a pizza topping, on burgers, or with crackers and cream cheese.

Fresh from the garden: JALAPEÑOS

Makes six 8-ounce jars | *35 calories, 0g fat, 110mg sodium; per tablespoon*

2 pounds jalapeños

2 cups apple-cider vinegar

4 cups sugar

1½ tablespoons sea salt or pickling salt

Fill a canning kettle two–thirds full of water and bring to a boil. Wash, rinse, and sterilize the canning jars and lids.

Slice the peppers crosswise into rings about ¼ inch thick. Don't bother to seed them.

In a nonreactive pan, combine the vinegar, sugar, and salt. Set over low heat and stir until the sugar is completely dissolved.

Pack hot, sterilized jars very tightly with sliced jalapeños. Bring the syrup to a boil and pour over the peppers, leaving ½ inch of headspace at the top of the jar. If needed, use a fork to keep the peppers pressed into the jar as you fill it. Seal the jars and process 15 minutes in a boiling-water bath. Extra syrup will keep for months in the refrigerator.

— *Recipe by Shelby Heeter*

Green Tomato Relish

Instead of the typical sweet concoction, this preserving recipe contains no sugar at all. It resembles a thick salsa, and you can use it as you would salsa—in quesadillas and tacos, mixed into guacamole, or as a chip dip. Stir a few dollops into refried beans or cooked rice. Put it on a hamburger or grilled steak, or mix a little into fried potatoes or hash. This recipe takes full advantage of the late summer and early fall harvest: in addition to green tomatoes, red peppers, onions, garlic, and apples are all called for. Relishes in general are quite forgiving, so don't be afraid to adapt the recipe to what your end-of-season harvest has to offer.

Fresh from the garden: GREEN TOMATOES, ONIONS, BELL PEPPERS, APPLES, GARLIC, JALAPEÑO, CILANTRO | *Makes 3 pints* | *10 calories, 0g fat, 60mg sodium; per tablespoon*

2 pounds green tomatoes, cored and chopped

1 pound yellow or white onions, chopped

¾ pound red bell peppers, cored and chopped

½ pound tart cooking apples, such as Granny Smith, cored and chopped

6 cloves garlic, finely chopped

1 cup apple-cider vinegar

1 tablespoon Kosher or sea salt

4 jalapeño peppers, cored, seeded, and finely chopped

2 tablespoons chopped fresh cilantro

1 teaspoon ground cumin, optional

Combine the tomatoes, onions, peppers, apples, garlic, vinegar, and salt in a large, nonreactive saucepan and bring to a boil. Reduce the heat and simmer, stirring occasionally, until thickened, about 1 hour.

Stir in the jalapeños, cilantro, and cumin and simmer for 5 more minutes. Briefly purée the mixture (in batches if necessary) in a blender so that it is still somewhat chunky.

If canning, return the puréed relish to a boil, then ladle the hot mixture into hot, sterilized jars, leaving ½ inch of headspace. Process 15 minutes in a boiling-water bath. Store in a cool, dark place.

— *Recipe by Susan Brinkley*

End-of-Garden Vinegar

This flavored vinegar makes a wonderful impromptu gift. Because vinegar is thoroughly acidic, any edible part of a plant can be added for flavor and color. The color will fade eventually, but even dull greens are lovely. Choose a tall, decorative, clear glass bottle for the vinegar. What size doesn't matter much, so long as you have enough vinegar to fill it. And it should have a tight-fitting lid or stopper.

Fresh from the garden: HERBS, EDIBLE FLOWERS, SMALL VEGETABLES
Makes 1 bottle | *0 calories, 0g fat, 0mg sodium; per teaspoon*

Branches of colorful and decorative fresh herbs (golden sage, African Blue basil)

Edible flowers on their stems (calendulas, flowering thyme)
Whole, slender, colorful vegetables (red chiles, small carrots)

White rice vinegar or white-wine vinegar, or a mixture, enough to fill the bottle

Gently submerge herbs, flowers, and vegetables in a sink full of cold water to lift off bugs and soil. Sterilize a tall, decorative, clear-glass bottle.

Lift herbs, flowers, and vegetables from the water and shake well or pat dry. Cut the herbs and flowers to different lengths so each will show to advantage in the bottle. Slide into the bottle one by one, shaking the bottle as needed to move each piece into place. Slowly pour vinegar into the bottle through a funnel, trying not to dislodge or crush anything. Fill to within ½ inch of the top and cap or cork the bottle tightly. Cover with brown paper to keep out the light. Keep in a cool, dark, dry place until time to use or give away.

— *Recipe by Sylvia Thompson*

Tarragon Mustard

This spread is fast and fun to make, especially when you've grown the mustard seeds yourself. Prepare a batch a week in advance, if possible, to let the flavors mellow.

Fresh from the garden: MUSTARD SEEDS, TARRAGON, CORIANDER SEEDS
Makes a generous ³/₄ cup | *10 calories, 0.5g fat, 35mg sodium; per teaspoon*

¼ cup plus 2 tablespoons mustard seeds (scant 2 ounces), preferably 3 parts yellow or brown and 1 part black

½ cup plus 1 tablespoon white-wine or champagne vinegar
1 teaspoon dried tarragon leaves
¾ teaspoon ground coriander

¾ teaspoon sugar
½ teaspoon salt
³/₈ teaspoon ground cumin

Put about half the seeds in a small food processor or mortar. Pulse or crush the seeds until they are the desired consistency, from coarse to fine as powder. Pulsing in a processor will produce a finer grind than crushing the seeds with a pestle. Add the rest of the seeds and the remaining ingredients with ¼ cup plus 2 tablespoons water and blend well.

Turn the mixture into a small, heavy saucepan and cook over low heat until it starts to simmer, about 5 minutes. Use a pestle or heavy wooden spoon to crush and stir constantly. Cool. If the mixture seems too thick, thin it with equal parts vinegar and water. Pour the mustard into a decorative jar and cap tightly. Write on the label: Keep refrigerated.

— *Recipe by Sylvia Thompson*

How to dry herbs

Late summer is a good time to harvest herbs for drying, before dropping temperatures cause parsley leaves to toughen, basil to wilt, and tarragon to yellow. Pick a day that's expected to be dry and sunny.

First, gently hose off the foliage, including the undersides of leaves, being careful not to splatter dirt up onto the plant. Give the plant a couple of hours to dry. Meanwhile, get out string or twine, and locate a place to hang the herbs to dry. Look for a dust-free spot without direct sunlight or dampness, and away from cooking oils or smoke. A spare bedroom or closet is perfect.

Gather the herbs and tie them into small bunches. Hang them up, making sure there is space between each bunch so air can circulate all around. If it doesn't, you may wind up with moldy herbs. An oscillating fan set on low will keep the air moving.

The length of time it takes for an herb to dry depends on the relative humidity as well as the thickness of the leaf and its water content. Check herbs every couple of days. You'll know they're dry when they crumble easily between your fingers. Store them in an airtight jar in a dark place.

— Ken Haedrich

Herb Sugar

What could be easier than stirring herbs into sugar and packing the mixture into jars? Sage, lemon thyme, peppermint, and lavender are particularly good choices. This is a wonderful gift for herbal tea lovers.

Fresh from the garden: HERBS
Makes 1 pint | *15 calories, 0g fat, 0mg sodium; per teaspoon*

3 thick sprigs of fresh herb leaves,
    such as sage, golden lemon thyme,
    peppermint, or lavender

2 cups sugar

Bruise the leaves of the herbs with a mortar and pestle or the back of a wooden spoon in a bowl until you can smell them—just enough to release some of their oils. Slowly pour in the sugar, stirring with the pestle to blend the sugar and the herbs' oils. Pour into a jar and cap tightly. Place the jar in a cool, dark, dry place. Every 2 to 3 days, pour out the sugar—it will be moist—and stir to distribute the herb's flavor, then return leaves and sugar to the jar. It will take about 2 weeks for the flavor of the herbs to be fully absorbed by the sugar.

— *Recipe by Sylvia Thompson*

Spiced Plums

Use any sweet, meaty-fleshed dessert plums that are in season and perfectly ripe. Spiced plums are a welcome side dish in winter, when fresh summer fruit is only a memory. Pair them with ham, pork, or rich poultry like duck or goose.

....

Fresh from the garden: PLUMS
Makes approximately 5 quarts or 8 to 10 pints, depending on the size of the plums | *80 calories, 0g fat, 5mg sodium; per ½ cup*

....

5 to 6 pounds plums	4 cups sugar	3 cups apple-cider vinegar
Whole cloves, one for each plum	1 cup light brown sugar	2 cinnamon sticks, broken

....

Fill a canning kettle two–thirds full of water and bring to a boil. Wash, rinse, and sterilize the canning jars and lids.

Wash the plums and prick the skins with a sterilized needle to prevent them from bursting. Push a whole clove into each plum.

Combine the sugars, vinegar, and cinnamon in a large saucepan and bring to a boil. Add the plums and cook for 2 minutes; remove the plums from the heat and cover. Let the plums stand in the hot syrup for 20 minutes.

Pack the plums into sterilized pint or quart jars. Strain the hot syrup, and then pour it over the plums and seal the jars. Process for 25 minutes in a boiling-water bath. If the jars do not seal properly, store them in the refrigerator and eat within 2 months.

— *Recipe by Meredith Ford*

Peach Preserves

Nectarines can be used for this recipe as well—and you don't have to peel them. The actual cooking takes place after 24 hours of macerating, so start a day before you want to make the preserves.

Fresh from the garden: PEACHES

Makes five 16-ounce jars | *50 calories, 0g fat, 0mg sodium; per tablespoon*

8½ to 9 pounds ripe but not mushy peaches, to yield 6 pounds after peeling and pitting

4 pounds sugar, about 9 cups

1 pouch liquid pectin, if necessary

Blanch the peaches to remove the skins. Bring 6 quarts of water to a boil. Have a large bowl of ice water close to the pot. Put some of the peaches in the boiling water, just enough so they have a little space between them (you will have to blanch them in batches). Boil for 1 to 2 minutes, or until the skin can be easily slipped off the fruit. Test one to be sure. Immediately plunge the peaches into the ice water to stop the cooking. When the fruit is cool, slip off the skins and place the peaches in another bowl. Continue blanching until all are done.

Cut each peach to the pit horizontally around the equator, then cut the fruit vertically into 1-inch wedges, letting them fall from the pit. Using a stainless steel bowl, glass bowl, or a plastic container that will fit into your refrigerator, alternately layer the fruit and the sugar, starting with peaches and ending with sugar. Cover and refrigerate for 24 hours, or up to 3 days.

When you're ready to proceed, put clean jars in a pot, cover with water, and bring to a boil.

Strain the fruit through a colander into a heavy, nonreactive 8-quart pot. Set the drained peaches aside. Scrape any undissolved sugar from the bowl into the pot, and give the syrup a stir so the sugar won't stick during cooking. Cook the syrup over medium heat until it reaches 230°F (110°C) on a candy thermometer, 20 to 25 minutes, skimming the foam from the top.

Add the drained peaches to the hot syrup and continue to cook over medium heat, stirring and skimming frequently, until it thickens and the fruit turns translucent or the mixture reaches 221°F (105°C). (This may happen at a slightly lower temperature.) As peaches cook, they tend to stick and burn, so turn the heat to low as they thicken, and stir frequently. If the mixture begins to look as if it is caramelizing, stop cooking.

Test for jelling by freezing a small amount on a plate for a few minutes. If the preserves are not setting, add one pouch of liquid pectin. If they are almost set, use less. Return to a boil, and then turn the heat to low, because continued boiling will break down the pectin.

Immediately ladle into sterilized canning jars and affix lids. Either process the jars in a boiling-water bath for 10 minutes, or let them cool and refrigerate them.

— *Recipe by Fran Gage*

Pear Preserves with Crystallized Ginger

The ginger in this dish accentuates the flavor of the pears. You'll need to let the fruit sit and macerate for 24 hours, so plan accordingly when you decide you want to make the preserves.

Fresh from the garden: PEARS
Makes five 16-ounce jars | *50 calories, 0g fat, 0mg sodium; per tablespoon*

9 to 10 pounds pears, to yield
   6 pounds of fruit after peeling
   and coring

4 pounds sugar, about 9 cups
3 tablespoons finely chopped crystallized ginger (1½ ounces)

4 tablespoons freshly squeezed
   lemon juice
1 pouch liquid pectin

Peel the pears and remove the stems and cores. Cut the fruit into 1-inch chunks. Using a stainless steel bowl, glass bowl, or a plastic container that will fit into your refrigerator, alternately layer the fruit and the sugar, starting with the pears and ending with the sugar. Cover and refrigerate for 24 hours, or up to 3 days.

When you're ready to proceed, put clean jars in a pot, cover with water, and bring to a boil.

Strain the fruit through a large sieve or colander into a heavy, nonreactive 8-quart pot. Set the drained pears aside. Scrape any undissolved sugar from the macerating container into the pot, and give the syrup a stir so the sugar won't stick during the beginning stage of cooking. Cook the sugar syrup over medium heat until it reaches 230°F (110°C) on a candy thermometer, about 20 minutes. Add the pears, chopped ginger, and lemon juice, and continue to cook, stirring and skimming frequently, until the mixture reaches 221°F (105°C), another 25 to 30 minutes. Stir in the pectin, return to a boil, then turn the heat to low, because continued boiling will break down the pectin.

Immediately ladle the preserves into sterilized canning jars and affix lids. Process the jars in a boiling-water bath for 10 minutes, or let them cool and refrigerate them.

— Recipe by Fran Gage

Black Cherry Preserves

Sweet dark cherries make luscious preserves that look like rubies. A jar of these with freshly baked scones in a napkin-lined basket makes a lovely welcome gift.

....

Fresh from the garden: SWEET CHERRIES, APPLE
Makes 1 pint | *45 calories, 0g fat, 0mg sodium; per tablespoon*

....

3 cups pitted sweet black cherries 1¼ cups sugar	1 large tart apple, peeled, cored, and cut into ½-inch dice	2 tablespoons freshly squeezed lemon juice ¼ teaspoon pure almond extract

....

In a medium bowl, toss together the cherries and 1 cup of the sugar and allow the fruit to macerate for 1 hour. Stir occasionally.

In a large frying pan over moderately low heat, combine the apple, the rest of the sugar, and the lemon juice, and cook, stirring constantly, until the apple pieces are very soft and translucent, about 10 minutes. Turn the heat to moderately high and add the cherries with any accumulated juices. Continue cooking and stirring for about 15 minutes. The mixture should become very bubbly.

Turn off the heat and put a tablespoon of the preserves in a saucer, and place the saucer in the freezer for 5 minutes. Draw your finger through the juice. If the surface wrinkles, cooking is complete; if not, continue cooking for a few minutes more.

Stir in the almond extract and pour the preserves into a pint jar. Cool to room temperature, cover, and refrigerate. The preserves will keep for up to 1 month.

— *Recipe by Edon Waycott*

Apple Butter

You can substitute apple butter for the butter and sugar filling in your favorite cinnamon roll recipe. If you have a dehydrator, you can make wonderful fruit leather with apple butter. And, of course, it's delicious served on hot buttery toast or biscuits. If stovetop cooking, which requires frequent stirring, seems too time-consuming, try using a slow cooker. Directions appear below.

Fresh from the garden: APPLES
Makes about 3 quarts | *20 calories, 0g fat, 0mg sodium; per tablespoon*

Apples, any combination of tart and sweet varieties	½ teaspoon ground cloves	1 cup apple-cider vinegar
4 cups sugar	½ teaspoon cinnamon	
	½ teaspoon ground allspice	

Wash the apples and remove the stem and blossom ends. There is no need to core or peel them. Slice each apple thinly into a nonreactive pot, and add 1 cup of the sugar and ½ cup water. Cook over medium heat, stirring often to prevent scorching, until the apples are soft. (Covering the pot will lessen the risk of scorching and will speed up cooking time a little.)

Run the softened apples through a food mill or a sieve, and return the pulp to the pan. Stir in the remaining 3 cups sugar and the rest of the ingredients and cook over low heat, stirring frequently, until the mixture is thick enough to mound up on the spoon.

Fill hot, sterilized jars with the hot apple butter, leaving ¼ inch of headspace. Wipe the rims clean, and seal with two-piece lids. Process for 10 minutes in a boiling-water bath. Remove jars, allow to cool completely, label and store.

SLOW-COOKER METHOD | This recipe will easily fit in any 5-quart slow cooker. After cooking the apples with ½ cup water to soften them, and then running them through a food mill, add the rest of the ingredients and cook the apple butter on the high setting with the lid off until it is the right consistency. This can take as little as 2 or 3 hours or closer to 6 or 7, depending on how juicy your batch is and how thick you prefer the finished apple butter. Stir the mixture thoroughly every 30 minutes or so, to prevent it from sticking to the sides. When it's ready, fill the jars and process as described at left.

— Recipe by Pier Jones

Lemon-Geranium Strawberry Jelly

Store-bought strawberry jelly is fine for this shortcut recipe because the flavor of the lemon geranium will play the starring role. Rose- or mint-scented geraniums would be lovely here as well.

Fresh from the garden: LEMON GERANIUM LEAVES
Makes 2 half-pint jars | *50 calories, 0g fat, 5mg sodium; per tablespoon*

2 cups strawberry jelly
¼ to ⅓ cup (depending on strength) loosely packed thin ribbons of fresh lemon geranium leaves

2 large, flat, fresh lemon geranium leaves, or 2 fresh sprigs if leaves are small

Sterilize the jars, preferably wide-mouthed ones. Combine the jelly and ribbons of leaves in a small, heavy saucepan. Cover and melt over lowest heat without simmering—set it on a heat diffuser, if you have one. Heat for about 20 minutes, and stir frequently.

Place a whole leaf in each hot, sterilized jar, and pour the liquid jelly through a strainer into the jars. If a large leaf has curled up, coax it open with a chopstick. Wipe the rims of the jars and set on the lids. The jelly will keep in the refrigerator for at least 3 weeks. To store unrefrigerated, process in a boiling-water bath.

— *Recipe by Sylvia Thompson*

Preserved lemon

A preserved lemon is simply a lemon that is salted and immersed in lemon juice. As the salt permeates the lemon, its tartness mellows and its skin tenderizes. The whole fruit takes on a zesty, salty flavor. Once preserved, the lemon will keep for several weeks. Preserved lemons contribute a sharp, briny flavor to foods, much as olives or capers do.

Preserved lemons are traditional in Mideastern cuisines but are easily adapted to American cooking. They work best when incorporated into simple dishes.

To preserve one lemon, you will need two. Cut one lemon in half and squeeze the juice from it. Slice the other lemon lengthwise in quarters. Measure out ¼ cup coarse or Kosher salt. Sprinkle the cut surfaces of the quartered lemon with one tablespoon of the salt. Reassemble the lemon and place it in a small jar, just big enough for the lemon quarters to fit inside. Sprinkle the remaining salt over the lemon and pour the lemon juice into the jar. Then seal the jar and shake it well. Store it in the refrigerator for at least a week, shaking it daily.

HOW TO MAKE THE MOST OF PRESERVED LEMON

- Slice a lemon quarter very thin, rind and all, and add it to potato salad, chicken salad, blanched fresh shelled peas, or asparagus with olive oil.

- Finely chop a lemon quarter and sprinkle over green salads or olives marinated in oil and herbs.

- Slice the lemon quarters in half lengthwise and when roasting chicken, duck, Cornish hens, or lamb, add the slices to the roasting pan during the last 10 to 15 minutes of cooking, turning the slices once. They will absorb the flavors of the roast and caramelize in the pan juices.

- Add sliced preserved lemon to braised meat dishes. Cut the slices crosswise into thin pieces and serve with the roasted or braised meat.

- To combine preserved lemon with pasta, slice a wedge paper thin and toss with pasta of any shape, garlic, chopped herbs, and olive oil. This is a good meal to prepare when you don't have much time.

—Amanda Hesser

Lemon Verbena Jelly

This subtly flavored jelly is good with scones or toasted brioche, or in the center of thumbprint butter cookies. Or warm it until it melts and brush it over pound cake or use as a glaze for fruit tarts. A small dab also makes an elegant and fragrant sweetener for tea.

Fresh from the garden: LEMON VERBENA

Makes five 6-ounce jars | *50 calories, 0g fat, 0mg sodium; per tablespoon*

2 cups packed, coarsely chopped
　　fresh lemon verbena leaves
6 strips (½×3 inches) freshly grated
　　lemon zest

¼ cup freshly squeezed lemon juice
4 cups sugar
3 ounces liquid pectin

Fill a canning kettle two-thirds full of water and bring to a boil. Wash, rinse, and sterilize the canning jars and lids.

Put the lemon verbena leaves, lemon zest, and 2¼ cups water into a medium saucepan. Bring to a boil over moderate to high heat, and then turn the heat to simmer and cover the pan. Cook for 15 minutes, then remove the pan from the heat and allow to stand, covered, for several hours. Pour the infusion through a strainer into a large, deep saucepan. Press on the leaves to extract all flavor, then discard the leaves and zest.

Stir in the lemon juice and sugar and bring to a full boil over high heat. Add the pectin and return to a full boil, stirring constantly. Continue to boil for 2 minutes, stirring. Remove from the heat and skim the foam, if necessary. Ladle the jelly into hot sterilized jars, filling the jars to within ¼ inch of the top. Wipe the rim, and seal with sterilized lids and rings. Process for 10 minutes in a boiling-water bath, remove, and allow to cool completely before labeling and storing.

— Recipe by Edon Waycott

Freeze corn for sweet flavor

Done right, frozen corn brings the flavor of summer to your table year round. There are a few key elements to capturing that true sweet corn flavor: use just-picked corn, work quickly, cut it correctly, and choose a good variety. Garner as many family members to help as you can, to keep things moving along.

FRESHNESS IS PARAMOUNT

For the best flavor, process only corn that has been picked that day. If you're not picking your own, choose only those ears with stem ends that are still moist and green, not dried.

Bring a large pot of water to boil, then shuck and desilk the ears. As quickly as possible after they've been shucked, plunge the ears into the boiling water and blanch for about 5 minutes. Then remove the ears and dunk them in a pan of cold water.

DON'T CUT TOO DEEPLY

When the ears are cool enough to handle, cut the kernels from the cobs. Hold the cob upright in one hand, and cut off strips of kernels with a sharp, medium-length knife, from the cob's tip to its stem end in a downward motion. Resting the cob in a low cake pan is a good way to catch the kernels. The secret to flavor perfection is to cut off only the top half of the kernels. This eliminates the hard ends of the kernels and woody bits of cob. Then, using the back of the knife blade, scrape the cob lightly to remove the milky juice and germ from the part of the kernel that is left on the cob. The juice and germ add to the eating and keeping qualities of the frozen corn.

Spoon both corn and juice into freezer containers or bags and immediately place them in the coldest part of the freezer to "flash" freeze the corn. Always label the package with the date and contents. When solidly frozen, corn will keep longer than a year, but it's best if used within a year of processing.

THE VARIETY OF CORN MATTERS

Older varieties of corn freeze much better than new sugar-enhanced varieties. New varieties retain their sweetness longer, but lack the complex flavor and good texture of older varieties, fresh or frozen. Look for the old shoe peg corn called Country Gentleman, the good yellow heirloom Golden Bantam, the old favorite white Silver Queen, and another yellow variety, Seneca Chief. Some new varieties, such as How Sweet It Is, mimic the flavor of older varieties and freeze well.

— *Sylvia Gatzy*

Seasonal Menus

SPRING

A Spring Dinner

Garden Party Nibbles

SUMMER

Appetizers on the Patio

High Summer Celebration Dinner

WINTER

Vegetarian Feast

FALL

Harvest Supper with Friends

Equivalency Charts

LIQUID/DRY MEASURES

U.S.	Metric
¼ teaspoon	1.25 milliliters
½ teaspoon	2.5 milliliters
1 teaspoon	5 milliliters
1 tablespoon (3 teaspoons)	15 milliliters
1 fluid ounce (2 tablespoons)	30 milliliters
¼ cup	60 milliliters
⅓ cup	80 milliliters
½ cup	120 milliliters
1 cup	240 milliliters
1 pint (2 cups)	480 milliliters
1 quart (4 cups; 32 ounces)	960 milliliters
1 gallon (4 quarts)	3.84 liters
1 ounce (by weight)	28 grams
1 pound	454 grams
2.2 pounds	1 kilogram

OVEN TEMPERATURES

°F	Gas Mark	°C
250	½	120
275	1	140
300	2	150
325	3	165
350	4	180
375	5	190
400	6	200
425	7	220
450	8	230
475	9	240
500	10	260
550	Broil	290

Recipe Index by Chapter

Pasta, Grains & Beans — **174**

Main Dishes — **202**

Index

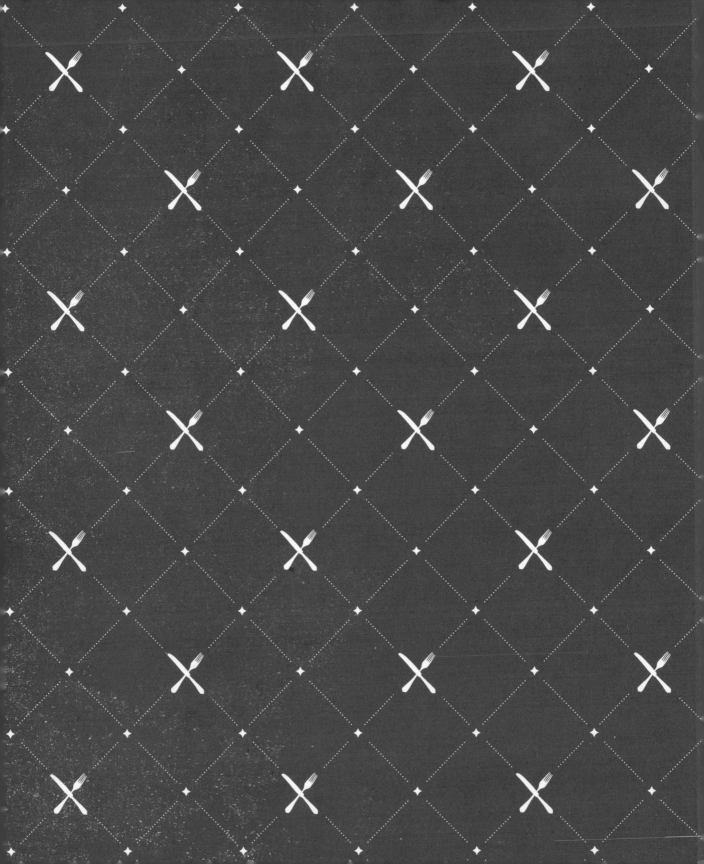